EMBROIDER
EVERYTHING
WORKSHOP

The Beginner's Guide

by diana rupp

illustrations by sybille schenker · photographs by jim franco

WORKMAN PUBLISHING · NEW YORK

DEDICATION

To my fiancé Brandon Eggena.
I could not have done this without you.

Library of Congress Cataloging-in-Publication Data
is available.

ISBN: 978-0-7611-5700-7

Cover design by Janet Vicario
Design by Sara Edward-Corbett
Cover photo by Janette Beckman
Additional photography and illustration credits
on page 251.

Workman books are available at special discounts when
purchased in bulk for premiums and sales promotions
as well as for fund-raising or educational use. Special
editions or book excerpts can also be created
to specification. For details, contact the Special Sales
Director at the address below or send an e-mail
to specialmarkets@workman.com.

Workman Publishing Company, Inc.
225 Varick Street
New York, NY 10014-4381
www.workman.com

Printed in China
First printing September 2011

10 9 8 7 6 5 4 3 2 1

Acknowledgments

I would like to thank everybody who helped me produce this book, namely:

My friend and agent extraordinaire Matthew Elblonk of DeFiore and Company. I am so lucky to have you in my corner! Megan Nicolay, Sara Edward-Corbett, Liz Davis, Janet Vicario, and everybody at Workman for the opportunity to publish this book and for making it a success. Illustrator Sybille Schenker for her gorgeous illustrations. You are not only incredibly talented, you are a woman of your word, which is a beautiful thing. Anna Jane Grossman and Jessica Vitkus for helping me get words onto paper.

Liza Bley, Whitney Crutchfield, Sarah Bennett, and Hillary Amber Fry for making the projects not once, not twice, but however many times it took for them to be just right. I especially want to give a high five to Liza Bley for being my right-hand lady through thick and thin. I majorly heart you. Please move back to NYC!

Jim Franco for agreeing to shoot this book, for making everything look so good, and for being a lot of fun to be around. You are awesome and I seriously owe you!

Dr. Patrick and Bonnie Eggena for letting us shoot at the farm and for all of your love and support. Ditto for Kendra, William, Basia and Nika, Sandy and Bernie, Vickie and Mel. I am so happy to be a part of the family!

Much love to my family, too: Marnie, Petr, Zoe, Robin, Jeanie, Alex, Zach, Mel, and Patch. You guys are the BEST.

To all of my friends and BFFs, including Christine Brenneman, Dan Golden, Jennifer Huh, Emily Woodburne, SB (again), Shawn Manley, Kristin Skibbinski, Doug Ng, Stacie Tabarez, Rich, Deb, Owen and Reese Williams, Michelle Courtois, and Sebastian Pearson. I love all y'all.

The students at Make past, present, and future, for all of your inspiration and continued support. I can't wait to embroider with you!

Of course I'd also like to thank my dog Rita for being there during all the really hard times yet again. Thanks to you, I am always in the company of a friend.

Last, but not least, I'd like to thank my Mom for encouraging me and for wanting the best. If it weren't for you, I would never have picked up a needle and thread.

Contents

The Projects

Let's Make

How Ambitious Are You Feeling?
* Keep Reading * Ready to Dig In?

FOR WEARING

FOR KIDS

FOR HOME

FOR GIVING

Get Pinned * Hand Sewing Tips * Stitches to
Finish What You Started * Other Odds and
Ends * Presentation Touches * Cleaning

Introduction

I love to make things more beautiful. Yes, I also enjoy making beautiful things out of nothing, but to me, so many things are beautiful to begin with. A totally unadorned handkerchief that belonged to my granny is beautiful. So is a piece of crimson thread. And a blooming flower. So, what if that handkerchief had a crimson tulip stitched on its corner? Well, that would just knock it out of the park.

In truth, making things more beautiful is my job—or at least, I help other people make things more beautiful. In 2002, I founded Make Workshop, a school and atelier on Manhattan's Lower East Side. I'm proud to say that, over the years, I've taught thousands of people to crochet scarves, tailor their own clothes, print on fabric— you name it. The only problem is that I can fit only so many people in my studio at one time! My hope is that this book provides you with everything you'd get if you popped in for an embroidery workshop at Make. It may even teach you more.

You don't need *Project Runway*–worthy skills or a degree in fine art to turn a not-so-exciting dish towel, a plain dress or skirt, a shabby sweater, or a pair of plain cotton panties into one of the coolest, more beautiful things you own. You just need some embroidery—and that's what gets me so excited to share it with you.

It was a little daunting to figure out exactly what to share in this book only because there's an incredible amount of embroidery knowledge

The park is my favorite place to stitch on a sunny day.

that exists in this world. If you were so inclined, you could literally get a college degree in embroidery—no, I'm not talking about a diploma from Lillian's Needlepoint Wondermart at the mall. In my next life I just might enroll in the amazing two-year program at the Royal School of Needlework, an English school that was founded in 1872; its first president was one of Queen Victoria's daughters. But you don't need a degree in order to stitch beautiful things—I've seen some of the most lovely images embroidered by small children who were just learning to sew.

Embroidery doesn't just make things look more beautiful and better than ever: I truly believe it can make the embroiderer feel better, too. The act of embroidering can be so calming that it has actually been found to help people with high blood pressure. It's a craft that regularly seduces everyone from nursing home residents to kindergartners to princesses and football players (for more on that, see "Twentieth-Century Needlepointing's Celebrity Odd Couple," page 51). What's more, the financial investment is minimal. Threads and needles cost little more than pocket change, and if you can't find inspiration in fabric you already have in your closet, canvases are pretty inexpensive as well.

And did I mention that you can get wow-worthy results without a ton of practice, physical exertion, or time? It's kind of like that old commercial where a mom makes instant cookies but pats flour on her face so her family thinks she slaved away.

My Life in Stitches

I think that we all have some kind of creative itch to scratch—even Kim Jong Il dreams of directing movies—but my mom likes to say that I was born with a particularly strong predisposition to make things with my hands. My grandmother's mother was a milliner. My dad's father was a painter and woodworker and was always making crazy marionettes and balsa wood planes. And my mom? She made everything from diorama Easter eggs to hand-churned butter (made from milk from our very own cow, Betty) to our clothes. One of my favorite family memories was of a Christmas where all gifts exchanged were handmade.

So if my hands are always busy, it's probably because so much about my childhood and family life was about making things. Today I can knit and sew up a storm, thanks to my very first introduction to the wonders of needles when my maternal great-grandmother, Hallie, aka Granny, first showed me how to do a running stitch on a scrap of cloth.

Granny was born in 1898. She was definitely from another time, and she might as well have been born on another planet. A wonderful planet, in my estimation. Her home was filled with porcelain tea sets and flouncy curtains and china doll collections. For a girly little sprite like me, visiting her was like going to heaven.

My mom, as I mentioned, was a gifted seamstress and was constantly producing adorable-but-practical clothes for me and my siblings. She even made sure my dollhouse residents had good fashion sense! Before I could even read, my mom helped me fiddle around on the sewing machine, and Granny had me decorating tea towels, pillowcases, and hankies with embroidered flowers and sweet drawings from the Aunt Martha's brand of iron-on transfers that I still use and love today.

With Granny, I was able to take boring things and make them so, so special—more beautiful. Really, is there anything less interesting to a kid than a tea towel? Even as an adult, I think they're pretty dull when unadorned. As a child, however, this simple object came to life thanks to the little strawberry my tiny hands learned to stitch. It was pretty darn easy: I followed an outline, and the backstitch took me about ten seconds to learn (you'll learn it just as fast—promise!). And that made me even prouder of my accomplishment. I remember bringing it to school for show-and-tell. Suddenly, every kindergartner wanted a tea towel. Granny had

bestowed on me the superpower to make the ordinary into the extraordinary.

Next, she showed me how a little decorative stitching could add a whole new level of excitement to a Mom-sewn pinafore. With that little embroidered element, Mom's handiwork and mine became a collaborative piece.

As I got a little older, though, I put down my embroidery hoop and threw myself into machine sewing. I became a denizen of Southern Cali's secondhand shops: As my skills improved, it seemed that there was no garment that couldn't be altered into something worthy of the pages of *Vogue*. (*Vogue* as *I* felt it should be, of course.) And, the more I dove into the world of seams and hems and necklines, the less I thought about embroidery.

I didn't stop getting excited by great stitchwork, however. Once you've done hand embroidery, you really appreciate the result because you know the time that went into completing it. When I graduated from high school, my mom gave me an embroidered quilt that Granny had made. It's a crazy quilt: The patchwork is held together with all kinds of textured embroidery stitches. I was amazed at how just a few colored threads could be manipulated to make such amazing designs on an otherwise ordinary object.

When Granny died, I inherited a box full of hankies that she'd embroidered. In a moment of missing her, I went out and bought a hoop

My Granny Hallie (above); Granny's crazy quilt was decorated with hundreds of embroidery stitches (left).

and a pack of handkerchiefs (yes, you can still buy them—and for cheap!). I spent the evening curled up on the couch, decorating the edges with simple chain stitches. My mind idled, and when I snapped back to attention, half of my wardrobe was decorated with stitched flowers. And bicycles. And zigzags. I was hooked. Again. I bought a dozen of Aunt Martha's patterns at Jo-Ann's—iron-on line art depicting everything from crocodiles to Corvettes to apple trees—and re-immersed myself into that creative place I'd inhabited as a kid. As much as I love the precise and rich world of sewing, there's a major spot in my heart for handiwork that can be done sitting up in bed, without any whirring machine drowning out *Talk Soup* on the tube.

use a preprinted pattern, or just stitch something off the top of your head is entirely up to you. (You'll have the skills to do all of the above and more before you finish the first half of this book.)

Your work can be a reflection of your personality, just like any art. You can stitch the needlework equivalent of paint-by-numbers and

Students learn to stitch at Make Workshop in New York City.

Embracing the Blank Canvas

Embroidery can be as technical and intricate as sewing on a machine or by hand, but it's also far more forgiving. Because most embroidery is purely decorative work, you'll rarely have to worry about how something is going to fit or whether or not straps will come loose. Most of the time, a mistake only adds to the charm of the final product. (Indeed, Amish women intentionally stitch an error in their work because they don't want God to think they're trying to make something as perfect as Him.) Whether you design your own needlepoint canvas,

produce something really spectacular. You can be the type of painter who does photorealistic work, or you can do something more organic and free-form. Picasso and Van Gogh and Warhol broke the rules; why can't you? And while those museum heavyweights don't usually come up in discussions of embroidery, they're not-so-distant relatives. New York's Museum of Art and Design has devoted several exhibitions to needlework, shedding light on some of today's most amazing textile artists. At their 2007 show *Pricked: Extreme Embroidery,* I watched one visitor after another marvel at the masterpieces on display, from Shizuko Kimura's muslin-and-thread "life drawings," done from live models, to works by Laura Owens, a trained painter, who creates flowering trees that are above and beyond anything I've ever seen made with a pencil or a brush. I was honored that the museum asked me to teach embroidery classes in conjunction with the exhibit. After seeing all the incredible embroidered work the show had to offer, I was not at all surprised that so many people were inspired to try their hand at it themselves—all my lessons sold out.

A sampling of samplers

School Is in Session

At Make, my embroidery classes lure in all sorts. There are new moms who want to appliqué onesies and college kids who want to add personal touches to thrift-store finds. There are people who are simply looking for a new way to pass the time on their train commutes to and from work.

In each intro to embroidery class, students produce a sampler that shows off all the stitches they're learning. The best part of teaching embroidery is seeing how each person's sampler turns out. Every student uses the same supplies, but by the end they've each stitched little works of art that are unique—totally theirs.

This book is designed to give you all the skills, practice, and secrets that you'll need to start your own stitching adventure. In the first half of the book, you'll learn about the history of embroidery and some of the different schools of stitching that have developed over time and in different places. Among other things, I'll also tell you exactly what supplies you're going to need (I promise: The investment is minimal!) and how to do the basic stitches used in the major schools of embroidery: freehand, needlepoint, counted thread, and smocking. Need some inspiration? Worried about how to thread a needle or pick out the right kind of fabric? We'll cover all that, too. This section of the book is useful before you hit the projects in the second half of the book, but you can also use it as a cheat sheet if you decide to do your own thing.

If you're like me, you might skip straight to the projects; they are really the heart of this book. Embroidery is fairly easy as far as stitchwork goes, but it's way easier when you know what you're doing. Reading this first section will give you the skills you need. It'll also give you great trivia to offer up during your next craft night. For instance: Did you know which famous football player wrote a book about the joys of needlepoint? I want to make sure you can stitch *and* be Mrs. or Mr. Popular at parties.

The projects are designed to help you figure out what kind of stitching most appeals to you— and what branches of the stitch tree you want to explore. Maybe you're turned on by the rich history of bargello work, or maybe you're excited by some of the quick projects and you'll finish making all your holiday presents by October. There's also the question of your mood at project time. Do you want to veg out and follow a pattern to a T, or do you want to riff on a design and make it your own? Are you excited to experiment with embellishing printed fabric or would you prefer a blank canvas?

I had so much fun making all the projects you're about to dig into—I really do have the best job in the world. I hope that you'll have an equally good time whipping up your own creations, whether they're inspired by mine or inventions of your own. My goal is to help you get down all the basic skills you need for embroidery success—and I think you'll master them in a jiffy. Now go forth and make something more beautiful. Something unique—and totally yours.

The Beautiful Bayeux

As you embroider, you're becoming a part of a rich tradition of needlework that extends millennia into the past—and continues into the future. That's right: You're going to be part of embroidery history! Some of the oldest pieces of art that exist in this world are textiles that were created by artisans who spent their lifetimes stitching to make fabrics sturdier, to make things more beautiful, or to pass on information. The best example is the Bayeux Tapestry, which was made by unknown stitchers in the eleventh century; it tells the story of the Norman conquest of England and the relationship between William the Conqueror and Harold, the last Anglo-Saxon king of England. The 70-meter-long embroidered piece, which now lives in Normandy, remains an important document for those who study eleventh-century military history, tactics, and fables (the borders of the tapestry are emblazoned with images taken from Aesop). So who is to say your little tea towel won't one day tell people about daily life in the twenty-first century? Thanks to the durability of textiles, there's a good chance your piece of embroidery will outlive many of the diary entries, drawings, and computer files you've made.

A detail of the Bayeux Tapestry

10 reasons why I embroider

Needlework has busied hands around the world for ages, largely because there's so much to like about it. In my opinion, to know embroidery is to love embroidery. Here are some of the reasons why I'm so thrilled to be able to introduce it to your fingers.

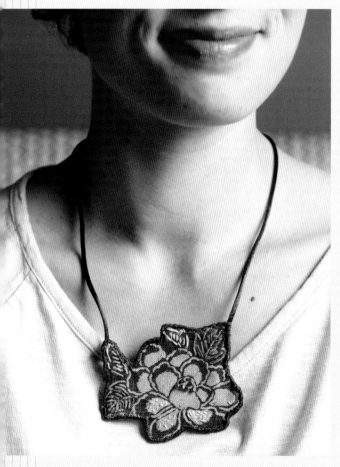

1 There's no right or wrong.

A mistake isn't really a misstep: It's just something that leads you down a path you didn't see before, right? Sure, but a hand-knit sweater loses some of its appeal if it unravels while you're wearing it. Embroidery, however, *is* foolproof—and that flattens the learning curve quite a bit. Yes, there are certain traditions or practices or styles, but it's largely about decoration, which means that a skipped stitch or a twisted thread on a dish towel won't make the thing less useful. Heck, an unplanned stitch could actually add something new and wonderful to the piece. With your average embroidery project, there are no seams that might rip and leave your grocery bag torn or your skirt at your ankles on the subway platform. (Oops! Good thing you're wearing those cute embroidered knickers, page 94).

2 I feel like a kid with a coloring book.

I think that coloring books are appealing no matter what your age, if only because sometimes having a few parameters is all you need to kick off your creative thinking. Because there's such an abundance of beautiful prepainted canvases and transferable patterns out there (please turn to the envelope in the front of this book!), I am always inspired; I never have that "where do I begin?" feeling I sometimes get when I'm staring at a blank document on the computer screen or a fresh page in my sketchbook.

3 It's soothing.

I once read about a doctor who found a unique way to bring down his own blood pressure: He took up needlepoint. He's not the only one who has seen—and felt—the correlation between stitching and calmed nerves. Whether I'm following an intricate pattern or just stitching lines on a sampler, I'm always comforted by the repetitive motions and the simple act of creating something. Embroidery quiets the chatter in my head and allows my mind to wander in the best kind of way. All the stress melts away when I curl up on the sofa with my dog/friend Rita, flip on *The Bachelor,* and busy myself with my stitched project du jour. (And it's better for my health than the tub of popcorn I'd likely devour were my hands idle!)

4 It's both an art and a craft.

I've heard it argued that crafts are all about creating something with a purpose, with certain functionality: a stool with legs, a shirt with armholes, and so on. Art may be a bit harder to define. But any way you look at it, embroidery is a skill that can be used in either realm—it's the great uniter. As with drawing, you can always build up your embroidery skills—but that doesn't mean that a child isn't able to create something beautiful on his first try. You might create something that has a use, or you could create a MoMA-worthy wall hanging. Whether you call it "craft" or "art" is up to you. I think it can be both.

5 It travels well.

I'm not a lady who packs a steamer trunk on every weekend trip. I prefer to travel light and keep things simple, which is why I love how portable embroidery is. Many of the projects in this book can fit into a small handbag. If I thread a needle before I leave home and tuck a pair of embroidery scissors and a few different flosses into my tote (a total weight of *maybe* 5 ounces), I'm guaranteed to keep myself occupied during those empty moments on the bus or at the dentist. What's more, it's always a good conversation starter—stitching in public means that you just might find yourself with something of an audience observing your every move. Yes, it's hard to be famous. But embroidery calls for such sacrifices.

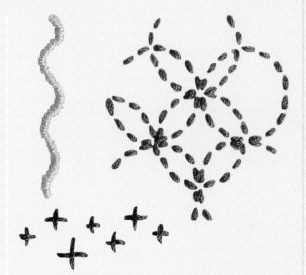

6 I make awesome personalized gifts.

When it comes to birthdays, weddings, and showers, I've been known to go a little over the top on the present front. I see every occasion as an excuse to tackle some kind of project. There's only one problem: While I love nothing more than making things for my friends, the cost of supplies can start to add up. And sometimes I just don't have the kind of time needed to knit a complete sweater or sew a cute skirt. Embroidery is the solution. I can take almost anything—a vintage hanky, a cool secondhand tuxedo shirt, a plain bib—and quickly personalize it by stitching on some initials or appliqué flowers. The result is something unique that will likely outshine anything on the registry. And while that's not really the point, it's a fun challenge!

7 I can see artwork in a new way.

I'm very inspired by my friend's aunt who is into needlepointing famous works of art. A walk through her house is like a guided tour of the world's museums. There you see *Mona Lisa* on a pillow; here, one of Van Gogh's *Sunflowers.* When you work on a piece like this, you really learn every line, color, and shadow that the artist painted. It's like taking an art history class every time the tapestry needle leaves your bag—and it's a way of collaborating with some of the world's most famous artists!

8 It's the secret to reviving old clothes.

I am a very loyal clothing owner. I have a collection of vintage cotton-print dresses, some of which I've owned since high school. Thanks to embroidery, I've made many a tired garment live well beyond its natural lifetime. I was able to save a circa 1960s Lily Pulitzer sundress with a couple of strategically placed appliqué flowers. Other longtime residents of my closet have enough lazy daisies embroidered on them to give a girl hay fever. But here's the best part: The Salvation Army is often chock-full of designer duds that have been retired because of an unsightly red wine stain or moth hole. With even just an ounce of embroidery know-how, it's possible to cover up those problem areas. The end result will be far more exciting than anything you'll ever find in a boutique.

9 Even practice pieces are frame-worthy.

Around the world, museums house embroidered works of art that were nothing more than samplers or practice pieces. But those practice pieces facilitated and represented a major exchange of information. Instead of scouring the web for new patterns to learn, embroiderers in need of inspiration invented and learned stitches by copying the designs of others. The resulting samplers might not have been meant for public view, but they're darn pretty. Same goes for my doodle cloths, which are like diaries of all that I've learned. Even in this connected age (I could spend *days* learning new stitches on embroidery sites), I find it exciting when I see another embroiderer's samplers. Inevitably, he or she has stitched something that I want to run home and try myself.

10 It gives me an excuse to shop . . . without breaking the bank!

In my New York City apartment, I have no room for snow globes or any of the other cute tchotchkes that I used to load up on when I traveled. But if I pass by any kind of bead or yarn shop, I always stop in and get a little something that I know I'll work into a future project. My finds are usually affordable and they're always unique additions to my home landscape. A button on an appliquéd pillow winks at me and reminds me of a little shop I visited in Paris a few years back; I made a sampler out of silk threads on an antique linen tea towel that I bought in the Czech Republic when I was visiting my sister and her family. Even if I'm just wandering around my own neighborhood and I get the urge to shop, I always manage to find a place that has some kind of material I can work into a project. I've found that friends are particularly generous when they happen upon an amazing yarn or string of beads during their travels—maybe it's because they know there's a good chance it'll be regifted to them in the form of whatever I happen to be stitching when their birthdays come along.

Embroidery, at its most basic, is about using needlework to embellish material. The most common application is fabric embroidered with thread, but pretty much anything goes. I've seen people stitch their way through paper, leaves, leather, even rocks. My point is simply that if you can touch it, you can probably stitch it. And if you can put it through a needle, go ahead and try working with it. A thousand years ago, girls in China started weaving their hair into images of Buddha to show their piety. So try ribbon. Go right ahead. How about cassette tape or dental floss? Really, the sky's the limit.

In this book, I've chosen to focus on a few major areas that fall under the embroidery umbrella. Once you can conquer these bad boys, you should be able to take on any stitching challenge that comes your way.

Freehand Embroidery

Freehand embroidery is a term that refers to stitching that isn't regulated by the weave or underlying structure of your fabric. Some kinds of embroidery are only suitable to some kinds of fabrics—different fabrics have different weaves or knits, different amounts of spaces between the threads, and so on—but nearly every kind of cloth or canvas is suitable for freehand work. Your image and your thread (I generally

Japanese silk embroidery is a stunning example of freehand work.

use stranded cotton embroidery floss) take center stage with freehand embroidery, and the fabric is rarely covered completely. Because the background is complete even before you touch your needle, freehand embroidery can be relatively quick. The iron-on patterns I used to stitch onto tea towels as a kid? That's freehand embroidery. The intricate stitched flowers that have decorated Japanese kimonos for a thousand years? That too. Many of my mother's linens have freehand monograms on their corners. Very fancy! That was Granny's doing, of course.

There are many, many schools of freehand embroidery. Three of my favorites are:

crewel

overembroidery, Richard Saja's work

sashiko

* **Crewel:** Wool embroidered freehand onto sturdy fabrics—usually cottons or linens. Crewel became all the rage when England, under Queen Elizabeth I, began trading with India. The British were likely inspired by imported Indian hangings painted with all kinds of flora. The Indians may have been copying ideas that the British had brought to them to begin with, and the British were undoubtedly influenced by fashions from China. It might be one of the most well-traveled of all the styles of freehand embroidery.

* **Overembroidery:** Embellishing printed fabric with freehand stitches. This could mean stitching a pattern that complements what's already there, like adding some little lazy daisies to a floral printed fabric or outlining images with running stitches; it could also be the stitched equivalent of graffiti to contrast the existing pattern. I'm a fan of the work of Richard Saja, a stitcher who has gained recognition for his weird and wacky overembroidery on toile, which is a linen cloth printed with one-color line drawings of French pastoral scenes. Saja stitches his own visions over these scenes. A milkmaid, say, may suddenly sport fishnets or a Mohawk or a clown nose. It's one form of embroidery where there's endless opportunity to let your imagination do cartwheels.

* **Sashiko:** A centuries-old Japanese style of quilting that usually is done with matte white twisted cotton thread on indigo-colored fabric. Intricate geometric patterns are made using running stitches. I love the contrast of the bold, intricate lines and the simple color scheme.

Appliqué

Appliqué involves using standard embroidery stitches to fasten one textile to another for decoration. This can mean layering many different fabrics on top of one another in a way that isn't so different from quilting. Or it can be as simple as applying a piece of felt to a bib or patching a pair of jeans. Types of appliqué work include:

✳ **Broderie perse:** Embroidering printed fabric to a base fabric. Traditionally this has meant arranging snippings of chintz flowers or birds however you please, but, defined more broadly, it could mean any kind of appliqué where you are using printed fabric pieces as your building tools.

✳ **Crazy quilting:** A traditional form of quilting that involves securing any desired combo of patchwork pieces together using embroidery stitches. There are no rules. They're not so much crazy as they are just totally fabulous.

broderie perse

✳ **Fon:** Brightly colored solid fabrics appliquéd together to create little scenes. They have been produced in Benin, Africa, for three hundred years, usually depict silhouettes of people and animals, and are said to consecrate important events. Important events are still worth a bit of embroidery no matter where you are or what time you're living in.

crazy quilting

fon

smocking

printed canvas work

bargello

Smocking

Smocking, a centuries-old method of gathering fabric, used to be one of embroidery's most practical techniques. This was in the pre-elastic-waistband era of clothing. Way back when, smocking was used as a method to create a degree of elasticity in clothing, while also prettifying the garment. The gathered stitches are executed over a grid of connected dots, with pearl cotton or embroidery floss on a lightweight-but-stable fabric—usually cotton.

Needlepoint

Needlepoint is any kind of embroidery where the stitches cover the background surface completely, resulting in a durable piece that can work well as a seat cover or a pillow or an eyeglass case. Most needlepoint is stitched on canvas, but it's possible to do it on any sturdy evenweave fabric. Wool, silk, cotton, or blended yarns can all be suitable for needlepointing. There's a massive array of stitches you can use, but the primary stitch used is the tent stitch. Types of needlepoint include:

✳ **Printed canvas work:** This is embroidery that is stitched on top of an image that has been screen-printed or hand-painted onto canvas, like the amazing design shown here (above, middle) by renowned illustrator Charley Harper (my fave!). *Printed canvas* starter kits can be found at any needlepoint or craft store, but you can also buy plain canvas and paint your own (for tips, see "Painting on Canvas," page 79). I find this to be one of the most soothing forms of embroidery. It's really the stitching version of Paint-by-Numbers. Kits are frequently sold with the appropriate colored yarns, but I often feel that the work is a bit more "mine" when I choose my own colors. Why settle for a basic gray pigeon when it could be stitched in hot pink?

✳ **Bargello:** Named for a series of cushioned chairs from the Bargello Palace (now the Bargello Museum) in Florence, Italy, *bargello* is also called Florentine work. This needlepoint style is believed to have come to England by way of Hungary in the 1300s. The stitches are worked vertically, can span one or several cross-threads, and are usually worked staircaselike, so as to create geometric, zigzagging stripes. It is often stitched using heavy wool or silk (wool is more standard) on canvas, but any evenweave fabric will work as a base as long as it's sturdy enough to support the yarn.

whitework

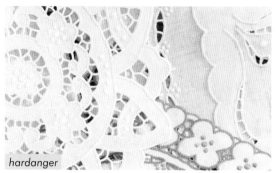

hardanger

Openwork

Openwork is embroidery where some areas of the fabric are removed—either by cutting it away or by removing threads from the weave of the fabric. Cutwork is when areas of fabric are cut away. The cut edges are reinforced with tightly spaced blanket stitches. Drawn thread work involves pulling out the warp and/or weft threads in some areas while binding or weaving the warp and weft threads in other parts of the patterns. Types of openwork include:

✳ **Whitework:** This is a traditional kind of cutwork embroidery in which white fabric (usually linen), is stitched with white thread (also linen). Some of the unstitched areas are cut away. This makes the patterns stand out despite the fact that there is little color differentiation.

✳ **Hardanger:** This drawn thread technique is named for an area of Norway. It's worked with pearl cotton on evenweave fabric and can be classified as an openwork method but follows a counted thread chart (see pages 64–69 for more on counted thread). It's quite gridlike, with open areas cut away

and surrounded by *kloster blocks,* which are simple groupings of satin stitches. Other areas are wound or woven together in order to create barlike crisscrosses.

Beadwork

Beadwork, as its name would suggest, is all about using beads to highlight your stitching. It can be done freehand using running stitches, backstitches, or couching—just add the beads when you bring the thread up on the right side of the fabric. (It's important to use a beading needle, which is uniform in size from top to

beadwork

cross-stitch

holes per inch both horizontally and vertically; the stitches follow a charted design and usually do not completely cover the fabric. Stitches are kept consistent in size, and each stitch is worked over the number of cross-threads determined by the chart. Types of counted thread work include:

✳ **Cross-stitch:** This genre of embroidery includes any counted thread pattern where the primary stitch is cross-stitch, which looks like an X. It is usually done with embroidery floss, and the look is very reminiscent of something you'd imagine in *Little House on the Prairie*. Cross-stitch can be done on any evenweave fabric, but it can also be fun to use non-evenweave fabric with a grid pattern printed or woven into it—gingham, for example. Counted cross-stitch done on gingham even has its own name: Chicken Scratch.

bottom, so that the bead doesn't get stuck on the eye.) Almost any kind of bead would work, but I like the delicate sweetness of little seed beads.

There's also a burgeoning school of embroidery called bead-point, which involves threading a bead onto every stitch (or selected stitches) of a needlepoint piece before returning the needle back through the canvas.

Counted Thread Work

Counted thread work is done on evenweave fabric where there is an even number of threads and

blackwork

✳ **Blackwork:** This kind of stitching is defined by largely repetitive patterns used to fill design areas. It's a style of stitching that originated in Spain prior to the 1500s and was most likely influenced by the geometric motifs of Arabic design. The stitching is usually worked solely with black thread (usually pearl cotton or a stranded cotton or silk) on white or cream evenweave fabric.

PART 1

The Basics

CHAPTER 1

Gearing Up

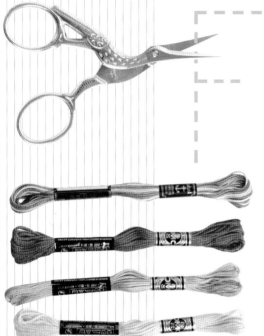

rom one fine thread a work of art is born. In other words, *tenui filo magnum texitur opus.* So reads the motto of DMC (Dollfus-Mieg & Compagnie), a longtime titan in the world of embroidery floss. The beauty of this phrase is that it really captures the simplicity of stitching. To embroider is to draw with thread—and, as with drawing, the fundamental tools are straightforward. People have literally been embroidering for thousands of years, and today you don't need much more to embroider than what could've been found in an old hominid's sewing box. A priceless work of stitched art can be made for mere pennies. It all just boils down to two things: a needle and thread. Even fabric, at its most basic, is just a weave of threads.

As basic as embroidery is, there are plenty of tools that may ultimately make your life easier as you become more skilled or ambitious. Whether or not you're a new embroiderer, you can put together a decent arsenal of supplies and materials at a craft store for darn cheap. If you buy your supplies online, all the essentials can most likely be sent together, in one small box, as a one-stop shipping miracle.

The Ultimate Embroider Everything Kit

If you have a bargain-basement drugstore sewing kit—or one from a hotel front desk!—for reattaching buttons and patching your jeans, you may already have a few of the things you need to embroider. (Go, you!) A few extra tools, however, can elevate you to a slightly more advanced level.

✳ **Needles:** You'll need a wide assortment of needles, because the one you choose to use for a particular project will depend on your fabric and thread. Stainless steel needles vary greatly in terms of point, length, width, and eye size. Go ahead and splurge—you can get packs of them for just a couple of dollars. Each pattern in this book specifies what needle to use. The ones you'll use the most are a size 9 embroidery needle and a size 20 tapestry needle, which are standard and easy to find. (For more information, see "Needles," page 8.)

✳ **Needle threader:** The most familiar type is contructed out of tin and stamped with the image of Queen Victoria. Pick up a higher-quality version (the three-for-a-dollar variety tends to break the first time you use it)— DMC makes one with hooks that can handle a variety of threads, including medium- to heavy-weight yarns.

✳ **Thimble:** Worn on the index finger of your dominant hand, these are used for pushing the needle through fabric without poking yourself. Some people love them, and some think they're silly. I find they're useful when working with heavier fabrics. Usually made of metal, thimbles are covered with dimples, or knurls, that grab the end of the needle while you push it through fabric. You can get them for nearly nothing (sometimes they are packed in a hotel sewing kit), or you can invest a little more and start a collection of interesting vintage or souvenir ones. One stitcher I know picks up a porcelain thimble whenever she comes across a tourist shop in a new city.

✳ **Needle pullers:** These small, textured rubber disks are useful, as their name would suggest, for pulling needles through thick fabrics. In a pinch, an uninflated balloon can also do the job.

✳ **Embroidery scissors:** These dainty little clippers are indispensable. Classic embroidery scissors are shaped like a bird, but the non-bird-shaped ones work just as well. I like the 4-inch scissors made by Gingher: They come with a lifetime guarantee and (bonus!) even a mail-order sharpening service.

✳ **Embroidery floss:** Start out with a half dozen of your favorite colors of stranded cotton plus a few basics like white, red, and black. An individual skein costs only 35 cents or so, but many craft stores sell inexpensive packs of assorted colors, which is a smart way to start your thread collection. (For more information, see "Threads," page 10.)

✳ **Hoop:** Made of wood, plastic, or metal, a hoop sandwiches your fabric in order to give you a taut work surface. On fabrics that are prone to wrinkling, bunching, or drooping, a hoop can be a lifesaver.

Some people swear by them, others don't use them at all—it's up to you. I find myself using a 9-inch hoop most often. (For more information, see "The Scoop on Hoops," page 16.)

✳ **Water- and air-soluble fabric marker:** Dritz makes the Dual Purpose Marking Pen, which has blue ink on one side and purple ink on the other. The blue ink washes out easily, and the purple ink evaporates into the air. Poof! They're one of the best ways to transfer images onto fabric.

✳ **Heat-transfer pencil:** The "lead" in this pencil is made from a special-formula ink that reproduces when heat is applied. How does it work? Simply trace a design onto paper and then transfer it to fabric using an iron.

✳ **Tracing paper:** Translucent paper is used for tracing and then transferring designs. Buy a tablet of tracing paper from an art supply store.

(continued on page 6)

The Ultimate Embroider Everything Kit

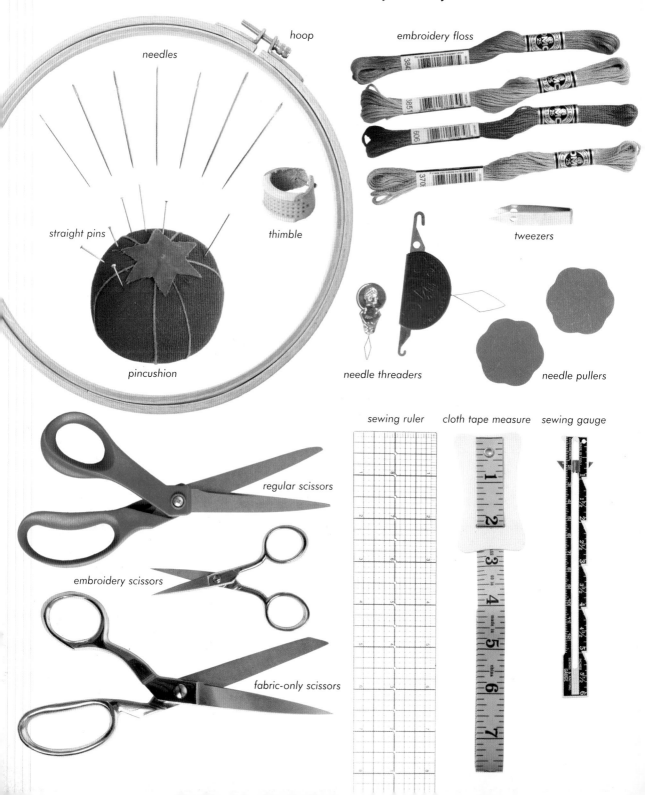

hoop

embroidery floss

needles

thimble

tweezers

straight pins

pincushion

needle threaders

needle pullers

regular scissors

sewing ruler

cloth tape measure

sewing gauge

embroidery scissors

fabric-only scissors

fusible interfacing

stabilizer

fabric marker

heat-transfer pencils

bookbinder's awl

hobby knife

seam ripper

rotary cutter

magnetic board and stand

cutting mat

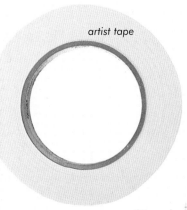

artist tape

tracing paper

quilting ruler

(continued from page 3)

* **Straight pins:** You'll need these for securing transfer paper and appliqué pieces, among other important tasks. I like to use standard, all-purpose dressmaker pins. Stay away from pins with colored plastic heads—they'll melt any time you use an iron.

* **Pincushion:** A pincushion keeps pins and needles safe and poised for action. A traditional tomato-shape cushion does the job.

* **Seam ripper:** Mistakes happen to the best of us. Good thing the seam ripper is here to save the day! On the wrong side of the fabric (the underside of your work, so as not to disturb the visible surface of the project), use the sharp hook of the seam ripper to cut every few stitches until you can pull everything out. Please, please, please, also use the seam ripper to snip your thread ends. Even if you're tempted to use your embroidery scissors to cut those rogue threads, think twice. I've seen far too many canvases and fabrics get snipped by accident. No fun!

* **Tweezers:** It's always good to have a pair of needlework tweezers on hand for pulling out a stitch that isn't behaving properly or gently tugging out a piece of the waste canvas you will sometimes use as a grid when doing counted thread work. The Nordic Needle tweezers shown on page 4 are spring-tempered, have precision points that grip wayward threads especially well, and have a lifetime guarantee.

* **Sewing ruler:** Most needlework measurements are in eighths of an inch, so you'll want an 18-inch transparent ruler that has eighths clearly marked. Use a ruler to center your patterns, and measure and mark fabric.

* **Cloth tape measure:** This flexible tool is for measuring soft, curved areas like your bust, waist, and hips, or soft furnishings such as a pillow. The standard length and width of a tape measure is $60 \times \frac{5}{8}$ inches, although there is a 120-inch version for home decor projects. Make sure your tape measure doesn't stretch—measuring tools should be as accurate as possible.

* **Sewing gauge:** Technically a sewing tool, this handy 6-inch ruler is small enough to fit in a wallet. It's invaluable for measuring stitch length and checking placement on the fly. Don't leave home without it!

* **Fabric-only scissors:** These should be reserved for only cutting fabric. Stainless-steel dressmaker shears made by Gingher are my favorite fabric scissors (in addition to a rotary cutter; see below). Invest in a pair of 7- or 8-inch shears.

* **Regular scissors:** These babies are for cutting paper and anything else (besides fabric and thread) that comes your way. Most likely you have a pair of these kicking around your house somewhere. Having them in your kit will keep you from using your embroidery or fabric-only scissors instead, which would be very, very bad.

* **Rotary cutter:** Like a pizza cutter for fabric! You'll be psyched to have one of these when you're cutting a lot of straight lines in fabric. (I find it a must-have for projects like the Book for Baby on page 133.) The most popular size blade—and the size I use—is 45 mm.

* **Cutting mat and ruler:** These vinyl boards will keep Grandma Ethel's wood inlay table from getting marred by any of your trusty blades. Look for a mat that is "self-healing." This means that its molecules will re-fuse after you slice it, extending its life for many, many uses. An 18×24 inch cutting mat and a 4×24 inch quilting ruler will be big enough for the projects in this book, but bigger sizes are also available. The mat and ruler are often sold as a set with a rotary cutter.

* **Hobby knife:** Bet you didn't think embroidery involved knives! This little guy will help you trim edges and cut your paper patterns with the accuracy of a pro.

* **Bookbinder's awl:** Stitching through paper is so much more fun when the holes are pre-punched! This type of awl can be found in the bookmaking section of any craft or art supply store.

* **Magnetic board and stand:** With any kind of charted work such as cross-

stitching or needlepoint, it can be easy to lose track of what line or color you're working. I find the easiest way to not lose count is to use a magnet to fasten the pattern onto a metal board and folding stand (mine is made by LoRan and costs about $10). It comes with a magnet that acts as a pointer so that I can keep track of where I am on the page. I find this is also a good way to keep my chart crisp and clean—I lost a lot of good charts to the crumpling effects of the far corners of my embroidery bag before learning this lesson.

✳ **Fusible interfacing:** Sold by the yard in fabric stores, interfacing has the texture of a dryer sheet. Iron the adhesive side to the underside of fabric and it will help to prevent fraying and create a protective layer that will reinforce your embroidery stitches.

✳ **Stabilizer:** Sometimes you need extra support to keep stitches in place while you're embroidering. This is especially true when you're working on fabric that has any stretch to it, or fabric that has a tendency

to pucker. Stabilizer keeps everything copasetic. There are several kinds of stabilizer with different properties that may be appropriate for certain projects but not for others. Sulky is a popular brand that makes stabilizers (Wash-Away and Heat-Away) that can dissolve with water or heat. They also make Cut-Away, a permanent stabilizer that aids during the actual stitching and protects the finished product against the evils of the washing machine. However, for the projects in this book that require stabilizer, I recommend a fourth variety, Tear-Away, which stabilizes the project while you are working and can be easily removed after stitching. The standard rule is that if a fabric stretches, use Cut-Away. If it doesn't stretch, use Tear-Away.

✳ **Artist tape:** A white archival tape is perfect for binding the edges of needlepoint canvas. Acid-free, it leaves no sticky residue and is repositionable, making it the go-to tape for many needlework tasks like taping a finished design to mat board. The most useful size is ¾ inch wide. Look for rolls of it at any art supply store.

Shopping in the Flesh

While the web does indeed offer up a wide variety of embroidering supplies, I prefer to frequent specialty embroidery shops when I need to replenish my kit. Call me old-fashioned, but there's nothing quite like running my fingers over the rainbows of threads or sitting and learning a new stitch with the shopkeeper—he or she is most likely a veteran needleworker who'll offer up the kind of camaraderie that can be hard to find in even the most active online crafting forum.

I also find that I'm often disappointed when I buy threads based on color cards or images on my computer screen. You just can't judge a color until you've seen the thread itself. Another advantage of playing with threads in the store is that you can press or twist together various skeins to see which hues look best when combined.

To keep things simple, start out by getting only what you need to use for the practice board (located between the first and second parts of this book, just before the projects). Learn the stitches and/or make your first sampler, then build your collection of supplies from there.

Annie & Company in NYC's Upper East Side

✳ **Iron and ironing board (not pictured):** A steam iron and firmly padded tabletop ironing board are handy to have to keep fabric surfaces—and stitched projects—on the straight and narrow.

Needles

Not all needles are created equal. They can be long or short, blunt or pointy, big-eyed or small-eyed. So many options! You'll need to channel your inner Goldilocks in order to find the one that's just right for any particular project. (For more, see the chart "Mesh + Needle Size + Thread" on page 16.)

Because your needle is so crucial when it comes to stitching (it is called needlework after all), you should stock up on all the different types. Go crazy, because they're really inexpensive. Otherwise, you may end up making things difficult for yourself. I'm reminded of the old saying, "a stitch in time saves nine." Basically, solve the problem of not having the correct needle tomorrow by picking up a variety of needles today.

The study of needle-ology requires an understanding of the three basic needle attributes:

eye

point

An Eye for an Eye

The eye of the needle needs to be large enough to comfortably accommodate your thread of choice—a thick thread and a small-eyed needle will likely result in frayed strands, crossed eyes (the ones on your face), and headaches.

Size Matters

Needles come in sizes 1 to 28. These numbers don't refer to length. Rather, the larger the number, the smaller the needle. You can often get multiple sizes in one pack. The appropriate size depends on your thread and the type of fabric you're stitching or the size of the mesh you're working on. A small needle may refuse to puncture a thick fabric; a needle that's too big will leave unsightly holes in your project or could even get stuck in fine weaves.

sharp   blunt

Getting to the Point

Most needles have two ends. One end is the eye end; the other has a sharp finger-pricking tip. Some needles, however, are dull—but don't feel bad for them! Blunt tips are useful for smoothly drawing thread between the cross-threads of a fabric where the gaps naturally occur (rather than through the fibers); sharp needles are needed to puncture tighter weaves and are necessary for precise and detailed stitching.

Here are five of the most common types of needles. I recommend that each be represented (in various sizes) in your stitching arsenal—so you're prepared when the next embroidery urge hits.

embroidery needles

tapestry needles

chenille needles

sashiko needles

beading needles

✳ **Embroidery needles**, aka crewel needles, are sharp-pointed, medium-length (around 1½ inches or 40 mm long) needles with large, easily threaded eyes. They're suitable for working fine or medium threads on most kinds of fabric. They come in sizes 1 to 12. I've recommended a size 9 embroidery needle for many of the projects in this book.

✳ **Tapestry needles** are blunt-tipped, which makes them suitable for needlepoint canvas and specialty needlework

fabric such as Aida cloth (page 12)—the dull point slips easily into the open grid of holes made by the intersecting horizontal and vertical woven threads without splitting fibers. Sizes range from 13 to 28, and are selected according to the mesh size of the canvas.

✳ **Chenille needles** are sharp and have large eyes that make them ideal for heavier threads. They are good for working thick thread such as pearl cotton on densely woven fabric. They are available in sizes 13 to 26.

✳ **Sashiko needles** are usually about 2 inches long and very sharp. Their length and sturdiness make them ideal for executing sashiko stitch patterns in which the stitches must be straight and uniform. They are also great for sewing running stitches on non-sashiko projects.

✳ **Beading needles** are long and lean and are the same width from top to bottom; their thinness helps them get through beads that have very small holes. They are very flexible and should be used only for beadwork.

Needle History 101

What did the inventors of the wheel and the creators of the Internet have in common? They were wearing clothes. And those loincloths and Izods couldn't have been made were it not for another crucial bit of technology: the needle. Archaeologists have found needle artifacts that date back as far as 40,000 B.C.E. Today needles are made of steel, but our ancestors made theirs from bone, horns, and stone. Ancient Mayans, Aztecs, and other native peoples used needles made from the spines of the agave plant. This was a particularly clever way to sew: The fiber that is naturally attached to the agave plant's spines acted as thread.

stranded cotton floss

sashiko thread

pearl cotton

tapestry wool

Persian wool

crewel wool

stranded silk

Threads

In so many kinds of sewing, thread is meant to be nearly invisible. In embroidery, however, thread gets to take center stage. There's an almost dizzying array of texture, weight, fiber, and color to choose from, and each type has its advantages. The most important thing? It needs to be able to pull easily through your needle and through your fabric. If you feel like you're forcing the thread through the needle or the canvas, try another type of thread or an alternate thread weight.

In each project, a particular type and brand of thread is called for. As you start experimenting on your samplers, see what it's like to do the same stitch using different threads that vary in weight, fiber, and texture. Soon you'll start to figure out for yourself which ones seem most appropriate for certain kinds of projects. When you do, don't be afraid to try a thread that's a little different than what's called for in a pattern—as long as you are mindful of how the thread will interact with the needle and fabric. For guidance on pairing thread with your needle or with your canvas, check out the handy chart "Mesh + Needle Size + Thread" on page 16.

Here are the basic kinds of thread you're most likely to come across during a romp through your local craft store:

✳ **Stranded cotton floss** is made up of six fine strands or threads, about nine yards long, loosely wound into what's called a *skein*. It's suitable for most embroidery and needlepoint projects. DMC is the go-to brand; you can usually buy skeins individually or in packs of complementary and assorted colors.

✳ **Pearl cotton** is a 2-ply thread with serious sheen. As with tapestry wool (below), you do not separate the strands before using it. It comes in sizes 3, 5, and 8, with 3 being the lightest and 8 the heaviest. For the projects included in this book, I used both 3 and 5.

✳ **Matte embroidery cotton** is a tightly twisted five-strand thread that's not separated before stitching. Usually used on heavier fabrics and canvases, it's the preferred thread when doing sashiko.

✳ **Tapestry wool** is a twisted 4-ply yarn mostly used for stitchwork done on canvases. The strands are not separated prior to stitching. Anchor is my go-to tapestry wool brand.

✳ **Persian wool** is a double-ply wool that comes with three strands twisted together, and is used in crewel and needlepoint. Strands can be separated and/or combined for different effects. My favorite brand is Paternayan, which I used to stitch many of the projects in this book. Smooth and durable, it's sold in 8-yard skeins in more than 400 colors.

A Tale of Two Companies

For the last two decades, there have been two major names in the high-stakes embroidery thread biz: Coats & Clark and DMC. Like *A Tale of Two Cities,* the story of embroidery thread begins in both England and France.

THE THREADS OF THE UNION JACK

One of the greatest men in the history of embroidery? Napoleon Bonaparte. In 1806 he blockaded England, which meant that the country had no access to the silk it had previously imported from the East. In order to make do, the British silk thread supply company Coats & Clark started experimenting—producing twisted strands of cotton that behaved similarly to silk when used for weaving and hand sewing. In the 1880s, the company developed a six-strand soft-finished thread that could be used for machine sewing. A revelation! They called it Our New Thread, or ONT. The acronym is still the name of the embroidery floss made by Anchor—a sub-brand of Coats & Clark.

A FAMILY AFFAIR

In 1746 Jean-Henri Dollfus started a decorated fabrics company in order to capitalize on the trend toward Indian prints. Dollfus's nephew, Daniel Dollfus, took over the company at the end of the century. When he married, he added his wife's name to his own—a tradition at the time—and changed the company's name to Dollfus-Mieg & Compagnie, or DMC. Daniel Dollfus revolutionized the industry by using a thread-treatment technique called mercerizing: Cotton threads are passed through caustic soda, rendering them extra durable, strong, and silky. DMC's place in thread history was solidified by the endorsement of Thérèse de Dillmont—she was something of an embroidering celebrity in the late 1800s. She recommended the use of DMC cotton in her 1884 *Encyclopedia of Ladies' Handicrafts.* The book, which is still in print (now titled *The Complete DMC Encyclopedia of Needlework*), continues to be a helpful resource: Stitchery hasn't changed all that much since Thérèse's time!

✳ **Crewel wool** is a fine 2-ply wool that's loosely twisted. It's a kind of worsted wool—which means that the fibers of wool are combed so that they are all parallel and there are no funny kinks or breaks that would make it coarse. It is sturdier than "woolen" wool, which is not combed, and the result looks like a single strand of Persian wool. Appleton, though not called for in this book, is a popular brand that sells crewel wool in about five billion colors . . . or at least a few hundred.

✳ **Stranded silk** is similar in appearance to stranded cotton, but shinier. If you don't want to spring for the top-shelf stuff, you can get artificial silk, aka viscose rayon.

✳ **Knitting yarn** in this context is smooth wool or cotton yarn. If you've ever dabbled in knitting or crocheting, you now have a use for all those leftover skeins from old projects. (Make sure to steer clear of anything that is nubby or that varies in thickness.)

knitting yarn

Fabrics

There are three varieties of materials that you'll see most often throughout your embroidery career. These key fabrics are evenweave, non-evenweave, and nonwoven. Here's the lowdown:

Evenweave Fabrics

Evenweave fabric has an equal number of horizontal and vertical threads per inch. The number of threads per inch is called *the count*. The lower the number of the count, the bigger the holes and the coarser the fabric. The higher the count, the denser the weave and the finer the fabric. For any kind of counted thread work, evenweave fabric is a must. Think of it as the backup dancers of the fabric world: It's got serious skills and commands respect, but it should never upstage the image or pattern you're embroidering on your project. There are several kinds of evenweave fabric. Here are some that you may come across as you embroider:

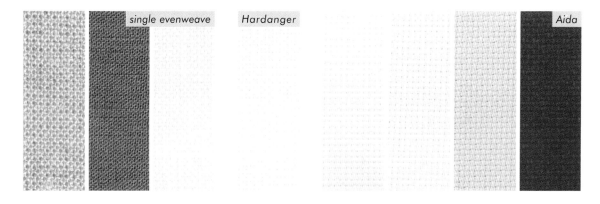

single evenweave   Hardanger   Aida

* **Single evenweave:** Like its name would suggest, this is a woven fabric with single strands of thread. It's commonly made of linen, comes in a variety of colors, and has somewhere between 18 and 30 threads per inch (aka 18- to 30-count).

* **Hardanger:** This is woven with doubled thread and usually is 22-count. It has a distinctive, blocky appearance and is usually used for counted stitch work, such as Hardanger embroidery, a Norwegian style of needlework.

* **Aida:** Usually made completely of cotton, Aida cloth has well-defined holes, making it a good option if you're doing counted cross-stitch. It's woven with multiple threads that make up the warp (vertical) and weft (horizontal) in each direction. It most commonly comes in 11- to 14-count. You might come across Aida with damask, which is fabric that includes decorative woven designs dotted with areas of Aida for your embroidering pleasure.

Non-evenweave Fabrics

This category contains pretty much everything you might have in your closet (with the possible exception of those leather chaps and that rubber catsuit). It's often used for freehand embroidery—work where the fabric will not be covered completely and therefore is integral to your design. Basically any woven, nonknit fabric falls under this umbrella: twill, satin, poplin, silk, wool, rayon, and so on. One of my favorite non-evenweaves is gingham, a medium-weight cotton that usually has a checked pattern woven into it: the crisscross of colored threads makes a grid easy for applying counted cross-stitch patterns. The checks, also with so many straight lines to follow, are ideal for practicing new stitches. Other patterned non-evenweaves can work, too, if you're following a counted cross-stitch pattern: Stripes, plaids, and even dots can act as the guidelines you need to keep your stitches evenly spaced and sized.

Nonwoven Fabrics

Nonwovens are any fabrics that are—you guessed it!—not woven, like leather, fleece, vinyl, ultrasuede, or lace. For the projects we're about to tackle, getting to know felt and knit nonwovens is most useful. Felt is made from small fibers (usually wool) that are pressed together so that they tangle and become solid. Knits are stretchy nonwovens made from interlocking loops of fiber (like the fabric used for making T-shirts). Ultrasuede, too, a synthetic ultra-microfiber fabric, is called for in at least one project.

non-evenweaves

silk

ticking

denim

poplin

cotton lawn

gingham

nonwovens

felt

knit

leather

Right vs. Wrong

Fabric has a right and a wrong side. The "right" side of a fabric doesn't have anything to do with right or left; it's the outside of the fabric or the side of the fabric that is meant to be seen. In some cases, one side of the fabric is printed or textured—this is easily identified as the right side. But in many cases, the two sides of the fabric are indistinguishable. In these instances, just pick one side that will be right and one that will be wrong and keep it consistent. You'll see references to the right side and the wrong side many times in the coming pages. In the project instructions in this book, the fabric sides are indicated by color: a color refers you to the right side, white is the wrong side.

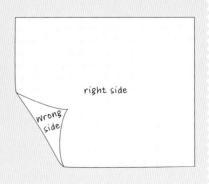

right side

wrong side

Selvage and Warp Threads and Weft, Oh My!

ny time you thread a needle in your life, there's more than likely going to be some fabric involved. It's hard to avoid the stuff—heck, you're probably wearing some right now!—and yet it's quite easy to never really consider its most basic properties. You don't need a Ph.D. in fabric in order to embroider, but understanding its basic properties will only help you as you stitch.

✳ **Weave** refers to the relationship of the threads to one another. If you ever made a looped potholder as a kid on a little square loom, you already understand the concept of "over, under, over, under." Most fabric that you use in embroidery was woven on a loom—except the loom was very big, threads were used instead of stretchy nylon loops, and it probably lived in China, not in Granny's den.

✳ **Warp threads** are the vertical ones that are placed on the loom to start out.

✳ **Weft threads** are woven perpendicularly through the warp threads. These threads run horizontally.

✳ **Selvage** refers to the natural edge of the fabric. It is a ½"-wide strip, with visible pinpricks, that looks different

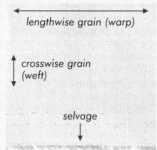

lengthwise grain (warp)

crosswise grain (weft)

selvage

from the rest of the fabric—created there as a boundary to keep the edges from fraying. The selvage runs along the sides, parallel to the warp threads. It can serve as a straight-edge guide when you're cutting fabric in which the weave is too dense—and the warp and weft threads too small—to be sure you are cutting on-grain. (For more, see "Cut to the Chase," below.)

✳ **Evenweave** is fabric in which the warp threads and weft threads are the same size and there are the same number of them per square inch. All the holes, created by the weft and warp threads, therefore, are uniform. Most counted thread embroidery work is executed on evenweave fabric.

✳ **Non-evenweave** is fabric made of warp and weft threads that may be of different sizes and/or more numerous in one direction than the other. It is possible to work counted thread techniques on non-evenweave fabric if you use cloth that has an even, geometric checked print on it, such as gingham or some plaids, or if you use waste canvas (see "Waste Not, Want Not," page 15), which will give you a grid that you can follow and then remove.

Cut to the Chase

or several projects, you'll need to cut straight lines that are "on grain." This means you need to cut exactly parallel to the direction the threads are woven. To do this, use a T-square or two rulers and lay one side flush against the edge of the

selvage (A). Only make cuts that are perpendicular or parallel to these lines, and make sure the selvage ultimately gets cut away. Cutting "off grain" will make things funky—and not in a good way. If you're using a scrap of fabric that has no selvage,

lay it on a flat surface, find a thread on one end and gently tug it while pulling the rest of the fabric in the opposite direction (B). If the thread pulls evenly, it will leave a straight line that you can use as a straight edge in lieu of the selvage.

A.

selvage

B.

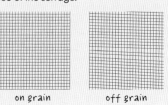

on grain   off grain

Canvas

If you're diving into the exciting world of needlepoint, you'll need to know a bit about canvases. Needlepoint, also sometimes called canvas work, is about using thread to fully cover a canvas, which is made of evenly woven cotton or stiff plastic mesh. Canvases are identified by different gauges—the gauge or mesh number refers to the number of threads or holes per inch. Mesh sizes are usually indicated following a hash mark, as in #18 for a canvas that has eighteen threads per inch. The bigger the number, the finer the mesh and the smaller the holes.

Plastic Canvas

Plastic canvas is a good option for beginner and/or kid-friendly projects; because of its rigidity it doesn't require a hoop or frame and the edges won't fray. You can cut it into shapes, which makes it ideal for making things like tissue boxes or coasters or earrings. Go crazy! The most common kinds of plastic canvas are semitransparent 7-mesh sheets, but I used a 10 mesh for the Color Theory Coasters on page 157.

Fabric Canvas

Fabric canvases are made from woven cotton; they're more flexile than plastic canvases. There are two main kinds:

✳ **Mono canvas:** Also called plain single canvas, this is made up of single threads creating evenly spaced holes. It is usually anywhere between 10 mesh (which means big holes that can accommodate thick yarns) and 18 mesh (for finer, more detailed work).

✳ **Penelope canvas:** Also called double canvas or double mesh, Penelope has pairs of threads. Because of its weave and double weft and warp threads, some holes are bigger than others. You can stitch over each pair of threads or you can go into the smaller holes to work finer details. Because its holes are smaller than on a mono canvas of a similar gauge, it's better at holding stitches solidly in place. It is available in mesh sizes 7 to 20.

Waste Not, Want Not

Waste canvas is a hard-working material, but while its cousins end up as pillows and wall hangings, waste canvas ultimately goes into the trash. But don't shed any tears for it; waste canvas is here to help you! It is used as a stitching guide for working counted thread embroidery, such as a cross-stitch. Made of starch-stiffened threads, you can tack this evenweave canvas onto your work to temporarily impose a grid over any fabric you choose (attach it using long impermanent basting stitches), and comes in 8.5, 10, 14, and 18 squares per inch. It acts kind of like a secret weapon: After you work a cross-stitch pattern on the waste canvas, use a damp cloth to help dissolve the starch and then pick out the canvas's threads using tweezers. Voilà!

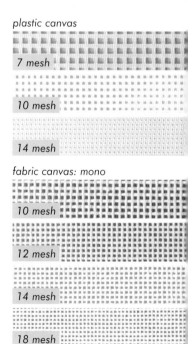

plastic canvas

7 mesh

10 mesh

14 mesh

fabric canvas: mono

10 mesh

12 mesh

14 mesh

18 mesh

fabric canvas: penelope

Mesh + Needle Size + Thread = A Delicate Combo

Once you've got your tapestry needle, design, and thread, you're ready to go, right? Not just yet. You still have to figure out how many strands of floss and what size needle you should use with your canvas of choice. After you've selected your canvas, start with its mesh size and read the table horizontally to determine the needle and thread size best suited to your stitch surface.

Canvas mesh HOLES PER INCH	Needle size	Embroidery floss	Persian wool	Tapestry wool	Crewel wool	Pearl cotton
7	15/16		5			
10	18		3	1		
12	20		2	1	5–6	3
14	20/22	6–9	2		5	3
16	22	4–7	1		4	4
18 to 20	22/24	3–5	1		3	4

The Scoop on Hoops

I used to turn up my nose at the very idea of hoops. Not for me, thank you very much. This was mostly because I like to travel light, and. I also didn't want to waste the handful of seconds it takes to put fabric in a hoop. My time is precious, darn it! However, as I became a more experienced stitcher, I started to see that a hoop *can* be an embroiderer's best friend.

We don't ask much of our fabric in embroidery—after all, you can use almost any surface, and mostly it just needs to lay there and look pretty—but we do appreciate it when it stays smooth and firm. When you want to stitch a gossamer handkerchief, for instance, a hoop comes to the rescue by providing the tension across the fabric to create a smooth stitch area. Some stitches, like the basic satin stitch (page 40) and chain stitch (page 34) are far easier to execute on firm fabric. Hoops are made of wood, plastic, or metal, and usually are fairly affordable. Even if you decide you feel more comfortable embroidering without one, it's not a bad idea to have one on hand just in case there's an embroidering emergency—hand me a hoop, stat! Hoops are also a nice way to display your work.

There are many different kinds of hoops, but at their most basic they consist of two rings, one that fits inside another. Whether you use wood, metal, or plastic is largely up to you. I like to use a high-quality birchwood handheld hoop made in Germany and imported by a company called Hardwicke Manor, but there are many brands and types out there for you to try.

Taking a Stand

Handheld hoops are great for riding on the train or cuddling up on the couch, but for large-scale projects, you may want to opt for a propped hoop that can free up both your hands. This way, you can keep one hand above your work and one below so that you can feed the needle back and forth. It makes the stab method (stitching in and out of the fabric, page 27) a lot faster.

standing floor hoop

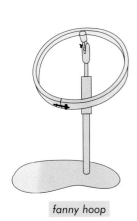

fanny hoop

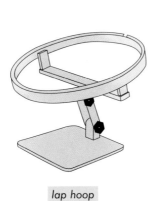

lap hoop

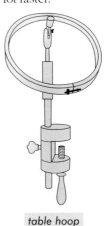

table hoop

* **Fanny hoop, or sitting hoop:** This embroidery apparatus involves a hoop attached to a stem that, in turn, attaches to a flat panel that is parallel to the hoop. The bottom panel of the fanny hoop slides under your bottom—which should be planted in a firm chair.

* **Lap hoop:** This embroidery tool, which resembles a makeup mirror, sits on a table or, as its name would suggest, on your lap. The advantage of working with a lap hoop is that it is portable; unfortunately, its portability also makes it more wobbly—and unstable—than its Fanny and Standing cousins.

* **Table hoop:** In this setup, the hoop is clamped to a table. Its screws can usually be manipulated to raise or lower the hoop. This is a nice tool as long as your work table isn't also your kitchen table, dining table, and desk: constantly screwing and unscrewing the thing so that you can serve dinner can get tiresome.

* **Standing floor hoop:** This style comes in various sizes; it may have one telescoping neck attached to a foot or a couple of legs to keep it sturdy. They're usually lightweight and can be easily moved and stowed out of the way during the hours of your day devoted to things other than embroidery.

Mrs. Pompadour and Her Tambour

Hoops and frames are sometimes called *tambours*, an old French word for *drum*, which refers to the drumlike nature of the hooped work. There's a famous eighteenth-century painting at the National Gallery in London called *Madame de Pompadour at Her Tambour Frame*. Madame is using a tambour frame that looks identical to ones that can still be purchased today.

Frames

There are certain delicate fabrics, like satin or damask, that can be marred by the friction and pressure of the two pieces of the hoop and are therefore better suited to square frames. Many other embroidery projects, especially needlepoint worked on canvas that is larger than 6 inches square, are best worked on a frame. There are two things to keep in mind when using one: First, make sure your canvas and your frame are both at least 2 inches larger than your finished piece. Second, you'll want to bind the raw edges of the canvas with artist tape to prevent them from fraying. Apply the tape before you put the canvas on the frame. To do so, cut a length of tape an inch or two longer than the edge you're binding, folding it in half lengthwise along the edge as you apply it, then trim away the excess tape at the ends (fig 1.1a). Use a bone folder, or even a butter knife, to smooth the tape and burnish it in place (fig 1.1b). There are two types of frames that most stitch artists use:

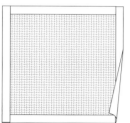

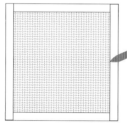

Fig. 1.1a   *Fig. 1.1b*

* **Needlepoint stretcher bars:** These inexpensive interlocking wood bars are easy to assemble—the sides of the frame simply slot together. They look a lot like artist's canvas stretchers, but you want the type that is made for stitching. Purchase them in pairs at needlework shops, craft supply stores, or online. Brass thumbtacks are used to attach the canvas to the edges of the frame.

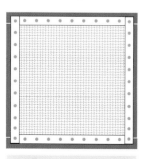

needlepoint stretcher bars

* **Slate frame:** This frame, which likely got its name because it resembles the chalk slates children used to use at school, has rollers on its top and bottom and stretchers on its sides. You hand-sew your work to the webbing on the rollers; then, using floss and large looping stitches, the fabric canvas is secured to the stretchers. For long pieces, you can adjust the canvas so it will scroll onto the rollers. Some slate frames do not have adjustable rollers, but the piece is fastened to the frame in the same way.

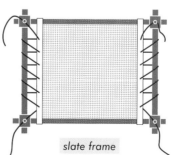

slate frame

Getting Organized

Embroiderers can travel light—conveniently, many of your embroidery projects will be small enough to tote around with you. There are downsides, however, to working with so many small and portable tools: threads get tangled, canvases can get dirty or pulled out of shape, and moving materials from place to place increases the chances of a needle accidentally falling to the floor—not good if you're working around your kids or pets!

flat zippered pouch

To keep things as orderly as possible, I store my supplies in a sewing or tackle box: My projects live in stowaway scrapbook boxes. These flat containers stack easily and are just the right size for projects. I recommend using transparent containers, like a flat zippered pouch (top right), so you don't have to open each one in order to see what's inside.

Most craft stores sell embroidery floss organizers. These small plastic cases have rows of dividers and come with paper cards on which you can wind all of your threads (middle right). You can also buy colored plastic cards that will fit in the rows. If you have multiple projects going at once, put each project's threads on like-colored cards so that you can quickly spot which threads you need. Winding the thread on the cards can be a Zen-like activity that results in a rainbow of thread packets. Pretty, pretty! Wind your paper cards loosely to avoid making creases in your thread.

case with dividers

Needles are wily and dangerous little things. After they're out of their packaging, I keep mine in a magnetic needle safe, which is a plastic container lined inside with magnets (bottom right). With no desire to be a human pincushion, I am happy knowing that any sharp wannabe deserters are in lockdown. If you're using one or more large-eyed needles for a project, here's a handy way to keep your needles in order when you're not using them: Insert a small safety pin through the eye of the needles and pin it directly to the fabric you're working on.

magnetic needle safe

Once you have your tools in order, it's time to get to work. So many colors and textures—so much possibility! In the next chapters, I'll give you a quick round-up of some of the (many) styles and techniques of embroidery and help you put everything together in order to "draw" with fibers and embellish, decorate, create, and manipulate fabric and threads. Ready, brave warrior?

CHAPTER 2

Get Ready, Get Set

o, you've got the gear. If you were getting set for a road trip, your car would be well oiled by now and filled with a tank of gas. Maps? Check. Potato chips? Check. iPod? Check. Now, if only you knew how to drive . . .

Welcome to Embroidery 101. Fasten your seatbelt, check your mirrors, and get ready to learn all you need to know in order to get behind the . . . needle.

But first things first—let's talk about things you need to think about before you even touch any fabric or canvas. That's right: Step away from the car!

Prepare Your Needle and Thread

Start Your Thread

Embroidery thread is packaged in two ways: a pull skein or a hank. It's important to figure out which type you're working with before you try cutting it so you don't end up with a tangled mess. Stranded embroidery floss, tapestry wool, and Persian wool are most commonly in *pull skeins*. Pull skeins are good to go: with the paper labels still in place, gently tug straight down on the cut end sticking out from the bottom of the skein (fig. 2.1).

Fig. 2.1

A *hank* of thread is a looped and twisted bundle of thread. Pearl cotton, matte embroidery floss, crewel wool, and many knitting yarns will come in a hank. With a hank, look for the double loop at the bottom of the thread. Cut the folded ends, then cut away the knot (fig. 2.2a). Slide the labels up slightly (but don't remove them) and pull each length of thread as needed (fig. 2.2b). As with pull skeins, the labels are keeping the thread nice and neat. Another option for extracting thread from both types of packaging is to wind it onto thread cards and store it in a case with dividers (see page 9).

Cut Your Thread

The thread or strand you start working with should never be longer than the length of your arm (fig. 2.3). I try to keep my working strands about 18 inches (roughly the distance from my thumb to my bicep). Strands longer than 24 inches have a tendency to tangle or fray after being pulled through the fabric too many times. Measure and snip.

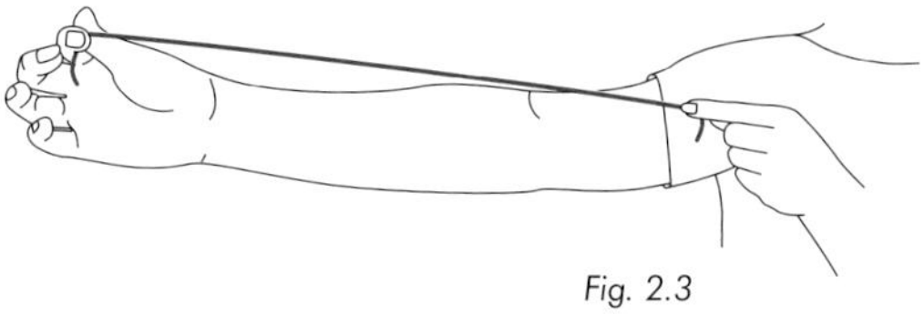

Fig. 2.2a   *Fig. 2.2b*

Fig. 2.3

Divide the Strands

Most embroidery floss is made up of several strands, or plies (indicated as *ply* on the packaging), that are twisted together—and many projects will require the use of only a few strands held together. To separate strands, pinch a couple of the threads between two fingers and grasp the others in your mouth. Hold the ends of the remaining strands in your free hand and gently untwist while you pull the strands away (fig. 2.4a). Continue until you have as many single strands as you need.

Fig. 2.4a

Once you have emancipated some working strands, lay them out and flatten them with your fingers. Separating them in this way will make the threads less likely to twist or tangle while you're working with them and your stitches will be neater. Then take however many you need for your project and recombine them (fig. 2.4b).

Fig. 2.4b

TIP: Pucker up! Here's my secret for keeping threads untangled: I use lip balm. Once I recombine the threads, I run them through my freshly beeswaxed lips in order to seal them neatly together.

Fig. 2.5

Thread Your Needle

You can't embroider without a threaded needle, and luckily, it's not such a complicated procedure. My personal system involves using my tongue to dampen the very tip of a freshly cut end of thread (no frayed strands, please). Then I find some good lighting and guide the moistened tip into the needle's eye (fig. 2.5). In particularly pesky situations, try rotating the needle: With machine-made sewing needles, one side of the eye is usually slightly bigger than the other.

Here are three tricks of the trade when it comes to needle threading:

✳ **Loop method:** Fold the thread over the shaft of the needle (fig. 2.6a) and then pinch the loop that forms. Slip the loop off the shaft and through the eye (fig. 2.6b). Voilà! Pull the thread until the short end of the fold is all the way through. This method works well with needles that are size 10 or larger.

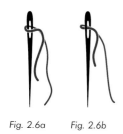

Fig. 2.6a   Fig. 2.6b

the loop method

✳ **Paper-strip method:** Cut a 2-inch-long piece of paper to the same width as the eye of your needle. Fold the strip in half lengthwise and then insert the thread between the two halves (fig. 2.7a). Pinch the thread and the paper together at the opening and push the fold through the eye (fig. 2.7b). Remove the paper, and the thread will remain. This works best with slightly larger needles.

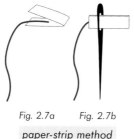

Fig. 2.7a   Fig. 2.7b

paper-strip method

✳ **Manual needle threader:** If you're really having trouble with this all-important first step, this disc-shaped doodad attached to a diamond-shaped wire loop will help you through hard times. The wire collapses easily to pass through the eye of the needle (fig. 2.8a). Thread the floss through the wire loop (fig. 2.8b), then pull the needle back over the wire (fig. 2.8c). The hooks on the sides of the threader may be used for thicker threads like wool and pearl cotton. As I mention in "The Ultimate Embroider Everything Kit" (pages 3–7) it's worth investing a couple bucks in a sturdy one if you think you'll use it a lot.

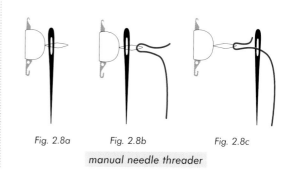

Fig. 2.8a   Fig. 2.8b   Fig. 2.8c

manual needle threader

Tie a Knot

Knots are verboten in the world of traditional embroidery, but I'm not a purist about such things. In my experience, they're not usually that obtrusive, as long as they're small and neat and are kept on the wrong side of your work. Here's how to do a quick stitcher's knot.

Fig. 2.9a

Note: These instructions are written for right-handed stitchers. If you're left-handed, reverse the instructions.

1. Thread the needle, maintaining a tail that's 2 to 3 inches long. With your left hand, hold the needle horizontally with the shaft pointing left and the eye, right (fig. 2.9a).

2. Place the tail on top of the shaft of the needle with its cut end pointing toward the eye. Pinch the tail end and the needle shaft with your right index finger and thumb.

Fig. 2.9b

3. Use your left thumb and index finger to wrap the thread that's near the point around the needle two or three times (fig 2.9b).

4. Pinch the wrapped thread between your left thumb and index finger and slide it toward the eye of the needle and down the length of the thread (fig. 2.9c). Don't let go as you slide—you're forming the knot as you go. Why hello there, little knot! Now you're ready to stitch.

Fig. 2.9c

Many embroiderers refuse to start their work with knots because of the bulk it might add, not to mention the messiness. Ideally, you want the back of your work to look just as neat as the front. There are several methods for starting your work without a knot. Keep reading.

How to Back Out of a Stitch

If you find, once you start embroidering, that you're not happy with a stitch—no problem. Just back out the offending stitch. To do so, unthread your needle (A), then use the point of the needle to pick out the thread (B)—make sure to catch all strands of the stitch, and be careful not to snag the fabric. Rethread your needle (facing page) and get back to work!

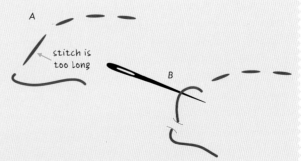

A

stitch is too long

B

Away Waste Knot

1. Put a small overhand knot at the end of the thread. No need for anything fancy—this waste knot is only temporary.

2. Insert the needle into the right side (also "correct" or pretty side) of your fabric or canvas at a point at least 1 inch from where you plan to start stitching your design. The needle should push through from above so that the knot is visible on the right side of the fabric.

3. Bring the needle back up at the point where you are going to start stitching. Work your next few stitches over the thread so that the thread is secured to the back of your piece (fig. 2.10).

Fig. 2.10

4. Cut the knot with embroidery scissors.

Waste Backstitch

Use this technique if the first stitches you're working are not suitable for enclosing the end of your thread.

1. Without knotting your thread, insert the needle into the right side of the fabric 1 inch from where you plan to start stitching. Leave a 3-inch tail on the right side of your work.

2. Make three or four backstitches (page 32) leading up to your starting point. They don't have to be pretty—they're not going to be around for long (fig. 2.11).

Fig. 2.11

3. When you are done working that area or that color thread, pick out the waste backstitches that you made with the tip of your needle (page 23).

4. Use that 3-inch tail you left to thread a needle.

5. Weave the tail through a couple of stitches on the wrong side, then carefully snip off any remaining thread with embroidery scissors.

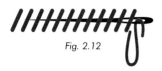

Fastening off

Fig. 2.12

When you finish your stitching, leave a few inches of thread at the end so you can weave the end through stitches at the back of your piece. This should keep the thread in place as long as no pet claws ever come near it (fig. 2.12).

Hooping Your Work

If you've decided that a hoop is the way to go (page 16), there are a few things to consider when you're selecting one. Pick a hoop that is large enough so that, if possible, no part of the design you are working is closer than one inch from its sides. When in doubt about the size, go with the larger-size hoop so that you can work big areas without constantly having to readjust the whole thing (which can cause unnecessary wrinkling of the fabric). Ideally, though, look for a hoop that is close in size to your design for maximum tension and ease of use. Let's get started—here are the four steps to hooping your work:

1. Loosening the screw on the adjustable outer ring to separate the two rings of the hoop (inner and outer).

2. On a table or other flat surface, place the smaller inner ring underneath your fabric, centering it beneath the middle of the area you plan to work (fig. 2.13a).

3. Place the outer ring on top of the inner ring, then gently pull the fabric taut as you use your palms to apply pressure to push down the outer ring (fig. 2.13b). Tug the fabric gently and evenly in every direction. Uneven pulling can cause the fabric's warp and weft threads to lose their perpendicular integrity.

4. Tighten the screw until the outer ring fits securely over the inner ring.

Note: The inner ring and the outer ring of an embroidery hoop may not be completely flush with each other (edges lined up and flat). That's fine as long as the fabric sandwiched between them is stretched tightly like a drumhead.

Extending the Hoop

If you're embroidering a corner or very near the bottom of your fabric, you might not be able to hoop your work. Solution? Use basting stitches (see "Basting Away," page 31) to temporarily attach a larger piece of scrap fabric to the wrong side (or back) of the fabric you will be stitching. Hoop the larger fabric and the problem is solved. When you're done, scrap the scraps, and voilà!

Baste your work to a larger piece for stitching ease.

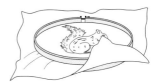

Fig. 2.13a

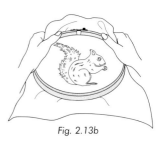

Fig. 2.13b

TIP: If you're working with fabric that can wrinkle or crease easily, or want to protect completed stitches that might fall under part of the ring, use twill tape or a long, 1-inch-wide swath of scrap fabric to wrap the inner ring. Then stitch the ends of the tape in place to keep it from shifting.

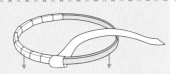

Always stitch with plenty of light and in a chair with good back support.

All the Better to See You With

No one wants to go around wielding needles in the dark. Someone might lose an eye! It's therefore crucial that you have enough glare-free light when you're stitching. This could mean leaving your shady room to show your embroidery what life is like on a park bench. Or it might mean just putting a daylight bulb in the lamp next to your favorite chair. I even know some embroiderers who carry book lights with them so they have enough light to stitch in cars (not while driving, of course). LED head lamps work well too, if you don't mind looking like a spelunker. If you're a righty, try to have the light coming over your left shoulder; and vice versa if you're a lefty.

Get Your Stitch On

A few years ago, my friend got me a supercool vintage armchair. Dozens of bottoms had clearly worked hard for decades to wear in the seat just for me. I didn't just sit in this chair: I moved in. I probably spent a week straight stitching in this amazing chair. I was all cozy and curled up in it with my back rounded and my feet folded at my side or tucked under me. Heaven!

Or maybe not. My body soon stopped feeling comfortable in any position. For every minute of comfort in the chair, I spent a day massaging my lower back trying desperately to stand without looking like a question mark. It was a painful lesson to learn.

Stitching might be a leisure-time activity, but if you're not careful it can be awfully hard on your body. Before you sit down to a project, figure out a sustainable work position. That might mean sitting at your desk with a good office chair—look for one that has good lumbar support and forces your knees to rest lower than your pelvis. (Ergonomic kneeling chairs or saddle seats, force your back into an S-curve, which is important to maintain if you don't want to end up looking like Quasimodo.)

But here's the real secret to keeping your body from aching: Take breaks! Your eyes and fingers need periodic rests just as much as the rest of your body does. Go for a trip to the fridge and back. Take the dog around the block. Treat yourself to a nap. Remember: Everything in moderation, even—dare I say it—stitching!

CHAPTER 3

Start Stitching

While there are many ways in which various embroidery techniques overlap, each one still requires a particular skill. Here, you'll learn the different kinds of embroidery used in the projects in this book as well as how to complete each of the stitch styles and how to follow a pattern. The schools of stitching covered here are:

* Freehand Embroidery
* Needlepoint
* Smocking
* Counted Thread

So let's dive right in and get to know some of the families that live in Embroidery Town.

How to Maneuver Your Needle
Stitching 101

There are two methods for making a stitch: the stab method and the sewing method. Which one you should employ depends on the stitch you're stitching.

The stab method is worked in two movements. After the thread is brought to the right side to begin (fig. 3.1a), push the needle through the fabric, down to the wrong side (fig. 3.1b), and then bring the needle straight back up again. The thread passes vertically through the surface.

To make a stitch that requires the sewing method, take the needle in and out of the fabric at a shallow angle and pull the needle through in one movement (fig. 3.2). The needle will not be pulled to the back side of the work.

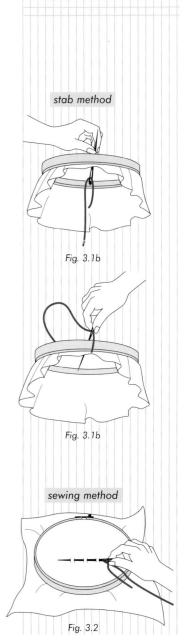

stab method

Fig. 3.1b

Fig. 3.1b

sewing method

Fig. 3.2

Freehand Embroidery

Counted thread embroidery and needlepoint, cover your ears. Okay, now that they're not listening, I can tell you the truth: Freehand embroidery is the most popular kid in the embroidery classes these days. It seems to be what a lot of people are most excited to learn. Yay you, freehand embroidery! Of course, I'm always rooting a bit for the underdog, too, and I'm such a nerd for needlepoint and counted thread work—the patterns and rules and lines are heaven to me. But sometimes I'm in the mood just to doodle with my needle. In these cases, I can do freehand stitching and make images where and how I please. If I feel like following a pattern, there's a never-ending amount available for stitchers. They can be preprinted heat-transfer patterns or ones of my own design.

Part of the beauty of freehand embroidery is the fact that you can strut your stuff with lots of different techniques and styles to make something beautiful, or you can use just one kind of simple stitch to create a masterpiece. What's more, patterns can be pretty forgiving: Follow it to a T or embellish it with your own ideas. Want to put devil's horns on a vintage pattern of a teddy bear? Some legs and arms on a pineapple? By all means! Really, the possibilities are endless.

Meet the Freehand Embroidery Stitches

As you start stitching, you'll begin to find that a new stitch may have as much of an effect on your piece as a new color. Indeed, I think that freehand embroidery stitches have a lot in common with the colors of the rainbow. We all know the basic members of the color family: red, orange, yellow, green, blue, and purple. But then there are all the subtle variations and in betweens. Same goes with stitching.

When it comes to freehand embroidery on fabric, the main families are:

* Straight stitches   * Blanket stitches   * Cross-stitches
* Backstitches   * Feather stitches   * Knotted stitches
* Chain stitches   * Satin stitches   * Couching stitches

Once you get to know one member of this family, the rest are really easy to relate to. If you can master these nine basic needle maneuvers, you'll be golden.

If you're just starting out, embroider on gingham. The checked pattern will act as a grid and help you visually keep track of how long and how far apart your stitches are, making it much easier to create perfectly even stitches right out of the gate. A 12-inch square of fabric should do you just fine. However, you don't have to feel bound by the suggestion: Any woven fabric will work. (For the moment, stay away from fabric that has any kind of stretch to it. There are ways of working on stretchy stuff, but we'll get to that later.)

Hooping the fabric (so you're working on a taut surface) will also make for better stitching; turn to "Hooping Your Work," page 25, for instructions. You'll also need a size 9 embroidery needle, a skein of cotton embroidery floss, a fabric marking pen or pencil, and a pair of embroidery scissors—if you compiled the Ultimate Embroider Everything Kit (pages 3–7), you should have everything you need except the fabric.

Before working your first stitch, remember to complete the four following steps:

1. Pull the free end of the skein of floss, as shown on page 21, and cut an arm's length (from wrist to shoulder).

2. Separate the recommended number of strands (try using 4 strands on the Practice Stitch Card) and tie a knot at the end (see page 23 for options).

3. Bring the threaded needle up through the fabric, working from back to front, or wrong side to right side, so the knot is anchored on the wrong side of the fabric.

4. When you run out of thread, repeat Steps 1–3.

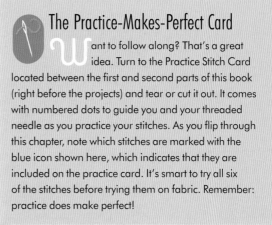

The Practice-Makes-Perfect Card

Want to follow along? That's a great idea. Turn to the Practice Stitch Card located between the first and second parts of this book (right before the projects) and tear or cut it out. It comes with numbered dots to guide you and your threaded needle as you practice your stitches. As you flip through this chapter, note which stitches are marked with the blue icon shown here, which indicates that they are included on the practice card. It's smart to try all six of the stitches before trying them on fabric. Remember: practice does make perfect!

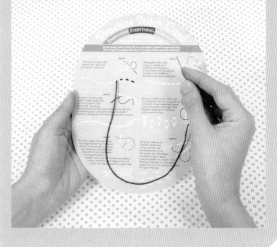

Straight Stitches

You could embroider from here to eternity using only this, the easiest, most approachable stitch, the straight stitch. A series of basic straight stitches are often used as outlines when embroidering a design on fabric. But a straight stitch can actually be worked in three ways: either as a single stitch (straight stitch), in a row (running stitch), or as a random grouping or cluster (seed stitch).

Get to know the family:

Straight Stitch

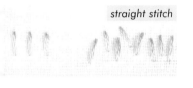

straight stitch

The straight stitch is as simple as an embroidery stitch can be. Insert the threaded needle into the back of the fabric and bring it to the front at 1. Insert the needle back down into the front of the fabric at 2, approximately ⅛ to ¼ inch up from 1 (fig. 3.4). A single straight stitch is extremely versatile, since it can be worked to any length and any angle with any thread.

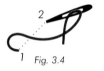

Fig. 3.4

Running Stitch

The running stitch is a row or line of straight stitches made one right after the other, "running" the needle and thread in and out of the fabric. Considered by many to be a foundation stitch of embroidery, the running stitch is great for outlining images and is actually the only stitch that is used for sashiko style embroidery (see Sashiko Top and Tunic, page 86). It should be worked from right to left using a long and sturdy embroidery needle (or, if you have one on hand, a sashiko needle). Running stitches should be approximately ⅛ to ¼ inch long or as desired—the key to creating a good running stitch is to make your stitches the same size and equally spaced, which is much easier said than done.

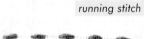

running stitch

The best way to achieve even stitching is to work the stitch like a quilter does, using the sewing method (see "How to Maneuver Your Needle," page 27): Rock the needle in and out of the fabric, always keeping the needle on the right side, or top surface, of the fabric. You should always be able to see the needle when you work the running stitch; it should never completely disappear to the back. Come up at 1, down at 2, then up at 3, without pulling the thread through to the underside of the fabric. Go down at 4 and up at 5 (fig. 3.5). Always take two or three stitches

Fig. 3.5

on the needle before you pull your thread through, looking at the parts of the needle where you see the fabric and making sure that the spaces are even. (When worked correctly, the length of exposed needle between the stitches should be equal to the length of the fabric on the needle.) Then pull the needle gently, easing the thread through so the fabric does not pucker.

Seed Stitch

A cluster of straight stitches placed randomly at contrasting angles and used to fill in a design area on a project—known in embroidery-speak as a *filling* or *filler* stitch—is called a seed stitch. (I actually think the stitches look like sprinkles, especially when worked with multiple thread colors, but I admit "sprinkles stitch" would sound silly.) To make the first stitch, simply go up at 1 and down at 2 (fig. 3.6). Maintaining uniform stitch length (as with the other straight stitches), continue to work stitches at varying angles, "traveling" across the stitching area in whatever direction you choose.

Fig. 3.6

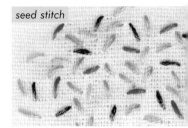

seed stitch

Basting Away

Basting is worked the same as a running stitch but with longer (¼- to ⅜-inch) stitches—and there's no pressure to make the stitches as even. It has gained quite a reputation for its rather impressive disappearing act—since basting is considered to be temporary, it's a stitch that you'll never actually see on a piece of finished embroidery work. Basting is usually done using an all-purpose sewing thread or a single strand of embroidery floss in a bright color that contrasts with your fabric surface. You might use a basting stitch to:

* Tack down a piece of waste canvas (page 15) to temporarily hold it in place while you're embroidering through it.

* Secure your canvas to the webbing in order to stretch it onto the scroll rods of a slate frame (see "Frames," page 18).

* Attach a piece of fabric to the edge of your work so that you can hoop it (see "Extending the Hoop," page 25).

* Transfer a pattern using tissue paper or stabilizer (see "Basting," page 77).

Backstitches

The backstitch family is closely related to the straight stitch family and resembles a row of machine stitching. In fact, it's the sturdiest of embroidery stitches around and is often used to sew two pieces of fabric together by hand (page 237). In every case, the needle moves "back" one stitch before it takes one stitch forward along the stitch line, hence the name. Unlike the running stitch, the backstitch is a continuous line, meaning there are no fabric spaces in between the stitches, and it will completely cover a solid line that was drawn or transferred onto the fabric. An ideal drawing tool, backstitches can be worked in straight lines, curves, circles, spirals, and more, and is often used in needlepoint and counted thread work.

Get to know the family:

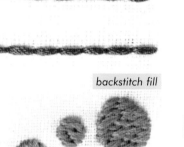

backstitch

backstitch fill

Backstitch

To start, sew a single straight stitch from left to right (up at 1 and down at 2), bringing the needle to the wrong side (back) of the work. Move the needle one stitch length away to the left and bring it up through the fabric at 3 (fig. 3.7). Make a straight stitch to the right and into 1 (the needle should enter the fabric in exactly the same hole). Repeat, and the resulting line of stitches will be continuous. You can make the backstitch long or short—it depends on the look you're going for, but all the stitches should be equal in length. You can also work backstitch closely together, for filling (left).

Fig. 3.7

Just Bead It!

Do you love beads? Of course you do. What's not to love? Adding shiny little seed beads to your embroidered work is a nice way to add some bling to any piece. All you need to do is thread one bead (or however many you want) onto your needle whenever you bring it up through the fabric to make a running stitch or a backstitch. Hold the bead down so it's snug against the fabric, and then just continue on with your stitching. Or go ahead and put on another bead! Word to the wise: Do not attempt to bead with anything but a beading needle (see page 9). If you use another kind of needle, there is a good chance that your bead will get stuck on the needle eye.

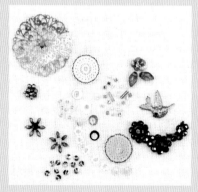

Beading adds sparkle to embroidery.

Split Stitch

This stitch, like the basic backstitch, is worked left to right. It's aptly named; to do it, you use the needle to split the thread. It's best worked with a soft, untwisted thread and multiple strands, since they are easier to split. Also known as the Kensington outline stitch, it can be used both for outlining and, when rows of stitches are worked closely together, for filling (split stitch fill, right).

split stitch

split stitch fill

Begin with one straight stitch, working from left to right (bringing the needle up at 1 and down at 2 (fig. 3.8a). Now bring the needle back up at 3, through the middle of the stitch you just worked. Pull the thread through and go down at 4 to make the next stitch (fig. 3.8b). Continue, piercing the previous stitch (fig. 3.8c). You want to be as accurate as possible: If you are stitching with four strands, make sure you split with two on each side of the needle.

A fun variation of this stitch is to use strands in two different colors. Split each stitch between the different-colored strands, always keeping the same color placement. The result is a multicolored stitch that can jazz up any outline.

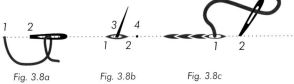

Fig. 3.8a   Fig. 3.8b   Fig. 3.8c

Stem Stitch (aka Crewel Stitch)

Stem stitch, as its name would suggest, is an appropriate stitch for making stems on flowers and is one of the oldest embroidery stitches, dating from ancient Egypt and Peru. It, too, is worked from left to right. To start, draw a line on your fabric. Make a single straight stitch on the line (up at 1 and down at 2). Now bring your needle back up just above the line at 3, centered between where your last stitch came up and where it went down (fig. 3.9a). Keep your working thread below the needle. Continue, making sure to keep all your stitches even in length. This stitch will produce a curved line, arching away from you. For a straight line of stitches, make the first straight stitch on a diagonal along the line you're working (fig. 3.9b). For a thicker line, bring the needle down just below the line. This will create stitches that are more noticeably diagonal. When properly stitched, stem stitch looks like a strand of rope. If your stem stitches start to look untidy, they're likely too long. Keep the stitches small and even to create a smooth and pretty line.

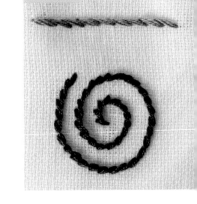

stem stitch

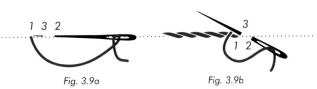

Fig. 3.9a   Fig. 3.9b

Chain Stitches

These are stitches that attach to one another just like . . . chains. Chains involve looping the thread (usually by putting it under the needle's tip) before putting your needle back into the fabric (see "Working the Loop-D-Loop," page 36). Most chain stitches are worked vertically either as an outline, in close rows as a filling, as a decorative border, or as a single "detached" chain. Members of this family can be challenging to stitch as they require an even thread tension—the loops should have a consistent shape or roundness. Pull too hard on the thread and you'll be out of the loop!

Get to know the family:

chain stitch

Chain Stitch

As a longtime knitter, this is one of my favorite stitches. A row of the interconnected stitches are like the embroidered version of a knit stitch.

This stitch is worked vertically from top to bottom so that the resulting stitches look like upside-down *V*s. Bring your needle up at 1. Take the needle to the right, creating a loop on the fabric, as you insert the needle at 1a (right next to 1). Bring the needle back to the right side of the work at 2, which will be in the center of the loop (fig. 3.11a). Pull on the thread while you use the thumb of your nondominant hand to hold the loop in place. Take another stitch at 2a (right next to 2), and up at 3, pulling to make the loop the same length as the previously worked stitch (fig. 3.11b). Continue as before, being careful not to tighten the thread so much that you lose the chain. To end the stitch, make one small vertical straight stitch over the final loop as shown (fig. 3.11c). (Guess what, that very last stitch was your first detached chain stitch! See next page.) The basic chain stitch is great for both straight and curved lines. Visually, it's a little thicker and less dense than running and stem stitches.

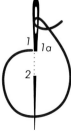

Fig. 3.11a

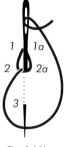

Fig. 3.11b

Fig. 3.11c

Detached Chain Stitch

To create little petal shapes, simply stitch a single chain as described in basic chain stitch, then finish it with a small vertical straight stitch (figs. 3.12 a–b). They can be worked in a neat line or in clusters in lots of directions (just make sure that they are close enough together that the thread on the wrong side of your work doesn't cause the fabric to pucker). When clustered together and stitched in the same direction, I think detached chains look like raindrops; when scattered randomly they remind me of seeds or falling snow. Make the finishing straight stitch a little longer for a slightly different effect—a bunch of them standing up straight resembles a cluster of tiny leaves or reeds.

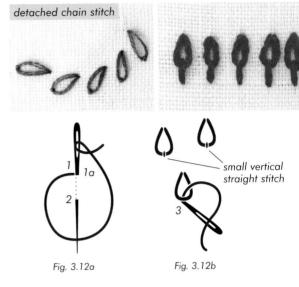

detached chain stitch

small vertical straight stitch

Fig. 3.12a   Fig. 3.12b

Ready, Set, Doodle

Before you drove on the highway for the first time, you sought out opportunities to tackle smaller challenges: a trip to the grocery store, a spin around the mall parking lot. Same goes with embroidery. Artists draw sketches; people who sew try patterns using muslin cloth first; we embroidering types create doodles on fabric.

In between parts 1 and 2 of this book (just before the projects), you'll find a Practice Stitch Card I've created to help you get the hang of some of the stitches we've covered. You'll have to get your own fabric to use as a doodle cloth. This will be the place for you to experiment with these new techniques. I usually use a linen tea towel. Go ahead and try them with different kinds of threads or needles to see what feels and looks right to you. Do you prefer the look of a chain stitch with three strands of floss or six? Are you more comfortable with a hoop or without one? It's also a good way to see what kind of fabric or canvas you're most comfortable working with.

The beauty of a doodle cloth is that it's really for your eyes only—and it isn't meant to be permanent. I often don't even bother weaving in the ends on mine. However, be forewarned: Doodles sometimes turn into masterpieces. Two stitches will

suddenly look like they were meant to be next to each other, or you may notice a color combination that's out of this world. More often than not, you may find that your whole doodle cloth is worthy of a frame, or perhaps you'll want to snip out part of it and appliqué it onto a shirt. Go for it! Take control of your doodle!

lazy daisy stitch

— French knots

Lazy Daisy Stitch

If the chain stitch started to spin in circles, it might look something like a lazy daisy (also called a *detached chain*). Bring your needle up at 1, then insert the needle back down into the same point creating a loop (fig. 3.13a). Before pulling the thread tight, bring the needle up one stitch length away. Draw the needle through the loop and pull the thread taut, creating a teardrop-shaped loop. Make one small vertical straight stitch at 3 to secure the loop (fig. 3.13b). To make the complete daisy, repeat the stitches to make six to eight petals at even intervals in a circle (fig. 3.13c). Optional: Finish with a single French knot (page 45) in the flower's center.

Fig. 3.13a

Fig. 3.13b

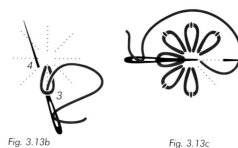

Fig. 3.13c

Working the Loop-D-Loop

When working looped stitches like blanket stitches and chain stitches (page 34), the needle stays on the surface of the fabric—you don't pull it to the back of the work. Use the thumb of your nondominant hand to hold on to the thread as you complete the stitch.

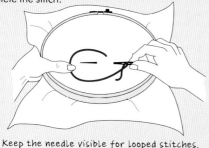

Keep the needle visible for looped stitches.

Blanket Stitches (aka Buttonhole Stitches)

You'll often see this stitch along the edges of a wool blanket, which is where it got its name. The stitch finishes the raw edge of the fabric, which prevents fraying, and it also does a really good job of keeping the edges flat. But there's so much more to the blanket stitch than blankets! It can be used in many other ways: purely decoratively; to seam two pieces of fabric together (as in the Old-Meets-New Gadget Cozies, page 205); or for sewing nifty-looking appliqué. Last, but not least, when blanket stitches are worked very close together, they're suitable for edging buttonholes by hand—this, not surprisingly, is why it is also known as the buttonhole stitch. How cool is that?

Get to know a member of the family:

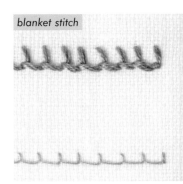

Blanket Stitch

This stitch is similar to the chain stitch in that the thread stays on the surface of the fabric and under the point of the needle, to create a loop. Before trying this stitch, draw two parallel guide lines ¼ inch apart with a fabric marker; if you're working on gingham there's no need, just follow the grid of the fabric. Working from left to right, bring the needle up at 1, pulling the thread to the right and using your thumb to hold it in place. Insert the needle down at 2 and bring it up at 3 making a vertical stitch (fig. 3.14a). Keep the thread flat and under the point of the needle as you pull it through. Practice having even spaces between stitches and a uniform length (fig. 3.14b). As with the running stitch, you never pull the needle through to the wrong side (back) of the fabric (fig. 3.14c). If your needle ends up there, start over. To finish stitching, take one horizontal straight stitch from left to right, bring the needle to the wrong side, and secure the thread there.

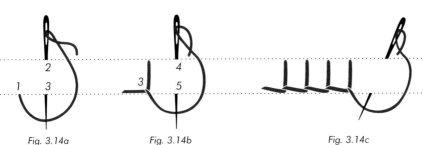

Fig. 3.14a   Fig. 3.14b   Fig. 3.14c

TIP: If you're having a hard time with the blanket stitch, try working it vertically instead of horizontally, that is, follow the basic blanket stitch illustrations but turning them so the line of stitching is vertical. Bring your needle through the fabric and lay the thread flat against it with the threaded needle toward you. Draw the thread to the right, using your thumb to hold it in place. Take a horizontal straight stitch into the fabric from right to left, at a right angle to the thread. Pull the needle through the fabric with the point of the needle on top of the thread. Repeat for a row of blanket stitches. Take one vertical stitch to finish.

The blanket stitch may be worked vertically.

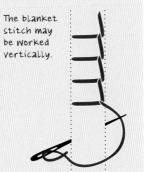

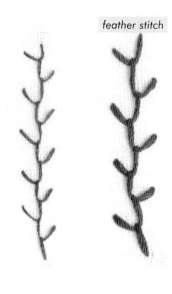

feather stitch

Feather Stitches

The feather stitch is all about loops worked from side to side, which makes it a cousin of the blanket stitch and chain stitch—but it definitely has a look of its own. The feather stitch is nice as a decorative border or as an ivylike flower stem or to fill in the texture of a stitched leaf. It's often used decoratively on quilts (it's a go-to stitch for a crazy quilt) and can be worked in a curved or straight line. In the days when nineteenth-century English smocks were all the rage, this was *the* stitch to know.

Get to know the family:

Feather Stitch

Start the basic feather stitch by drawing four vertical guidelines ⅛ inch apart on the right side of your fabric (again, if you're using gingham, there's no need; just pick four rows to follow). You're going to be working from top to bottom. Bring your needle up on the second guideline at 1 and then down on the fourth guideline at 2, with the thread under the needle point from left to right. Before pulling your needle all the way through to the wrong side, bring the point up diagonally at 3 on the third guideline (fig. 3.15a), making sure to loop the thread under the needle, and then pull through. Insert the needle on the first guideline at 4, at the same level as 3. Insert the needle into the second guideline at 5 (fig. 3.15b). Keep an even tension so the loops have a consistent openness and roundness. Fasten off with a small vertical straight stitch (fig. 3.15c). The stitch weaves back and forth like this from side to side. Once you get the rhythm of it, it'll be second nature and you'll be fine scrapping the guidelines.

Fig. 3.15a

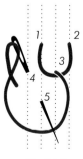

Fig. 3.15b

Fig. 3.15c

Closed Fly Stitch

Few stitches are better suited to making a leaf or a feather than a closed fly stitch. Draw the shape of the leaf and its center line before you start. The stitch is worked top to bottom. Begin by making one small vertical straight stitch at the top of the center line—up at 1, down at 2 (fig. 3.16a). Bring your needle up to the left at 3 and just under the top of the first stitch. Pull the needle through to the front. Bring it down at 4 on the opposite side of the center stitch. Before pulling the needle all the way through, bring the needle's point back up at 2 (fig. 3.16b). Now pull through, making sure that the needle point is above the looped thread that goes from one side of the leaf to the other. Begin again, starting with another vertical, but much shorter, stitch; down at 5 and up at 6 (fig. 3.16c). Continue to fill in the leaf (fig. 3.16d), and end with a vertical straight stitch (you may want to make that last stitch a bit longer than the rest—it's the stem!).

closed fly stitch

Fig. 3.16a

Fig. 3.16b

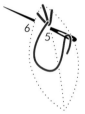

Fig. 3.16c

Fig. 3.16d

Hanky Panky

When I have a cold, my desk is littered with crumpled tissues: not pretty. But up until a few decades ago, handkerchiefs lived in every man's pocket and lady's purse. Besides being useful receptacles for tears and snot, hankies were personalized pieces—a way to distinguish oneself from the gray-flannel-, white-glove-wearing hoity-toity. People likely have been using cloth to wipe their brows or blow their noses for thousands of years; handkerchiefs first became common wardrobe items in Renaissance Europe—they were called *nopkyns*. (In prerevolutionary France, Louis XIV took the issue quite seriously: He used his royal prerogative to decree that all handkerchiefs be square.) They may not be so common now, but I still love to embroider them—it's a way to embellish something otherwise banal—and, quite frankly, old-fashioned. You can buy handkerchiefs in packs online (look for ones made of Irish linen), and secondhand stores sometimes have vintage ones perfect for stitching (just make sure to launder them first).

Satin Stitches

These stitches are the best for filling a design area for a smooth, satiny surface. They are usually worked over an outlining stitch (such as a split stitch or backstitch) to create raised areas of stitching for a 3-D effect. They can also be worked in multiple thread colors at different stitch lengths to create delicate shading. My favorite examples of satin stitches can be found on embroidered kimonos. Traditional Japanese silk embroidery is incredibly elegant and rich with color, and was my inspiration for the Peony Jewelry Box (page 183). If you're not a fan of silk, any type of thread will do, as well as any fabric. The design can be worked in needlepoint, too (we'll talk more about this later).

Get to know the family:

satin stitch

Satin Stitch

I find I almost always have to use a frame or hoop to do this stitch—too much slack in the fabric will make it nearly impossible to produce the kind of even stitches you want.

The first step is to thread your needle with a single strand of floss. Satin stitch uses more thread than many of the other stitches, so be prepared to reload your needle when you run out of thread. Next, use a fabric marker to draw a small rectangle (this is the easiest shape to stitch) on your fabric. Working from left to right, bring your thread up at 1 and then down at 2. When you bring the needle back up at 3, get it as close as you can to 1 (fig. 3.17a). Insert the needle equally close to 2 at 4, making a parallel vertical stitch. The goal is to get your stitches close enough so that none of the fabric below is visible, and all stitches are perfectly even in length and flat (fig. 3.17b). Continue making parallel stitches until you've covered the outlined shape. If you don't like a stitch, simply back it out (see page 23).

Fig. 3.17a

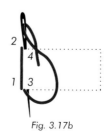

Fig. 3.17b

Fig. 3.17b

Padded Satin Stitch

This stitch is used to create a solid-colored area that is slightly raised. Draw a rectangle on the fabric as you did to practice the basic satin stitch, then work a split stitch (as shown) or backstitch along the border of your design using two strands of floss (fig. 3.18a). There are various schools of thought on how to pad your stitch, but my preferred method involves filling the area with straight stitches sewn perpendicular to the direction your satin stitches will go (fig. 3.18b). The understitches will not be seen—they are just there to give depth. When the area is filled with stitches, work satin stitch over the area using a single strand of floss, starting and ending just outside the split-stitched or backstitched border (fig. 3.18c). When you finish, the area should be completely covered with satin stitch.

padded satin stitch

Fig. 3.18a

Fig. 3.18b

Fig. 3.18c

Eyelet Wheel Stitch

This freewheeling stitch is a cinch—just don't get too dizzy while you stitch it! To make it, you'll want to start by drawing a circle on your fabric with a fabric marking pen or pencil, then make a mark in the center. Bring the needle up on the circle at 1, down at 2, up again at 1, down at 3 and repeat (fig. 3.18a–c). Continue around the circle taking stitches into the center.

eyelet wheel

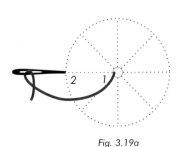

Fig. 3.19a

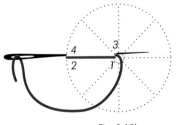

Fig. 3.19b

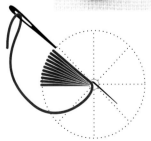

Fig. 3.19c

41

long and short stitch

Long and Short Stitch (aka Satin Shading Stitch)

When doing this stitch, I love using threads of three different tones in order to create areas of stitching on my work that seem to fade from one hue to another. To start, make one row of satin stitches from left to right, with every other stitch measuring half the length of the preceding one (up at 1, down at 2, up at 3, down at 4)—long then short, long then short, and so on (fig. 3.20a). For the subsequent rows (all of which should also be worked left to right), use only long stitches to continue the pattern. Bring your needle up one long stitch length below the bottom of the first stitch on the top row at 5. Bring it down at the bottom of the first stitch on the top row at 6, piercing the thread as you enter (fig. 3.20b). Continue this way to the end of the row. To complete the last row, make alternating short and long stitches to the edge of the area being stitched.

Try using successively lighter colors in each row to create a fading effect. Split the bottom of each stitch when you insert the needle to create a smooth blend from one color to the next. That being said, you can also work this stitch without splitting the stitch above it. Instead, bring your needle down through the hole where you began the stitch above it. This is called the *brick stitch* (see page 57) which should be worked in rows alternating from left to right and then right to left.

If Jane Eyre Had Been an Embroiderer...

"As I cannot write, I put this down simply and freely as I might speak to a person to whose intimacy and tenderness I can fully intrust myself." So begins the writing on a sampler made around 1830 by Elizabeth Parker, a young woman from East Sussex, England. Born in 1813, Parker was the daughter of a schoolteacher and a laborer, had ten sisters and brothers, and left home when she was thirteen. She then went on to become a nursery maid for families that treated her "with cruelty too horrible to mention." Her story gets darker: She tries to commit suicide but fails. How do we know all this? She spills it all in this sampler, which reads like a script for a Lifetime special. After stitching 6,699 cross-stitched letters in red thread, Parker seems to have gotten tired fingers. She ends in midsentence ("What shall become of my soul") halfway down the canvas. The sampler now lives at London's Victoria and Albert Museum.

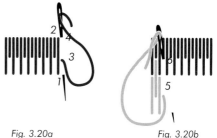

Fig. 3.20a   Fig. 3.20b

Appliqué

Combine freehand embroidery with fabric shapes, and you get appliqué! For the appliqué projects in this book, you'll either stitch felt to fabric or stitch over fabric shapes that have been stiffened with fusible interfacing (see page 7) to get a layered look.

Appliqué pieces can be secured to a piece of fabric using a fusible webbing such as Steam-A-Seam or a fabric glue, but I prefer to use stitching to keep the pieces in place. Cross-stitches, blanket stitches, running stitches, and feather stitches are all frequently used in appliqué. All you have to do is work part of the stitch over the attached piece, and part of it over the base fabric. You can also do a simple stitch conveniently known as the appliqué stitch:

First, prepare a needle with one strand of floss. Bring the needle to the right side of the base fabric at the edge of the appliqué. Make one small perpendicular stitch into the edge of the appliqué at 1. Bring the needle down through the base fabric at 2 and up again one stitch length away at the edge of the appliqué at 3.

Felt or other nonwoven appliqués need not have their edges turned under, because they won't fray. However, in traditional appliqué, the edges are turned about 1/16 inch to the underside as they are sewn. If you do not hem the edges, you can cut them with pinking shears (scissors with zigzag blades) to avoid fraying. Another alternative is to use dense embroidery stitches to cover the edges. If the appliqués have been adhered to the base fabric with fusible webbing, there's no need to turn the edges under unless you plan to wash the project. If you do plan to launder it, turn the edges under before applying the appliqués to the base fabric.

Cross-Stitches

These are most commonly seen in counted cross-stitch work and on samplers, but they can be done in freehand work as well. I find them to be quite versatile stitches, since they can be used to cover large areas, or can stand on their own—one lone cross-stitch against the world (or two, if you're embroidering the eyes of a boxer who has just been KO'd). If you're working with evenweave fabric, such as Aida cloth or linen, you can control the size of your stitches by the holes in the mesh, but if you're trying to do cross-stitch on non-evenweave fabric (where you can't see a grid), it's a good idea to draw two parallel guidelines (or use waste canvas, page 15) to make sure that your stitches remain even. You can also buy heat transfer pattens that are cross-stitch designs. Simply cover up the Xs with thread.

single cross-stitch

cross-stitch

Get to know the family:

Cross-Stitch

To work a single cross-stitch, make one diagonal stitch slanting 45 degrees from the bottom left at 1 to the top right at 2. (When working on evenweave fabric such as Aida cloth, the stitch can be worked over one or multiple mesh crossings—it depends on the size and look you're going for.) Bring your thread back up one stitch length down from 2 and up at 3, then make one diagonal stitch in the opposite direction (bottom right to top left) to 4 to complete a single X (fig. 3.21a). Always work the right-leaning diagonal first and the left-leaning diagonal second as shown here, so the light hits all the stitches in the same way. If you need to work several cross-stitches, work them in rows (fig. 3.21b), stitching the bottom diagonal from left to right, then the top diagonal from right to left.

Fig. 3.21a

Fig. 3.21b

TIP: Look at the wrong side of the fabric when working the left-leaning diagonal of your cross-stitch; it's much easier to find 3 by taking a vertical stitch down from 2. Work the cross-stitch from the underside of your work.

upright cross-stitch

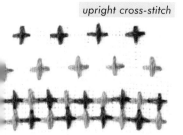

Upright Cross-Stitch (aka St. George Cross-Stitch)

This cross-stitch is placed upright on the fabric and looks just like a plus sign. To work a single cross, come up at 1 and down at 2, then up at 3 and down at 4 (fig. 3.22a). For a row, work a running stitch (see page 30) from right to left and then work back from left to right crossing each horizontal stitch with a vertical straight stitch (fig. 3.22b).

Fig. 3.22a

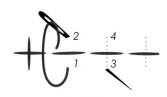

Fig. 3.22b

Knotted Stitches

Knots are not just for anchoring thread to fabric, nor are they just a negative consequence when your thread tangles; they're also made intentionally on the right side of the work for a textural 3-D effect. In fact, there's a whole family of knotted stitches, some of which are worked as isolated knots like the French knot, below, while others are in the form of line stitches most often used as intricate decorative borders. (Knotted buttonhole stitch, anyone?) The key to a nicely knotted stitch is even thread tension, which takes practice. Remember to hold the part of the stitch with the knot down firmly on the right side of the fabric with your thumb while you pull the working thread through with your other hand.

Get to know the family:

French Knot

A French knot can stand alone à la the stamen for the lazy daisy (see page 36), be stitched in a row to create a dotted line as in the Lacy Parasol (see page 186), or be closely packed together as a filling stitch, like the fluffy bunny's tail in the Book for Baby (see page 133). Whether you want to create one knot or many, the method is the same. Bring the threaded needle through to the right side of the fabric at 1. Hold the needle close to the fabric and wrap the thread twice around the needle (fig. 3.10a). Use your free hand to keep tension on the thread to hold the wraps in place (fig. 3.10b). Insert the needle very close to 1 (fig. 3.10c). Use your free thumbnail to slide the wraps against the fabric. Hold the wraps with your thumbnail against the fabric and, at the same time, pull the needle through to the back of the fabric. The raised knot should sit neatly on the surface of the fabric (fig. 3.10d). If you'd like a big, beefy knot, increase the number of times you wrap the thread around the needle or use a thicker thread such as pearl cotton.

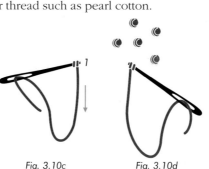

French knot

Fig. 3.10a

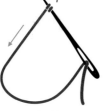

Fig. 3.10b

Fig. 3.10c

Fig. 3.10d

couching

Couching Stitches

In love with two kinds of yarn or thread and don't know which to use? Don't worry! Couching can solve your problem! It's a method of applying one yarn to fabric by sewing over it with another yarn. The first yarn is sewn into the fabric only at the beginning and end. This is called the *laid* yarn or thread. The laid yarn can be more than one yarn. It may be two threads together. Or three. Or whatever! (I recommend using just one or two yarns the first time you try it.) The one that is stitched over it is called the *couching* yarn. Many of the previously described stitches, including blanket stitch, cross-stitch, satin stitch, and more, may be used to couch a laid thread.

Get to know the family:

Couching

Thread the laid yarn(s) through one needle. (I recommend using a chenille needle and six strands of embroidery floss.) Draw the needle to the top of the fabric at 1. Use your thumb to hold the laid yarn against the fabric. It should come out of the fabric on the right, laying to the left (fig. 3.23a). Thread your couching yarn into another needle. The couching yarn should be finer than the laid yarn; try couching with two strands and see how you like the contrast. Bring it to the right side of the fabric one stitch length from the start of the laid yarn at 2. Then make one small straight stitch to 3 to secure it (fig. 3.23b). Bring the needle up at 4 and down at 5 (fig. 3.23c). Continue working until the laid yarn is completely sewn to the fabric with the couching yarn. The stitches should be evenly spaced and can be staggered (as shown above left) or worked into other patterns. At the end of the stitch line, bring the laid yarn to the back of the work and secure.

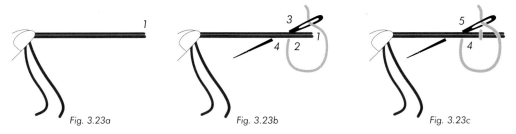

Fig. 3.23a   Fig. 3.23b   Fig. 3.23c

Couching is often used for borders, but if you want to use it to fill an area, curve your yarn back toward whence it came, using your thumb to pin it down so that it is parallel to (and touching) your first laid yarn. At the point where the yarn turns, make one horizontal straight stitch, from right to left (fig. 3.24a). (Make sure that the laid yarns lay flat against one another; none should overlap.) Continue couching the laid yarn using vertical straight stitches, and continue curving the yarn in a zigzag, with a single horizontal straight stitch placed at the point of each curve (fig. 3.24b).

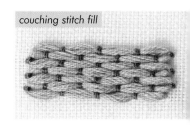

couching stitch fill

Fig. 3.24a   Fig. 3.24b

Samplers

A sampler is considered a step up from a doodle cloth (page 35): it's meant to be a practice piece, but traditionally it's worked in more thought-out patterns, and the final result is used as home decor. The word stems from the Latin *exemplum,* meaning "an example"—which inspired the French *essamplaire,* meaning "something to be copied or imitated." Before printed books with neat spiral bindings were available to the masses, people used samplers to record new stitches they saw or learned in order to create a sort of library of needlework to which they could refer and then pass on to the next generation of stitchers. Samplers were displayed in homes in olden times, but they were also carried from place to place— like from Europe to the Middle East and back again. This may be one of the reasons you can find some of the same embroidery stitch techniques developed in so many different corners of the world.

Samplers started to become popular in the fifteenth and sixteenth centuries. London's Victoria

American embroidered sampler, c. 1834–38

and Albert Museum has one that dates back to 1598; it's essentially a series of stitch experiments: patterns, pictures of animals and plants, borders, and so on. It's a good example of how samplers were used as a way to test stitches. They were also kind of like badges of honor—something to hang on the wall to show off one's mad needle skillz.

Samplers were often symmetrical or followed a particular pattern. In Victorian times, embroidering for the pure pleasure of embroidering was seen as a sign of vanity. (Imagine that!) This might be one of the reasons there was a vogue for creating samplers with purpose: Teaching young girls to stitch maps or proverbs or the alphabet was a way to kill two birds with one needle.

For your first sampler, try making parallel rows demonstrating the stitches we've covered in this chapter, each in a different color or all in one color. The end result will be a good reference as you choose stitches for future projects, but it'll also be a nice, small, decorative piece to display.

a sampler

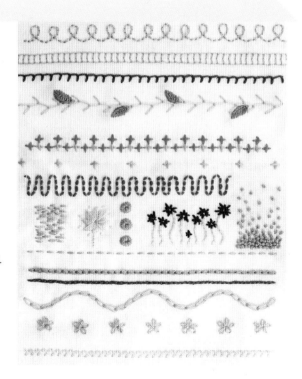

Not sure what to write on your sampler? Yes, you can work your favorite stitches, write your name, or the alphabet in your favorite font. But if you want to mix it up a bit, you could always . . .

✳ Stitch a bunch of *Z*s in different fonts and put it over your bed.

✳ Find a really fun tweet posted by you or a friend on Twitter and conquer all 140 characters with your needle.

✳ Write GOOD MORNING SUNSHINE backward and hang it so it faces the mirror in the bathroom.

✳ Stitch the first sentence from each of your favorite books.

the rupp rules for monograms

For years, I've put friends' initials on towels and pillowcases for their birthdays, weddings, or kids. I prefer to put full names, but sometimes two or three letters is all I have time for—what can I say, I have a lot of friends who have birthdays.

The letter ordering always seemed fairly obvious to me. I don't come from a formal family, so I'm pretty much a self-taught monogram embroiderer. I knew, for example, to put DJR on my skivvies when I was a kid at camp so that I could get my clothes returned from the wash. This was such a clever ploy it even helped me land Deb Jones-Richards's supercute culottes.

Some experts insist that women should have their first initial to the left on sheets, but men should have theirs first on cocktail glasses—supposedly because men don't buy sheets and women never drink. Others believe that both spouses should always use the husband's name, while still more find it in bad taste for a man to be included in any monogram at all.

But you know what? All rules are made up by somebody—you can even make up your own. Here are the rules I live (and stitch) by, submitted to you, dear readers, for posterity.

1 If you're going to make all the letters the same size, they should read first initial, middle initial, then last initial.

So, my friend Hillary Amber Fry would be HAF. This is the go-to monogram for anything owned by a child (think backpacks).

2 If someone has more than three names, just do one letter—the first initial of either the first name or the last name.

If a last name is hyphenated, I'll sometimes do the first initial of each last name with a hyphen in the middle, but this sometimes looks too much like a math equation. Four initials starts to look like it's a law firm or a dentist's office.

3 If a couple is married and share the same last name, it should be his first initial, then his last initial, and then her first initial.

The last name initial should always be in the center—and it can be larger than the other two. So Diana and Brandon Eggena would be BED. Martha and George Washington? GWM. Monograms originated in prefeminist society, which is why the husband's name traditionally goes first.

4 If the two people in the couple have different last names, well, they should each get their own darn monogram!

Alternatively, I sometimes will do just two letters: the first initial of each of their last names, for a simple and classy solution.

5 If the two people in the couple have the same last name but it's a hyphenated name, or if they each have two first names, or are named Kate and Kurt Kilgore, just stitch "His" and "Hers."

Readers, these are the rules I live by. But you can make up your own rules! Unless you forget whether your friend is Cathy-with-a-C or Kathy-with-a-K, I think you'll find most of your monogrammed gift recipients are thrilled to have something personalized at all.

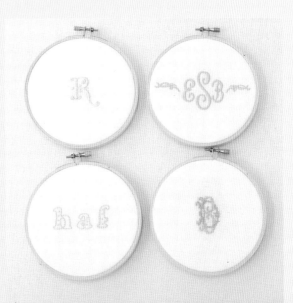

Needlepoint

How sturdy is needlepoint? Well, the chair seat my grandmother made in 1946 is still hole-free despite cushioning so many derrieres over the years. The point is, if it's done right, it can last for decades or even centuries. Archaeologists sometimes find scraps of needlepoint that have been around for thousands of years.

Needlepoint is made sturdy thanks to the fact that it's created so the canvas or evenweave fabric is completely covered by stitching. But beyond its resilience, I think we see so many examples of needlepoint because people enjoy the process. Needlepoint has an ineffable sort of appeal that can captivate the mind when the fingers are busy. People really tap into that meditative zone reserved for when you're doing something repetitive, tactile, and undemanding. And whenever you snap out of the zone, the excitement of seeing the progress made as an image develops lures you right back in. I truly believe that making things with your hands can bring as much serenity as any amount of time in the lotus position. So what are you waiting for?

how to start

Fig. 3.25a

how to finish

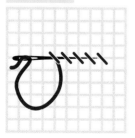

Fig. 3.25b

Meet the Needlepoint Stitches

Because needlepoint stitches are supposed to cover the canvas completely, the members of this family stick close together—but you might see some resemblance to relatives in other stitching families. (It's worth noting that needlepoint stitches for canvases may be used on evenweave fabric materials such as linen or Aida cloth; however, because some of the stitches we've already covered do not completely cover the fabric beneath them, not all embroidery stitches will work on canvas.)

Time to test out your stuff! Start by gathering a few supplies. Cut a 12-inch square of 10-mesh mono canvas with regular scissors. Tape the raw edges of your practice canvas with artist tape (available at any art or craft store) and write "top" on one taped edge with a permanent marker. You'll also need a skein of tapestry wool, a size 18 tapestry needle, and embroidery scissors. When starting, leave 1 to 2 inches of yarn to the back of the canvas. Catch the yarn end with the first few stitches and then trim away the excess (fig. 3.25a). When ending, bring the needle and yarn to the back of the canvas and weave the yarn through the backs of the last few stitches (fig. 3.25b). Cut the yarn short.

Twentieth-Century Needlepointing's Celebrity Odd Couple

"You do needlepoint!?" a friend exclaimed to me a few years ago. "But you're so cool."

Ouch! For whatever reason, most people buy into a needlepointer stereotype. It's usually some kind of prim granny busying herself while she's waiting for Charlie Rose to come on. I blame it on the fact that many of the preprinted canvases available for sale are decorated with stodgy images—maudlin landscapes or flowers that *look* like they belong on musty-smelling pillows. The thing is, you can needlepoint any image you want (see page 72 for tips on how). What's more, a lot of fierce, nongrannyish folks have tasted the pleasures of needlepoint (historical badasses Mary, Queen of Scots and her cousin Elizabeth I, Queen of England, come to mind).

So if folks approach you with comments like the one I got from my so-called pal, you can respond: "Maybe I'm so cool *because* I do needlepoint!" Indeed, you're in swell company. Check out these two famous needlepointers of the twentieth century.

GRACE KELLY

I'll always think of her as Jimmy Stewart's glam lady friend in *Rear Window*. Others remember her best as the Princess of Monaco. To some, however, she'll best be remembered for her beautiful needlepoint work. She was awarded the very first American Needlepoint Guild's Mary Martin award (named for another famous actress-turned-stitcher). "Sometimes my husband just doesn't quite understand when I say in the evening, 'I must do at least one more row before I will put my needlepoint down,'" Princess Grace told a reporter in 1974 at a needlepoint exhibition in Monaco. For her, stitching was a family affair: On vacations, she, her children, and her princely husband used to work on a needlepoint rug made up of squares designed by each member of the family. Today, the American Needlepoint Guild offers an annual Princess Grace Award for needlepoint pieces executed entirely in tent stitch.

ROSEY GRIER

Confession: I have a favorite professional football player—but don't ask me what team he played on. What do I know about burly Roosevelt "Rosey" Grier? After he retired, he became a bodyguard for the Kennedys, sang "It's All Right to Cry" on the *Free to Be . . . You and Me* album, and . . . wrote a book about his passion for needlepoint. I know, right? Naturally, he was especially into designs that featured athletic equipment.

On the back of his 1973 book, *Rosey Grier's Needlepoint for Men,* he wrote: "If anyone would have told me that I would go from football to needlepoint, I would have laughed in their face. In fact, the whole thing started as a joke, but it's turned into one of the most enjoyable and satisfying things I've ever done. I try to turn other guys on to needlepoint wherever I go—from the dude sitting next to me on a plane to the guy working behind the scenes on a movie set. 'Smile all you want,' I tell them, 'but if you try it once, you'll keep on coming back for more,' and that's the truth, brother."

I couldn't have said it better myself.

Easing the Tension

straight canvas and pretty stitches on a needlepoint project require even thread tension.

Pull too tight on your yarn and the canvas will warp (see the Continental Stitch, below); too loose and the

stitches will pucker and reveal the canvas beneath (see the Gobelin Stitch, below).

Continental Stitch

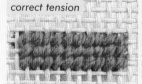

correct tension

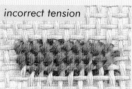

incorrect tension

Gobelin Stitch

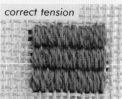

correct tension

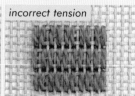

incorrect tension

Tent Stitches

The tent stitch is the most common kind of stitch used in needlepoint—indeed, you could needlepoint for the rest of your days with just this one little stitch. It's a simple one but requires some practice, nonetheless: too much tension or too much slack can cause areas on the stitch surface to pucker or warp (see box above). Done correctly, the tent stitch will produce uniform diagonal hatches that can be used to cover swaths of canvas.

There are several kinds of tent stitches; they're executed differently, but each looks the same on the right side of your piece (it's the underside where you'll notice a difference). You might find that one is easier for you to work than another. I recommend choosing a particular tent stitch based on the shape of the area you are working. Each individual tent stitch should always slant from bottom left to upper right—like an *accent aigu,* for all you Francophiles.

Continental Stitch

This stitch is worked right to left when done horizontally, but it can also be worked vertically. In either case, the stitch should start at the top right of the area you are working.

Start by making one tent stitch over one mesh or intersection of the canvas threads. Bring the needle up at 1, down at 2. As mentioned above, when this stitch is done correctly, the thread will look like a right-leaning diagonal. To make another tent stitch, bring your needle back up in the hole directly to the

continental stitch

left of 1 at 3, and then down at 4—to the left of 2 (fig. 3.26a). When you reach the end of the row, leave your needle and thread at the back of your work (fig. 3.26b) and then rotate the canvas 180 degrees. When the canvas is rotated, bring the needle back up at 1a, one hole above where your last stitch ended. Continue working the stitches right to left until you finish the row (fig. 3.26c). Then rotate the canvas back to the starting position to begin the next one.

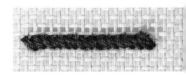

If you're working this stitch correctly, the wrong side of the canvas should have long sloping stitches that appear diagonally across two threads.

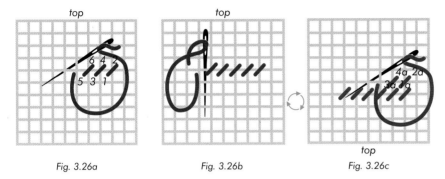

| Fig. 3.26a | Fig. 3.26b | Fig. 3.26c |

When the continental stitch is worked vertically, it should move from top to bottom (fig, 3.27a). After completing a row (fig. 3.27b), rotate the canvas in order to begin the next row of stitching (fig. 3.27c, same as with horizontal stitching).

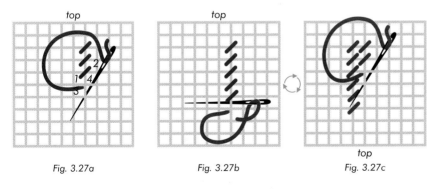

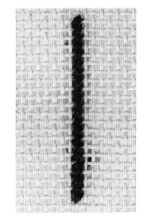

| Fig. 3.27a | Fig. 3.27b | Fig. 3.27c |

TIP: Canvas is often stiff enough that it feels comfortable to stitch without a hoop or frame. However, the shape of the canvas will likely distort if you use primarily diagonal stitches. This problem is easily solved by blocking your piece when you're done, a technique used to restore the shape of your piece when it's gone out of square (for more, see "Getting Things Straight and Flat," page 238). If you use a frame as you're stitching, you'll find that the canvas is more likely to keep its shape.

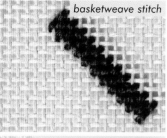
basketweave stitch

back of basketweave stitch

Basketweave Stitch

The wrong side of this stitch looks like a woven basket, hence its name. The right side looks like the continental stitch. So . . . why use a basketweave stitch if it looks identical to the continental stitch? Good question! Basketweave stitch is worked in diagonal rows, which is less likely to distort the canvas because it pulls the canvas evenly in both directions. The continental stitch, on the other hand, only pulls to the right, which can distort the canvas (see page 52). (But don't worry, it can be fixed with blocking, see "Getting Things Straight and Flat," page 238.) Stick to basketweave stitch when filling in backgrounds or large shapes, and use the continental stitch for tricky maneuvers in a tight space, such as filling in a small area or working a fine detail.

The basketweave stitch is worked diagonally from top left to bottom right. Make a stitch over one mesh or intersection, up from 1 at bottom left and down at upper right at 2. Leaving one hole empty, bring your needle up at 3 and down at 4 (fig. 3.28a). Proceed with another stitch like your first one, to the bottom right.

When you get to the last stitch of the resulting diagonal row, bring the needle up at 5 and down at 6 (fig. 3.28b), then work back to the top left. Stitches will be worked into the empty canvas holes of the previous row. Repeat these two rows working up and down the canvas (fig. 3.28c). When working down a row, your needle will be vertical and pointed down; when working up, your needle will be stitching horizontally.

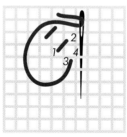

Fig. 3.28a

Fig. 3.28b

Fig. 3.28c

TIP: Let's be blunt: You don't want a superpointy needle if you're doing needlepoint or cross-stitch on evenweave fabric or canvas. The sharp point can pierce and split the fibers, causing an uneven stitch. A tapestry needle, which has a dull point, slides smoothly into the holes, between the fibers, exactly as it should. It really makes a big difference!

Backstitch

This is worked just like the basic embroidery backstitch discussed on page 32. Working from right to left, make one straight stitch up at 1 and down at 2, then come up at 3, one thread to the left of 1, and down at 1. Repeat to the left of the first stitch (fig. 3.29a). The backstitch can be worked horizontally, vertically (fig. 3.29b), and diagonally (fig. 3.29c) on the canvas as shown.

backstitch

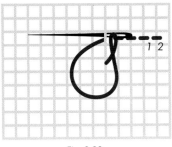
Fig. 3.29a

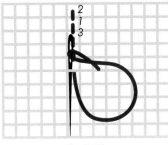
Fig. 3.29b

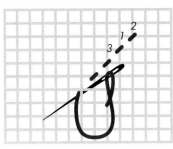
Fig. 3.29c

Gobelin Stitches

If your goal is to cover a large area of your design quickly and easily, Gobelin stitches are a nice, even, clean option. Doing them reminds me a little of the way I eat an ear of corn: start on one end, eat all the way to the other end, then go down to the next row of kernels and eat your way back to the starting end.

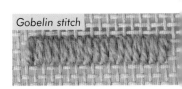
Gobelin stitch

Gobelin Stitch

With the Gobelin stitch, start on the right, making one vertical straight stitch that goes from bottom to top (up at 1, down at 2). It can span from one to five canvas threads. Your next stitch is worked exactly like the first one, stitching from bottom to top (fig. 3.30a). When you bring your needle down at your last stitch, you'll be ready to start the next row. To do this, just bring your needle up one stitch length below your last stitch at 1 and down at 2, and then work your next row from left to right (fig. 3.30b). The top of this row of stitches will share holes with the bottom of the row above it. Make sure your threads are untangled and untwisted; with this stitch, any kinks or overlaps in the strands will be quite apparent.

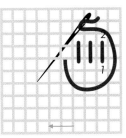
Fig. 3.30a

Fig. 3.30b

55

Needlepoint + Beads = Beadpoint

ften described as "backwards needlepoint," beadpoint is a form of beaded embroidery that was popular in Victorian England. It simply involves inserting a bead onto each tent stitch. The bead provides the color rather than the thread. Choose a bead that is large enough so it will not fall through the holes of your canvas. This may take some trial and error, but, generally speaking, seed beads work well with 14-count Aida cloth and canvas; for 11-count, use rocaille beads, clear seed beads with a metallic lining. Try stitching a bead here and there as a highlight on your needlepoint canvas, or you can cover the entire piece!

encroaching Gobelin stitch

Encroaching Gobelin Stitch

My favorite variation on the Gobelin stitch is the "encroaching Gobelin," a hard-wearing stitch used to fill in the backgrounds around the silhouettes on the Art of Conversation Pillows (page 149). To work the encroaching Gobelin, position the tops of your second row of stitching (2) to the left or to the right of the bases of the stitches in the preceding row (fig. 3.31).

Fig. 3.31

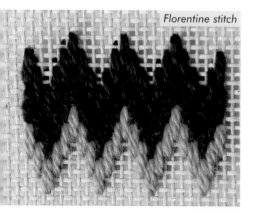
Florentine stitch

Florentine Stitch

This stitch is one of the main ones used when working bargello patterns, which consist of a very old European style of zigzagging stripe (see "Bargello," page xviii). Usually with bargello, you will work one zigzag row according to a pattern, and then you use that row as a model for the other lines of stitching. The shape can range from a simple zigzag to a more dynamic pattern resembling mountain peaks. Start in the center of your pattern with one vertical straight stitch, worked from bottom to top (up at 1, down at 2). The length of the stitch is up to you, if it's not dictated by the pattern you are following; it could just be the length of one box. Start your next stitch one square to the left and one square below the place where you first brought your thread up and make another vertical stitch spanning the same number of squares as your first stitch from 3 to 4. (Your stitch can travel more than one square if you want a more acute zigzag—just make sure that your stitch is adjacent to one square in the previous stitch.) Continue in this manner (fig. 3.32a), forming a row of *V*s. When you finish the row, go back to the center and extend the pattern in the other direction. Your next row of stitches should exactly mimic your first row above and below it (fig. 3.32b). The result will be a flamelike row of peaks and valleys. It's a particularly cool effect when each row of zigzags is worked in a different color.

Fig. 3.32a

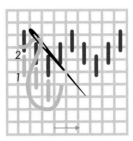

Fig. 3.32b

Brick Stitch

The brick stitch, a simple and decorative stitch, is worked in needlepoint the same way it is in freehand embroidery (see "Long and Short Stitch," page 42). Like the Gobelin stitch (page 55), the brick stitch is a straight stitch worked with vertical stitches across the canvas. It is useful for filling in large, solid areas in a project (it will create a textured background), and has a woven appearance when completed. The stitches are executed so they are even in length and alternate up and down in a zigzag (rather than being worked straight across). The resulting pattern recalls its very apt name: the alternating stitches resemble a brick wall or cobblestone path.

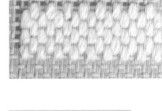

brick stitch

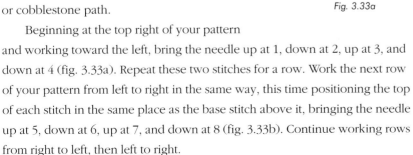

Fig. 3.33a

Fig. 3.33b

Beginning at the top right of your pattern and working toward the left, bring the needle up at 1, down at 2, up at 3, and down at 4 (fig. 3.33a). Repeat these two stitches for a row. Work the next row of your pattern from left to right in the same way, this time positioning the top of each stitch in the same place as the base stitch above it, bringing the needle up at 5, down at 6, up at 7, and down at 8 (fig. 3.33b). Continue working rows from right to left, then left to right.

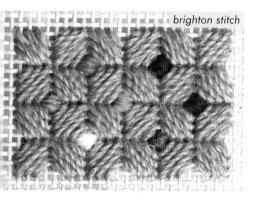

brighton stitch

Brighton Stitch

This stitch is made up of two blocks, each covering 16 cross-threads of canvas (or threads in evenweave fabric), and with one upright cross-stitch in the center. Each block is made up of five stitches. Start your first block at top left with one diagonal straight stitch that spans two diagonal meshes, angling from bottom right to top left (up at 1, down at 2). This will be the top left edge of your first block. Bring the thread up one hole below where your first stitch started at 3, and make one straight stitch over three meshes, ending one hole to the right of where your first stitch ended at 4. The third stitch comes up one hole below the start of your last stitch at 5, spans four meshes and ends one hole to the right of the previous stitch at 6. The fourth stitch starts one hole to the right of the start of the last stitch, spans three meshes, and ends one hole below the end of the last stitch (up at 7, down at 8). The fifth stitch spans two meshes starting one hole to the right of the previous stitch and ends one hole below the end of the previous stitch (up at 9, down at 10, fig. 3.34a).

The second part of the Brighton is a mirror image of the first part. Diagonal stitches span meshes—first two, then three, then four, then three, then two—angling this time from bottom right to upper left (fig. 3.34b). The first stitch starts at 11, three holes down and three holes to the right of where the last stitch ended. If you rotate your canvas 90 degrees clockwise, you can work this stitch as you worked the first block. Return to the original position when working the third block, and so on.

Start subsequent rows with a block of stitches sloping in the opposite direction of the block above it (fig. 3.34c). Likewise, every block is a mirror-image of the one next to it (fig. 3.34d).

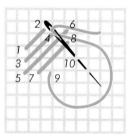

Fig. 3.34a

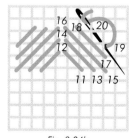

Fig. 3.34b

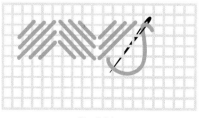

Fig. 3.34c

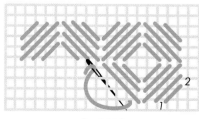

Fig. 3.34d

When you've covered the desired area, make one upright cross-stitch (see page 44) in the center of every four blocks of Brighton stitch. Look for the diamond-shaped unstitched canvas spanning two threads horizontally and vertically in the center. Work the cross-stitch up at 1, down at 2, up at 3, and down at 4 (fig. 3.34e).

The Brighton stitch produces a very textured effect that gives a canvas an almost quilted appearance. The upright cross-stitch may be worked in the same color as the blocks of stitches, or it can be worked in contrasting thread colors, as shown opposite. Pretty!

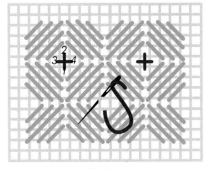

Fig. 3.34e

Following a Needlepoint Chart

There are two ways to needlepoint: use printed or painted canvas that already has the design on it, or a charted design, which is printed on a separate sheet of graph paper.

Coloring Between the Lines

Canvases often come with a picture silkscreened or hand-painted on them. A needlepoint kit will often contain a tapestry needle and all the color threads needed to work your piece, so everything's included. Following the pattern is much like doing a Paint-by-Number painting: Simply stitch areas following the color you see on the canvas. Light-colored stitches should always be completed before dark-colored stitches so that tiny, stray dark fibers aren't accidentally pulled up, sullying the lighter colors.

A brightly painted canvas awaits needle and thread.

Find Your Center

Before you start to needlepoint a design, it's important to find the center of your work. It will give you a point of reference when you count stitches and compare their placement to what the box chart or line chart indicates. To mark the center, fold the canvas in half horizontally and then vertically. Mark the fold point with an air-soluble marking pen. Use a very light touch. You'll want to make it discreet enough to be covered with stitching.

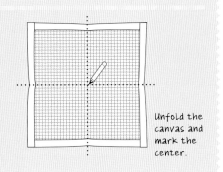

Unfold the canvas and mark the center.

On the Charts

Charted needlepoint designs are printed on an independent sheet of graph paper. The number of squares on the chart equals the number of holes in the needlepointed portion of your canvas. Stitches are shown one of two ways—either as colored-in squares used to represent each thread (this is called a *box chart*, below left), or with lines shown extending across the crossed threads of the canvas to resemble the actual stitches (known as a *line chart*, below right). Sometimes the marks are illustrated to represent the color of the thread you are recommended to use for the project. These charts are accompanied by a color key, in which each color is represented by a small box that identifies the color number and name of the thread to be used. Other times, thread color is represented in the design chart by symbols—like dots, squares, hearts, and other shapes—which are then demystified in the accompanying color key along with the thread numbers and/or names.

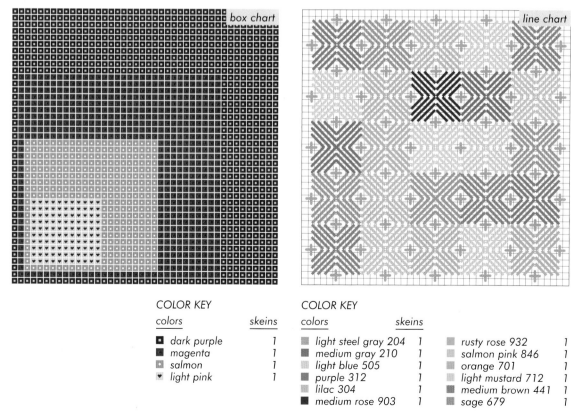

box chart

line chart

COLOR KEY

colors	*skeins*
▣ dark purple	1
▦ magenta	1
▢ salmon	1
♥ light pink	1

COLOR KEY

colors	*skeins*	*colors*	*skeins*
▦ light steel gray 204	1	▦ rusty rose 932	1
▦ medium gray 210	1	▦ salmon pink 846	1
▦ light blue 505	1	▦ orange 701	1
▦ purple 312	1	▦ light mustard 712	1
▦ lilac 304	1	▦ medium brown 441	1
■ medium rose 903	1	▦ sage 679	1

Smocking

What do little girls of today have in common with pre-nineteenth-century British laborers? A weird question, and one that I'd wager you haven't been asked recently. But the answer? Smocking.

Smocking is a method of using embroidery to gather fabric. Back in olden times, the technique was used in place of elastic (which wasn't invented until the nineteenth century). It was also an inexpensive way to do away with fastenings because it made garments stretchy. A shirt could be pulled over one's head and hands and revert to a normal shape once it was on the body. Smocked work shirts were particularly popular in England; laborers in each county wore smocks of a particular color. (It's believed that some smocked patterns indicated the profession of the person wearing it.) They were frequently passed down from generation to generation until they disintegrated.

The Smocked with Love Dress, page 125, showcases smocking at its best.

Today, smocking is used mostly for decoration on children's clothing. The advantages are numerous: It's durable because of the thickness of the gathered pleats; it's stretchy and therefore can go over big baby and toddler heads; it's more comfortable against the skin than buttons; and it's an inexpensive way to add character to a plain garment.

There are two kinds of smocking: English-style smocking and North American–style smocking, which is a kind of New World take on the more traditional methods. With English smocking, the pleats are made before you start embroidering. (Hardcore smockers may want to invest in a pleater, a handy machine that will do the pleating job for you.) English smocking is often recommended for beginners because pregathering makes the smocking stitches easier to work, so that's the focus of this little lesson.

With regular smocking, you make the pleats as you go. The Smocked with Love Dress on page 125 uses the regular smocking technique. There are several kinds of North American–style smocking that use patterns made up

FUN FACT: The word *smock* comes from *smoc,* an Anglo-Saxon sacklike garment worn by farmers as an outer layer to protect their clothing underneath. It evolved into loose underclothing for women, called *smickets,* a delightful word that no doubt should be brought back into general usage!

of rows of dots that are marked and stitched on the right side of the fabric. Sheets of specially made iron-on dots can be transferred to your fabric just as you'd apply an iron-on when doing freehand embroidery (fig. 3.35a). You can also draw your own dots using a water-soluble fabric marker. Just use a ruler to make sure all your spaces are even! Spacing is usually ⅛ to ¼ inch between dots and ⅛ to ½ inch between rows. The lines of dots should be aligned both vertically and horizontally with the warp and weft threads of the fabric (fig. 3.35b). Small-patterned fabrics, such as gingham or evenly placed polka dots, can also be used to guide your pleat-making if you want to forgo the iron-on dots.

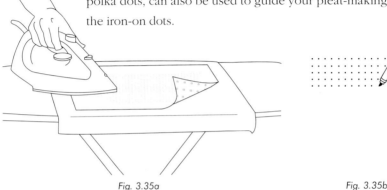

Fig. 3.35a

Fig. 3.35b

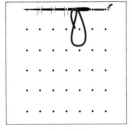

Fig. 3.36a

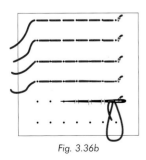

Fig. 3.36b

A Pleating Primer

Cut a 12-inch square of gingham fabric. The wrong side of the fabric should be facing up while you are making the pleats. Pleat-making is called *tacking*. First, make a knot at the end of your tacking thread (see page 23). (I usually use an all-purpose sewing thread in a contrasting color to the fabric, but, because the thread will be removed once your stitching is complete, there's no reason to stress too much if you don't have your fave thread on hand.) Mark the fabric with dots as shown in fig. 3.35b. Insert your needle just before the upper-right dot, and make one running stitch to the left, coming back up just after the dot. (Because you're working on the wrong side, the knot will be visible.) Continue in this way—with each stitch going down into the fabric before the dot and coming back up just after the dot—until the end of the row (fig. 3.36a). The result should look like a series of dots and dashes. Leave a 3-inch tail after the last dot on the wrong side. Continue in this way with all the other horizontal lines of dots, using a new thread for each row (fig. 3.36b).

To gather the fabric, simply pull evenly on the tacking threads, two at a time, and gently gather the fabric to the right as you go (fig. 3.36c). When you have the desired width, knot the two tacking threads together. Do this with each pair of tacking threads.

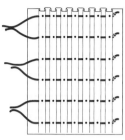

Fig. 3.36c

Meet the Smocking Stitches

There are a lot of fun smocking stitches, most of which are variations of basic freehand stitches that are worked through pleats on the right side of the fabric. Each stitch is worked through about one-third of the depth of the pleat.

Get to know a member of the family:

Honeycomb Stitch

This stitch is worked on the right side of the fabric, from the top to the bottom. It goes from left to right in a zigzag formation. Thread a size 9 embroidery needle with three strands of floss. Work with the regular method as shown or have your gathered fabric ready to go (see "A Pleating Primer," facing page).

honeycomb stitch

Bring the needle through the fabric with a knot at the back to secure the thread. Working from left to right and with the needle pointing to the left, bring the needle up at 1 and make one small straight stitch from left to right at 2, and another small stitch from left to right at 1. Pull up the thread to draw the two points together, enclosing one square of the gingham between them (fig. 3.37a). Reinsert the needle at 2 and come up at 3 on the row directly below (fig. 3.37b). Take a small stitch at 4 and another at 3, keeping the needle pointing to the left (fig. 3.37c). Pull the thread taut as before, so that points 3 and 4 are drawn together (fig. 3.37d). Continue along the row, repeating the two straight stitches up and down the two rows. At the end of the pair of rows, take the thread to the back and make a knot on the wrong side to secure it. Cut your thread. Make a knot in the end of the thread and bring your needle up three rows down from 1. Repeat pattern 1–4 to work another pair of smocked rows (fig. 3.37e).

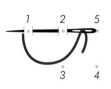

Fig. 3.37a

Fig. 3.37b

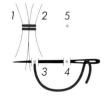

Fig. 3.37c

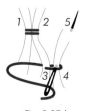

Fig. 3.37d

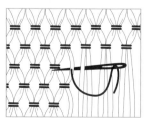

Fig. 3.37e

63

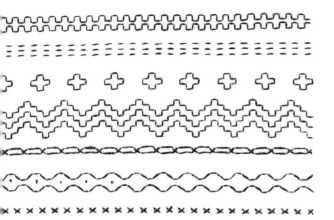

A redwork sampler is a study in counted thread embroidery.

Counted Thread

Growing up, I had an older cousin who was a big counted cross-stitch fan, and at every family gathering she'd be there with her needle and thread and a paper chart of lines and dots. To me, it looked like one big math problem. One Thanksgiving, however, she showed me how each square corresponded with one of the meshes on the fabric canvas. Aha!

Thanks to her, I quickly grew to love the orderly nature of counted thread work—a kind of embroidery that relies heavily on simple linear stitches like the straight stitch (page 30), running stitch (page 30), backstitch (page 32), and cross-stitch (page 44) worked in repetitive geometric patterns. The patterns are made by counting the threads of the fabric while following a charted design. Since the threads of the fabric are already woven straight up and down, you're always able to achieve perfect results without even trying. Perfection without effort? Sign me up.

Cross-stitch, blackwork, Assisi (named for the town in Italy where it originated), pattern darning, Hardanger, and pulled thread work are all well-known styles that belong to the counted thread embroidery family.

Counted thread work is usually done on Aida cloth (page 12) or similar kinds of evenweave fabrics, such as linen—anything that has countable threads that run straight up and down and form a grid (see page 12 for more information). The more threads there are for each inch of fabric, the "smaller" and more delicate the embroidered area will be.

It's also possible, however, to follow counted thread grids by treating the elements on printed fabrics just as you would the mesh on your fabric. Gingham, with its neat rows of checks, works really well for counted thread work, even if the fabric isn't technically evenweave.

Get Wasted

Waste canvas in action.

Using waste canvas is the best way to stitch counted thread designs onto a non-evenweave fabric (where there's not an obvious grid to follow): Just baste the waste canvas where you'd like the pattern to go, matching the warp and weft of the canvas to the grain of the fabric, fig. 3.38a), and then stitch over the waste canvas and through the base fabric (fig. 3.38b). Each canvas mesh and hole is followed, just as you'd follow the meshes and holes on an evenweave fabric. When you're finished, the waste canvas threads are carefully pulled out with tweezers (sometimes it helps to moisten the area first with some water to ease the process, see page 15), as in fig. 3.38c. The perfectly stitched design on the fabric surface remains.

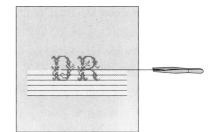

Fig. 3.38a   Fig. 3.38b   Fig. 3.38c

Following a Counted Thread Chart

Counted thread embroidery charts will list the mesh size of the evenweave fabric (the count of stitches per inch), as well as the correct needle and thread to use. Lines on the grid represent the number of squares of your gridded fabric, however, you can make a design bigger or smaller on your stitch surface. Use a fabric with a different size weave or multiply the number of squares you use for each stitch. Instead of having each thread span over one mesh, you can span two meshes so that your final cross will cover an area of four stitches; three meshes and it'll cover nine; four and it'll cover sixteen, and so on.

When charted designs are in color, the color indicates what thread color should be used. When a chart is in black and white, symbols indicate thread color. For both types of charts, a color key on the edge of the chart will tell you what thread color, floss numbers, and floss names to use for each color or symbol on the chart.

FUN FACT: Hands off my napkin! Before the days when you could purchase paper napkins by the hundred-pack and cheap cotton ones could be easily snagged from restaurants (or so we've been told . . .), people used unique counted stitch designs to set their table linens apart from everyone else's—lest someone try to snag one and pass it off as their own. It was like LoJack for linens!

TIP: Use a tapestry needle when you're doing counted thread work—they slip easily in the holes of evenweave fabrics while sharper needles get stuck in the mesh. However, when using waste canvas or a non-evenweave fabric, definitely go with a sharper needle that'll easily pierce the fabric.

There are two kinds of charted designs, box and line:

Box charts: Every box on the grid usually represents one stitch, but the boxes indicate the mesh of the weave, not the holes. In addition to telling you what colors to use, the key on the side of your chart might also tell you what stitch should be used in each area. Usually, a letter in the box will correspond to a letter in the key and to the name of the stitch. In cases when a stitch will cover more than one box, an outline around the boxes will indicate the boundaries of that stitch.

Line charts: The lines that make up a line chart represent the warp and weft threads of your fabric, and the boxes, therefore, are the holes between the meshes. Each stitch is shown individually as a straight mark spanning one or more meshes or threads. The type of stitch required for an area is indicated by how the lines are drawn; an X over one mesh will be a cross-stitch, a "+" is an upright cross-stitch, a straight line spanning several threads is a backstitch, and so on.

COLOR KEY

colors	skeins
■ dark red	1
♡ pink	1
◹ green	1

box chart

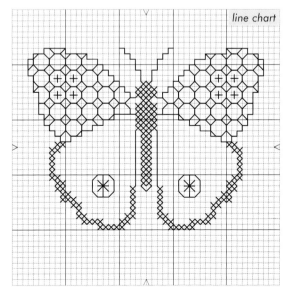

line chart

Get Centered

The first thing you have to do before starting any counted thread design? Find your center. I'm not talking metaphorically—what I mean is, find the actual center of the area you are going to work. The center point is extremely useful as you follow your chart; most charts have their center points marked. The chart's center and your fabric's center act as reference points as you literally count how many stitches you need to work in every direction.

To find the center, fold the fabric in half horizontally and then vertically. Lightly make a mark with an air-soluble fabric marking pen where the two folds meet.

Meet the Counted Thread Stitches

The main stitches you will use when doing counted thread work are cross-stitch (page 44), straight stitch (page 30), running stitch (page 30), and backstitch (page 32). These are the most basic embroidery stitches and the easiest to learn and do. If you haven't done so already, break out the Practice Stitch Card located between the first and second parts of this book. It will teach you how to do all of these stitches. You'll just need a threaded needle to get started.

Get to know the head of the family:

Cross-Stitch (aka Sampler Stitch)

The number-one most popular counted thread embroidery stitch is the cross-stitch. In fact, counted thread embroidery is often called counted cross-stitch. The Old Country Tea Towel on page 180 is a prime example of a counted cross-stitch project, as it involves the two best methods for working a cross-stitch: as a pictorial element (the heart) and stitched letters (the monogram).

In counted cross-stitch every single stitch is a cross-stitch worked singly or in rows. When working with an evenweave fabric such as Aida

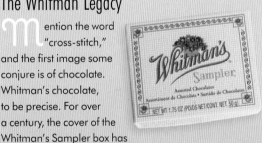

The Whitman Legacy

Mention the word "cross-stitch," and the first image some conjure is of chocolate. Whitman's chocolate, to be precise. For over a century, the cover of the Whitman's Sampler box has featured the Whitman's logo rendered in counted thread cross-stitches. In 1907 the company's president had a clever idea: Inspired by a stitched sampler in his home, he decided to present a sampling of chocolates in a box decorated with a sampler. For the bicentennial, Whitman's hired a noted embroiderer named Dorrit Gutterson to stitch a 16 x 28-inch sampler that related the history of Philadelphia, the company's hometown. Whitman's has had no small role in maintaining the heritage of counted thread work: In 1971 the company donated a collection of more than 575 cross-stitched samplers to the Philadelphia Museum of Art.

cloth or linen, you'll usually use one cross-stitch per box, but sometimes you might need to do a cross-stitch over several boxes in order to make your design the proper size, as with the Victorian Tic-Tac-Toe (page 189).

If you'd like some hands-on practice, follow the "Home Sweet Home" box chart on page 66 using embroidery floss in the colors shown. For fabric and needle suggestions, see page 16.

Blackwork

Like every form of counted thread embroidery, blackwork uses straight stitches in different combinations to make patterns. They can be repeated to fill large or small areas or used to add texture to pictorial designs.

Although this form of embroidery gets its name from working black thread on white fabric (hence "black" and "work"), the same exact patterns look just as nice in and on any color. In fact, working these patterns in red would be called . . . *redwork*. All of the patterns worked on the Dashing Vest and Tie on page 91 are classic blackwork patterns, stitched in red.

Blackwork designs are usually illustrated with a photograph of the completed pattern along with a line chart (see "Following a Counted Thread Chart," page 65). Unlike most embroidery stitches, many blackwork patterns do not have a name to identify them. Instead, the patterns are either assigned an arbitrary number by the designer, or they are given a descriptive name, such as "thistle" or "Tudor rose."

Here are three typical blackwork patterns (figs. 3.41a–c) for you to try out. Cut a 12-inch square of 14-count Aida cloth. Use a skein of embroidery floss in a contrasting color, a size 24 tapestry needle, and a pair of embroidery scissors to follow along. If you like these patterns, I have good news: There are hundreds more!

FUN FACT: Blackwork, or "Spanish work," was popularized in England during the sixteenth century when Catherine of Aragon brought blackwork shirts with her from Spain. Portraits of both men and women in the Elizabethan period often have blackwork embroidery stitched upon their sleeves, cuffs, and collars. In fact, the Holbein stitch (aka the double running stitch) is named for the painter Hans Holbein the Younger. Keep an eye out for blackwork the next time you're visiting a museum or watching an episode of *The Tudors*!

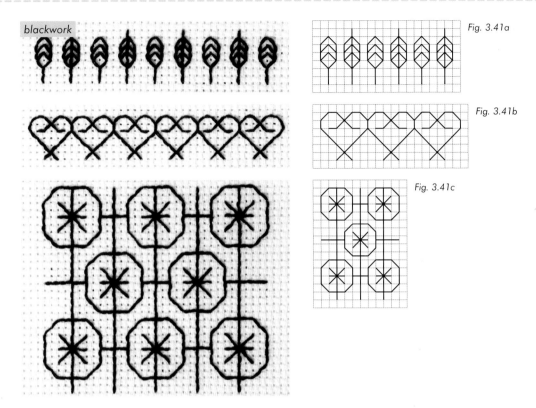

blackwork

Fig. 3.41a

Fig. 3.41b

Fig. 3.41c

Two Steps Forward, One Step Back

Has something gone awry with your work? Don't sweat the small stuff! Here are some common embroidery stitching missteps along with how to straighten your stride and sprint on ahead.

Problem: I missed a stitch!
Solution: No biggie. If the pattern is going to still make sense visually without that one stitch, then I say keep going and don't stress. If not, turn your work to the wrong side and use a seam ripper or embroidery scissors to snip the back of the stitches. Then use a tweezers to pick out the rogue threads. Yes, it's sad to see your work ripped out, but it's sadder if a pesky mistake is going to bother you every time you look at your finished project. The more you practice stitching, the fewer times you'll skip a stitch in the future.

Problem: My thread is tangled!
Solution: Turn your work upside down so that your needle and thread dangle down. The thread should untangle just like when you let go of a twisted swing to let the chains unwind. (Your needle shouldn't fall off, but keep an eye on it just in case.)

Problem: I just can't do the stitch.
Solution: Change your point of view. Either put it down and try again a little later, or see if you can do the stitch upside down: Try rotating your fabric 180 degrees and work it that way, or try executing the stitch at an entirely different angle (try turning the canvas 90 degrees) or in a different way. Hey, you're allowed to make up your own stitches just as much as anyone else!

how to start an embroidery group

ometimes embroidery is best undertaken on a cozy evening in front of your 42-inch plasma. But it sure doesn't stop there. Embroiderers band together online and in real life to share needling secrets, show off their work, and host stitch-ins. Check out Hand-Embroidery.Meetup.com to look for embroidery communities in your area. Or, if you're eager to launch your very own embroidery group, here are eight ideas to get you started:

1 Make a home online.

A website is a great way to show off your work, and you can also use it to attract embroiderers to your brand-spankin'-new weekly stitching group. Post pictures of your creations each week. At the very least, create a homepage with basic contact information and relevant keywords so that like-minded people searching online will find you. Check out Tumblr.com or Blogger.com if you want to make a quick and easy free blog on which you can upload pictures and info.

2 Go viral.

Start a Facebook fan page for your embroidery group. Anytime a fan comments on your page, each of her 300+ friends will read about it in their newsfeeds. Now imagine what would happen if you had five, ten, or fifty fans posting to your page. You don't have to be a math whiz to know your embroidery group will gain a ton of exposure—and reach new potential members.

3 Connect on craft forums.

Craft forums are great places to meet local embroiderers and recruit them to your group. You can reach thousands of potential members on sites like Craftforum.com, Craftster.org, and Getcrafty.com. These online communities also come in handy when you're having trouble with your padded stitch or want to learn one of the hundreds of kinds of stitches that I couldn't fit in these pages!

4 Play Show and Tell.

You can find a heck of a lot of stitching camaraderie on the Internet. There are countless sites where you can show off your stitching skills and drool over the talents of other embroideristas. Needlework-tips -and-techniques.com has a "Show and Tell" page where you can upload a photo of your latest design and the story behind it. One of my favorite sites, Feeling Stitchy, has an embroidery group on Flickr where thousands of members upload pics. Or if you look really good on camera and want to share your latest beadwork stitching tricks, try uploading a homemade tutorial on YouTube. (If you regularly host a real-world stitching group, remember to plug it at some point during your vid.)

5 Network like nobody's business.

You never know who might have an embroidery hoop handy, so e-mail everyone you know—friends, coworkers, relatives, and neighbors—to ask if they embroider or if they'd like to learn. Entice them by attaching an image of one of your masterpieces. And don't forget to ask them to forward your message to anyone else who might be interested. Timing is an important consideration: I once invited people over to make some simple embroidered ornaments and cards at Make Workshop a week before Christmas. There were so many RSVPs that I had to invest in folding chairs.

Network outside of your social circle, too. Try chatting up anyone checking out the embroidery section at a bookstore (quite a hopping place!) or any familiar faces at your local craft store.

6 Open an EGA chapter.

Looking to join a national network of hardcore embroiderers? Anyone can start his or her own chapter with the Embroiderers' Guild of America at www.egausa .org. Or you can bring your own embroidery group on a field trip to the EGA location of your choice. EGA chapters across the country hold workshops, offer judge certification programs, and host lectures with renowned needleworkers.

7 Pick a theme.

You may not know a lot of embroiderers, but you must know people who have other interests. Music? Travel? Gadgets? Pick an overarching theme for your group, or pick a new one each week. For example: At your music-lovers group one week, have everyone embroider their favorite song lyric onto a sampler. Then create appliqué versions of each member of the Beatles the next. Or pick a technology-inspired project each week (iPod cozies week one, stitched pictures of computers week two...). Or pick a style of embroidery from a different country each week. What's that—you're going to do the Florentine stitch? And you're serving Tuscan wine? Where's my invite? This is also a good way to get the word out about what you're doing. If you have a group where you just make homages to old cameras, local sites and newspapers will likely eat it up—and more press will mean more attendees. Also, you can use it as a hook to tip off specialty sites. The heavily trafficked tech site Gizmodo has posted pictures of embroidered computer motherboards. It'll drive a lot of traffic to your site, and to your group, if you can get them to link to a swell picture of that cleverly cross-stitched Polaroid camera you just whipped up.

8 Find a space.

If your home is hardly bigger than your bed (a common situation here in New York City), community centers, libraries, and parks are prime (and spacious) locations for embroidery meet-ups. Or you can scout out a local sponsor to let you hold your meetings at their shop. With the chance to attract new customers and the potential for good PR, fabric stores, art galleries, or restaurants would be happy to host your meetings— especially if you promise to embroider their business name on your sweet new embroidery team uniforms!

CHAPTER 4

Getting Designs onto Fabric and Canvas

Before I get my stitch on, I always try to have some idea of what I'd like my finished product to look like. (Okay, not always—sometimes I just pick up a needle and go at it, Jackson Pollock–style.) Needlepoint canvases often come preprinted (you can also paint your own). Cross-stitch patterns can be followed from a chart. But with freehand embroidery especially, it's more than a little helpful to have your image applied directly onto the fabric before you start working. This goes for commercially printed patterns with heat-sensitive ink as well as for those that originate in my own little cells of gray matter. Ergo, before I pick up my needle, I (almost!) always have to deal first with transferring the design using one of these hand methods.

Iron-ons

About half my childhood was spent ironing—and I loved it. No, really! Granny Hallie always had a handy supply of hot-iron transfers that I could embroider. She gave hers to me, and I give mine to you (in the envelope at the front of your new all-time favorite craft book—nudge, nudge, wink). Iron-ons are simply line drawings that you can transfer to almost any fabric. With freehand embroidery, your stitches can follow the lines of the transferred image. The purplish lines left behind by the transfer ink won't fade, so you'll want to use stitches that will cover the transfer. The disadvantage of this method is that if your fabric is a dark color, the purple won't show up well; but it's perfect for anything on the lighter side.

The transfers I used as a kid were Aunt Martha's (that's the name of a company, not a relative). Aunt Martha's patterns have been around since the 1920s; I'd bet good money that you've bought or worn or wiped your hands on more than a couple of items with an Aunt Martha's design on it. Style-wise, these transfers are still living in the Truman era, and that makes them extra cool, if you ask me. They have a superinnocent, vintage feel to them. And their variety is impressive—there are so many designs. If you can dream it, they have a cute transfer of it: A dog with a cowboy hat and a lasso? An elderly couple square-dancing? An adorable cat doing bookkeeping? Check, check, and—amazingly—check! Look for them at any craft store or online at

Aunt Martha's transfers

Wash Up

Before you start your project, wash and dry the fabric or garment in the same way you plan to do after it's embellished (we're only talking fabric here; if you're stitching on Aida cloth or needlepoint canvas, there's no need to rub-a-dub-dub). If you plan to machine-wash your project down the road, it's a good idea to preshrink your fabric. Washers, and especially dryers, are harsh and you never know how the work is going to hold up when put through the spin cycle. In fact, it's a good idea to do a few stitches on a test piece and wash that too, just to make sure that nothing bleeds or stretches. Long story short, I'd suggest treating all of your stitched pieces with serious TLC. I hand-wash most of my work using a smidgen of Woolite and cold water. After removing excess moisture with a towel, I lay it flat to dry. Alternatively, you can take your handiwork to a dry cleaner. If you do use machinery, put the washer on its gentlest setting and then set the dryer to cool. But, if you never plan to wear or wash the project, don't worry about this step.

Ironing Pointers

* Use a padded ironing board. I have a little tabletop one that doesn't take up much closet space. Ironing on the floor or on a towel or table never works out well.

* If you are really into your ironing board cover, put a piece of scrap fabric on top of the ironing board to protect the surface. Otherwise, there's a very good chance that the image will transfer onto the board cover itself.

* Not all fabrics are iron-friendly. If you're unsure whether yours is or isn't, test a little piece to make sure it doesn't melt. What's more, keep in mind the fabric around the area you are going to be stitching. When embroidering on cotton panties I've very often ironed too near to the lace trim, causing it to melt. No fun!

* Never leave a hot iron unattended! This might be a no-brainer, but it's worth repeating. (Gosh, maybe I should stitch that on a sampler!)

TIP: Ideally, you want to test an iron-on pattern on a scrap of the same fabric you'll be stitching. Commercially produced hot transfers will come with a test pattern just for this purpose. (See ours on the pattern sheets in the envelope at the front of this book.)

ColonialPatterns.com. They come in envelopes that cost about a dollar and each pack contains multiple reusable patterns and a good dollop of nostalgia.

Once you've picked out your iron-on, cut it out, leaving at least a ½-inch border around the image. Place your fabric on your ironing board, right side up. Usually you preheat a dry iron on the cotton setting for a heavyweight fabric and on the wool setting for a lightweight fabric. Iron the fabric in the area where you will transfer the design to preheat it, as hot fabric stamps more quickly. Place the transfer facedown exactly where you'd like it to go and pin the design to the fabric. Press the transfer onto the fabric for five seconds and take a peek by carefully lifting an edge of the pattern to see if it's working (A). If the lines are faint, reapply the iron in five-second intervals. Make sure to heat the whole area, but try to move the iron and transfer as little as possible, to prevent blurring. Peel away the pattern to reveal the transferred design (B). Now get stitchin'!

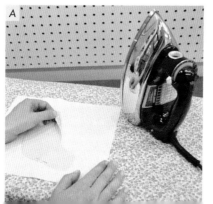

A

B

Heat-Transfer Pencils

I've yet to find a satisfactory kind of DIY iron-on transfer paper of Aunt Martha's ilk. So when I have a non-Auntie-M line drawing I want to embroider, I use a heat-transfer pencil. Heat-transfer pencils come in several colors, but I've found that red shows up best. As with other iron-on processes, this is a good option only if you're using a light-colored fabric. (For dark-colored fabrics, you'll want to use the basting or dressmaker's carbon methods on pages 77 and 78.)

Heat-transfer pencils are easy and convenient, but there are a few steps involved.

Material Girl

*D*o you have a closet? Oh my gosh, me too! How about a drawer of dish towels? A blah shower curtain? Potential embroidery projects are all around you. If you're worried about experimenting on your own precious duds, load up on old clothes at any thrift store or yard sale—skirts, button-downs, hats, pants. . . . If you're a beginner, you might want to stay away from jersey, spandex, or other fabrics that stretch at least the first few times you stitch, but otherwise, the sky's the limit when seeking out surfaces to embellish.

1. Find a drawing or photo that you'd like to transfer. The picture could be an original drawing, something traced, lettering—the sky is the limit!

2. *If there's no text on your piece and/or you don't care what direction the image faces, then skip to Step 3.* If you want or need the image to be reversed, tape the drawing to a sunny window or put it facedown on a glass table and then shine a light through it from underneath. You may also reverse the image on a computer, or use a lightbox.

3. With a piece of regular tracing paper from a stationery or art supply store, trace the image using your heat-transfer pencil (fig. 4.1a). Make sure that the point is sharp and your line is clear and dark.

Fig. 4.1a

4. Place the drawing facedown exactly where you'd like it to go on the fabric and pin it in place. Set the iron to the appropriate temperature for the fabric you're working on (linen = hot, for example) and then iron the paper for ten to twenty seconds (fig. 4.1b). If all goes well, you'll now have your original image (in the right direction!) on your fabric of choice.

Heat-transfer pencils are permanent, so, as with iron-ons, you want to use stitching that will completely cover the lines (fig. 4.1c).

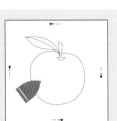

Fig. 4.1b

Fig. 4.1c

The Make Workshop "Free Martha" cross-stitch kit

Photo Heat-Transfer Paper

Yes, I'm a little obsessed with Aunt Martha's (see page 73). But sometimes you want to make your own darn picture of a feline CPA. Or perhaps you want to make a picture of that other "Aunt" Martha—Martha Stewart, that is. You might remember that way back in the early days of this century, Ms. Stewart had some problems with the law and ended up in jail. It was not a "good thing." But to make lemonade out of the situation, I started selling kits so that people could stitch T-shirts with Martha's image and the words FREE MARTHA. I did this using a photo of Martha, which I converted into a cross-stitch grid on my computer (see "Pretty As a Picture," page 79, for more on how to do this yourself). A stack of photo heat-transfer paper, a printer, an iron, and I was golden. The kits were such a success, they spawned a crafting empire that includes a TV show, magazine, and lines at Macy's, Michaels, and Home Depot. Okay, not quite, but a girl can dream . . .

Photo heat-transfer paper works very much like iron-ons. The major difference is that it leaves a kind of heavy film on the fabric—if you've ever dabbled in T-shirt decorating, you probably know what I'm talking about. Even the blank areas will have that starchy-filmy covering. As a result, I try to cut the paper as close to my design as possible—this minimizes the amount of space that's covered with the film. I like to use it only when I plan to cover the area entirely with stitches. Otherwise, the transfer paper shows through, and there will be an obvious discrepancy in texture.

Transfer-Eze 101

Transfer-Eze. (The name says it all!) Simply photocopy or scan and print the artwork directly onto the stitchable "film" sheets of Transfer-Eze. Peel off the paper backing and apply the Transfer-Eze directly onto your fabric, then stitch. When you're done, cut away excess Transfer-Eze and then soak your project in cold water to melt the remaining film—magic!

Water- and Air-Soluble Fabric Markers

When I was a kid there was a brand of marker called Magic Markers—but those things had nothing on water- and air-soluble fabric markers. I load up on these whenever I find myself at a Hobby Lobby. They're actually two markers in one: One end is blue and the other purple. The blue side makes a line that will come out with H_2O. Marks made with the purple side will be visible for a few days (maybe longer if it's brand-new), and then they'll fade completely. Magic, right? But wait, there's more! Clover also makes a marker that has a water-soluble pen on one end and an eraser pen on the other so that if you make a little mistake, you don't have to launder the whole thing.

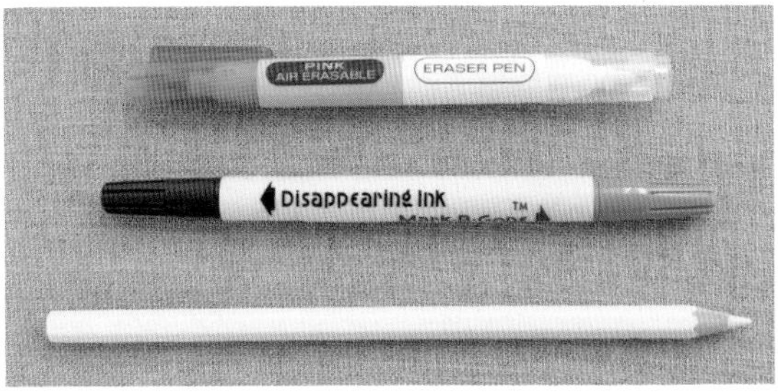

These are my go-to markers when I want to create a design freehand directly on the fabric. Alas, as with many of the other methods mentioned here, these usually won't show up on darker fabrics. Chalk, however, will. I try to stick to a tailor's chalk pencil in white—it's the least waxy and also the least likely to smudge (fig. 4.2a).

Create freehand designs by drawing directly on fabric.

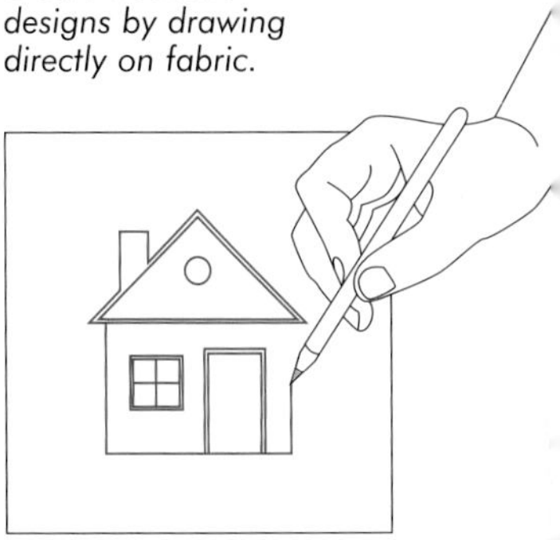

Fig. 4.2a

Basting

Basting is a technique for transferring an image without putting any kind of indelible mark on your fabric. It's also (at last!) a way to transfer images onto dark fabrics. First, trace your image onto a piece of tracing or tissue paper (fig. 4.3a). Then pin or baste it to the fabric (fig. 4.3b). Using an all-purpose sewing thread, make long straight stitches over the outline of the image (fig. 4.3c). This technique is also known as a *thread trace,* which makes sense. When you've basted all the lines, tear off the paper and either cover the basting with stitches or remove it as you go along (fig. 4.3d).

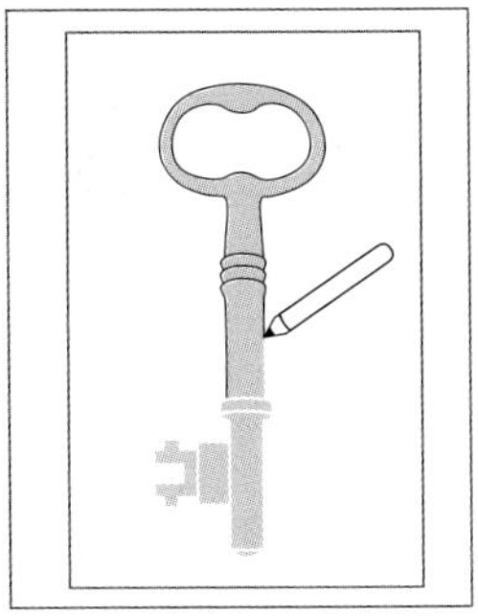

Fig. 4.3a

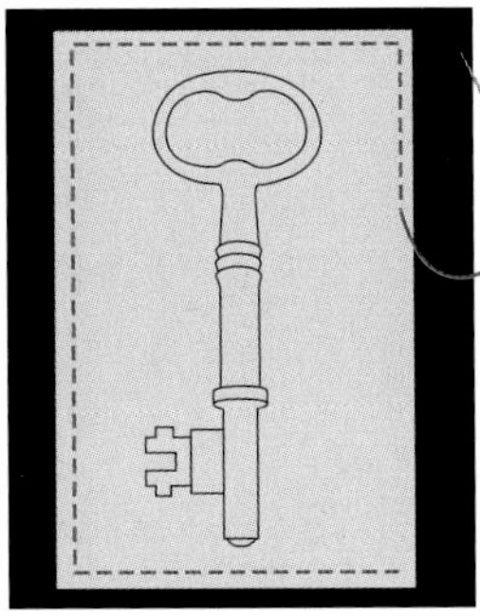

Fig. 4.3b

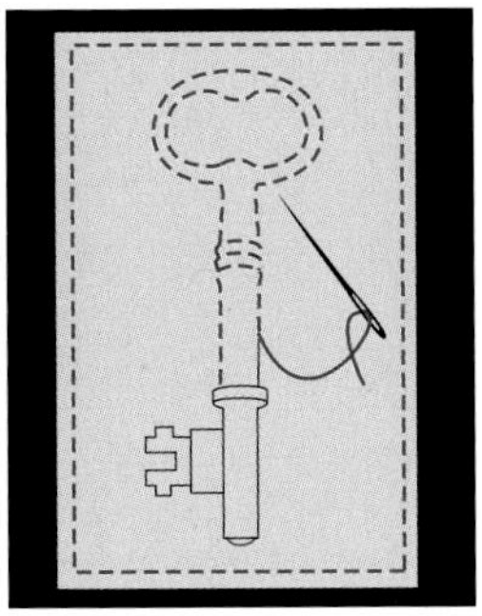

Fig. 4.3c

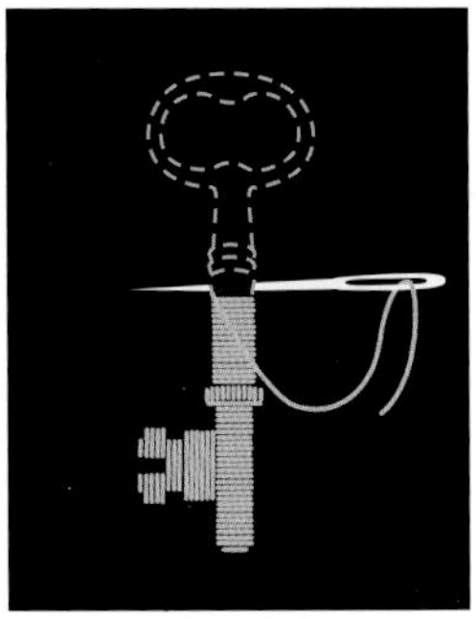

Fig. 4.3d

Dressmaker's Carbon

To use dressmaker's carbon, a chalky paper material used to transfer sewing patterns to fabric, you need to make a little sandwich: At the bottom you have your fabric, right side up; place the carbon paper, carbon side down, on top of that; and lastly, place your image, right side up. Pin the layers together. Using a tracing stylus tool or ballpoint tracer pen, trace over the lines of your image (fig. 4.4a). Carefully peel back the carbon paper to make sure the image has transferred. Remove the carbon paper and your image (fig. 4.4b) and begin stitching. Dressmaker's carbon comes in a variety of colors, but some work better than others. In my experience, white is the most reliable; and I much prefer using a tracing stylus instead of a pen or pencil. After you're finished embroidering, you can use a wet or dry cloth to gently wipe off the carbon lines.

Fig. 4.4a

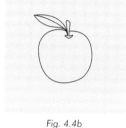

Fig. 4.4b

Stabilizer

There are some instances where you need to use stabilizer on the back of your work in order to create a firm, nonstretchy ground for your piece (if you're working on a knit fabric, for instance, see fig. 4.5). There's also removable stabilizer that can be used to transfer images onto any type of fabric which is especially helpful when working on dark colors with a printed or pencil heat transfer. Here are two main ways to use stabilizer to get images onto fabric.

The first involves tracing your image or ironing a heat-transfer pattern directly onto the stabilizer. Pin the stabilizer to your fabric and trace the outline of your design using basting stitches (see "Basting," page 77), then remove the stabilizer (fig. 4.6). This is done according to what kind of stabilizer you're using:

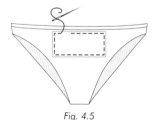

Fig. 4.5

Fig. 4.6

✳ Tear-away stabilizer is removed using your fingers or tweezers.

* Wash-away stabilizer dissolves in water.

* Heat-away stabilizer disintegrates with the heat of an iron.

Check the type of stabilizer you're using and follow the manufacturer's removal instructions.

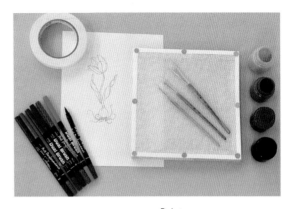

Painting on Canvas

Many store-bought needlepoint canvases are hand-painted, which makes them awfully pricey. Solution? Paint your own. All you need is a blank piece of canvas (cut at least 2 inches larger than your image on each side), a few tubes of acrylic paint, and brushes in a handful of shapes and sizes (I find that firmer stencil brushes work best). To copy an image, tape the canvas down on top of a color copy of the image and then trace it with a pencil. Tack the canvas to stretcher bars and fill in the outlines with paint. Or skip the tracing and paint from your imagination! If the acrylic paint seems to be clogging the holes of your mesh, thin it with a little water or use a straw to blow open the holes. For a more simple design, simply trace the image using a fine-tip permanent marker.

Paint your own needlepoint designs onto raw canvas.

Keep in mind what stitch, or stitches, you plan on using; if your entire piece will be worked in tent stitches, each cross-thread will need to be one color. The higher the mesh count of the canvas, the more detailed your image can be.

Pretty as a Picture

Any photo can be turned into an original embroidery pattern. Here's how:

Make a black-and-white photocopy of your picture, and then outline all the key lines in black permanent marker. (If you want, you can scan your photo, use a program like Photoshop to turn it into a black-and-white image, and then increase the contrast—that'll work, too.) If you're using a light-colored fabric, use either the heat-transfer pencil or water- or air-soluble fabric markers to transfer the pattern. If it's a dark fabric, try the

dressmaker's carbon method (facing page). When transferring, stick to following the lines; use stitching to create shaded areas.

Where Technology and Embroidery Meet

To convert an image into a perfect grid for your needlepointing or cross-stitching pleasure, there are a handful of options available online and on disc.

✻ PC Stitch is my go-to program for uploading images and plotting out grids. Using it, I create a grid that will work for cross-stitching. Symbols designate which thread colors go where. PC Stitch also lets me modify patterns and text from predesigned patterns and incorporate them into my own image. Available at PCStitch.com, this software works only on PCs.

At StitchesApp.com, transfer any image into a stitch chart.

✻ Stitches is a nifty program similar to PC Stitch, but created for use with Macs. Available at StitchesApp.com, it's a quick and easy way to upload a picture and transfer it into a printable PDF to follow for needlepoint or cross-stitch work.

✻ If you're Photoshop-savvy, you can create a perfectly functional pattern for either needlepoint or cross-stitch by lowering the color resolution and then using the Pixellate→Mosaic function to determine the size and density of your design grid. Then, you can match the colors to threads by sight, or you can find charts online that will point you to the particular DMC thread number that best corresponds to the RGB number of the Photoshop color.

✻ Visit Pic2point.com to explore a site that can convert your uploaded images into needlepoint patterns. You enter your mesh size, canvas size, and the number of colors you want and up pops a preview image of your canvas! You can then print out a needlepoint pattern (on regular paper) that you can copy onto canvas.

If you prefer avoiding the web, contact your local embroidery or needlepoint shop. The store likely works with a professional artist who will paint a canvas for you from a photo.

A Crash Course in Color

Mixing up color is a fun and easy way to customize a project. I like to think that I have a naturally good instinct when it comes to colors, but, in truth, there are certain combos that just go better than others. Sometimes when I'm unsure what colors to use, I turn to my trusty color wheel, which illustrates the relationships between different colors. You can buy one at a craft or paint store. Some color wheels have little windows cut out from each color tab so you can hold up different fabrics to see how they will look with the surrounding color.

The most common color combinations are *monochromatic*, *analogous*, and *complementary*. Knowing the basics about these three groupings of color will make you a little savvier when you're trying to figure out how to make your piece soothe the eye or snap to attention.

✳ **Monochromatic combinations** include variations on just one color, shaded a little darker or lighter. Stick with these very similar tones when you're hoping for something that'll look elegant and clean.

✳ **Analogous colors** look pleasant and cheery next to each other thanks to the fact that they live next to each other on the color wheel: Dark red, red, reddish orange, and bright orange are all considered analogous.

✳ **Complementary colors** are opposite each other on the color wheel. One is primary and the other is secondary; the secondary color is complementary when paired with the primary color that contains no element of that hue. So, orange, for example, which is made up of reds and yellows, looks striking with blue; blue is the one primary color that cannot be combined in any way to make orange. Many artists traditionally use a set of complementary pairs such as white and black, red and green, and yellow and violet (and you should, too!).

color wheel

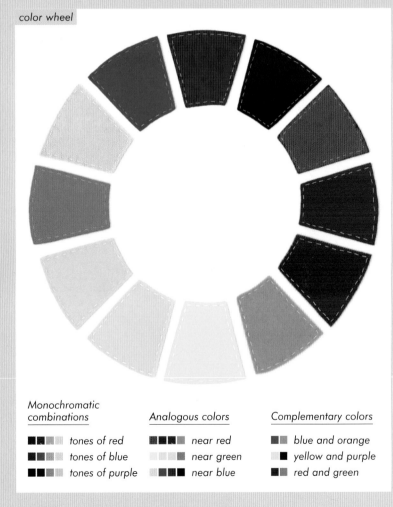

Monochromatic combinations	Analogous colors	Complementary colors
■■■■ tones of red	■■■■ near red	■■ blue and orange
■■■■ tones of blue	■■■■ near green	■ yellow and purple
■■■■ tones of purple	■■■ near blue	■■ red and green

Get Inspired

The most important tools for any aspiring needleworker are absolutely free: your eyes and your curiosity. Inspiration is everywhere. Using the techniques described in this chapter, any image can be translated into embroidery. Take note of patterns that you like and rip out appealing images from magazines. Look for motifs and color combinations that please you. It could be the trim of a favorite coat, a design on an old book binding, or an adored object that you'd like to see replicated on your favorite sweatshirt or dress (an old mixtape, perhaps). I like to keep a pad of graph paper in my purse for doodling geometric designs when I'm on the subway or on hold with the phone company—the gridded lines of graph paper are perfect for converting drawings into stitch patterns. In addition to your notebook and clipping file, you should also spend some time seeking out other people's projects on embroidery blogs and checking out their links to other bloggers (which can be found with a simple online search), or by perusing pictures of great stitched projects at websites like Craftster or photo sharing sites like Flickr.

The Scribble Game

Sometimes your imagination literally needs a little material in order to get the juices flowing. Ever play the game where you look at a cloud and see if you can see something fantastic in it? A bear holding an umbrella? Or a dolphin eating a banana?

Well, it can be a good idea to stitch with your head in the clouds.

A friend of mine comes from a family of artists. At the dinner table growing up, she and her siblings would take turns playing what they called "The Scribble Game." One of them would close their eyes and scribble a mess of lines on a piece of paper, then the others would turn the paper in every direction and try to make an image out of it by drawing on and around the scribble.

If you're stuck in an I-don't-know-what-to-embroider rut, try stitch doodling in this way: Make a few rows of stitches twisting and turning in random directions—you have to start somewhere. When you get to a stopping place, hold it up and see if there's anything unexpected to be found. What can you add? Rotate it. Notice any shapes? It could be as simple as adding a flower and a vase to a row of stem stitches, or it could mean filling in areas with satin stitches and "drawing" new lines to help accent a particularly fantastic shape or accent.

PART 2

The Projects

Let's Make

T ucked into the envelope in the front of this book are heat-transfer patterns to guide you through some of the freehand embroidery projects. Each iron-on transfer can be used about five times, so make sure to hold onto them after their first use. If you want to transfer a pattern onto fabric that is darker than the lines of the iron-on patterns, iron the pattern onto removable stabilizer first, lay it over your fabric, and stitch through it (see page 78).

I intentionally designed the 40 projects in this book to be as customizable as possible—the patterns are really only suggestions meant to guide and inspire. I suggest thread color and pattern imagery, but feel free to mix and match or add your own touches by drawing on the patterns with a heat-transfer pencil or improvising on your projects with thread. I truly believe that the best way to become a talented embroiderer is, simply, to walk around with your eyes wide open. You'll be surprised by how much decorative stitchwork you'll see in your everyday life—and how many everyday sights seem like they were meant to be embroidered on a pillow or a denim skirt. Try carrying around a notebook and/or a digital camera so that you can quickly capture images that excite you. Then develop and substitute your own patterns for the ones presented in these pages whenever the mood strikes. The shadow of a bike against a brick wall could be turned into a great silhouetted appliqué; birds on a wire are destined to be chain-stitched; that child with a pink umbrella and galoshes would look lovely on a fitted tee. Or maybe you're inspired to stitch a view from the window on your curtains.

How Ambitious Are You Feeling?

The projects in the pages that follow range from quite simple to pretty challenging; sometimes a project is challenging because it requires a lot of time and concentration, and sometimes it's challenging because it takes practice to get all the steps right, from transferring an image to stitching it to finishing it. Skip around and find what inspires you, or try the easy ones first. Totally up to you! I definitely recommend that you try at least one freehand pattern and one needlepoint or counted thread pattern. I'm pretty confident that these require the use of very different parts of your brain—so go ahead and see which side feels more comfy!

one skein of thread
beginner

two skeins of thread
beginner to intermediate beginner

three skeins of thread
advanced beginner

Keep Reading

When you approach the projects in this book, you'll recognize the following elements:

* **Materials:** Needles, thread, and fabric used for the project are listed at the beginning. When it comes to thread type, people have different preferences; some threads of similar weight and thickness are interchangeable. Don't feel afraid to swap out the designated colors for your own!

* **Patterns:** Fifteen of the freehand embroidery patterns in this book use the iron-on transfers I've included. Again, each of those iron-ons can be used as many as five times, so make sure to save them! In other instances, I'll explain how to make your own patterns. When image transfer processes are used that don't involve the patterns included in the envelope, I provide a quick how-to refresher, but you can always turn back to Chapter 4, "Getting Designs onto Fabric and Canvas," for additional study.

Needlepoint and counted thread projects come with stitch charts for you to follow. (The Art of Conversation Pillows on page 149 are an exception. Since there are only two colors there is very little chance for confusion, and it's much easier to paint the design than try to count out all the stitches.) Each chart in this book is labeled with arrows indicating the center of the pattern. Start from this point with one thread or yarn color and stitch as much of that color as you can.

* **Tools:** If you have already put together the Ultimate Embroider Everything Kit (see pages 3–7), you're ready to roll with the projects in the book. For each project, I'll point out what tools are musts and what tools are helpful to have on hand.

* **Techniques:** Each project calls for certain techniques that have been covered in Part 1. In the project instructions, I've listed page reference numbers for the pattern transfer, the various stitches worked, and the specific finishing methods you will use, just in case you need to flip to the pages to refresh your memory.

* **Variations:** Each project is meant as an initial inspiration, so take it as a suggestion: If you prefer dresses to skirts, embroider the folk art pattern on a dress—or a pillow, or a tapestry.

Ready to Dig In?

Whether you're a returning embroiderer or this is your first foray into stitching, I salute you. Whether you feel like dabbling with something quick and easy like the Bejeweled Blossoms on page 130 or really want to go whole hog and break a sweat in order to create something you can hand down to your kids' kids' kids (I'm thinking about the Family Tree Photo Album Cover, page 198, or Something Blue Hanky, page 225), I'm fully confident that there's something in this book for every level of devotion. Just remember everything I've mentioned about the longevity of stitchwork: Your needlepoint pillow will outlast us all. That means it's all the more important to give it your all—all your capacity for enjoyment, that is. It may sound a little cheesy, but I believe the love and happiness and excitement you put into every piece will show. I'm hoping that the following projects get you so psyched that those kids' kids' kids will look back on your work and know that you were having an awfully good time.

So let's get to it!

Sashiko Top and Tunic

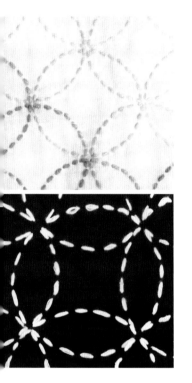

Sashiko (which means "little stabs") is a traditional Japanese embroidery and quilting technique for reinforcing fabric in areas that get more wear—like the shoulders of a field worker's shirt. Though originally designed for function, the results are beautiful—I've borrowed a design called "Seven Treasures of Buddha." Alternatively, try the design on a pillow, place mat, or old skirt that needs a lesson in Japanese.

Apply the design to the fabric

1. Transfer the sashiko design on page 88 using Transfer-Eze (page 76).

step 1

For Top

Repeat the pattern, laying sheets end to end to cover the stitching area.

For Tunic

Repeat the pattern, laying sheets side by side and end to end to cover the stitching area.

Using Sashiko Thread

Sashiko is even easier to do if you precut your thread into stitch-ready lengths. Here's how:

1. Open up the skein or coil of thread, and remove the paper label. Look for the knot that's tied around the thread and cut through all of the threads at this point.

2. Keep the cut threads folded in half. Hold either end and loosely braid the threads to keep them tidy. Draw out individual strands from the top of the braid as needed.

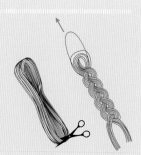

How to work the design

2. Stitch along the pattern lines in continuous diagonal wavy lines as shown. When stitching, hold the needle still and use a pleating action to work several stitches at a time instead of the standard in-and-out (the sewing method, page 27).

3. Continue stitching as in Step 2 until the entire transferred design has been stitched.

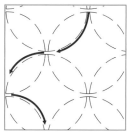

step 2

Finishing

4. Remove Transfer-Eze by soaking the embroidered garment in cold water. Blot with a towel and line dry.

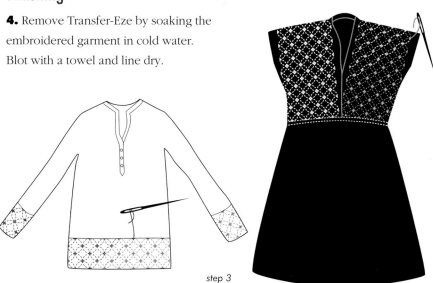

step 3

Dashing Vest and Tie

f you have an appreciative man—or are one—this is the project for you. Because counted thread embroidery requires patience—a lot of it. The good news: It's not very hard, and counting threads to create geometric patterns can actually have a relaxing, meditative effect. Let the weave of the fabric or waste canvas be your guide, since counting threads means you don't have to transfer a pattern. For a fresh perspective, I like to apply old techniques in new contexts. I chose to update a herringbone vest and cotton tie—garments that are a bit old-world to begin with. The result is refreshingly modern, featuring patterns you'd see in tiles or architecture.

Apply the waste canvas

To the vest:

1. The vest shown has four pockets with 4½" × ¾" welts. Using regular scissors, cut four pieces of waste canvas approximately ¼" larger on all sides than the welts. Baste them to the welts with the embroidery needle and thread.

step 1

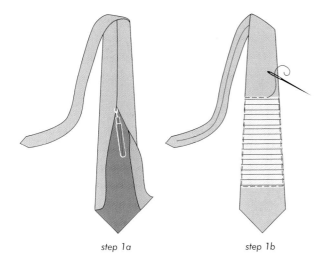

step 1a

step 1b

To the tie:

1a. Use the seam ripper to carefully open the center back seam of the tie. This allows you to stitch the front of the tie without having the wrong side of the embroidery show on the back. For a sampler approximately 5¼" high, open the center back seam 6".

1b. Cut the waste canvas to the width of the tie front (sample is 2¼") and 1" higher than the planned sampler. Baste it to the front of the tie with the embroidery needle and sewing thread. (Apply the waste canvas at least ½" above the start of the center back seam so that the wrong side of your stitching will be hidden; on this sampler, I began stitching 3¼" from the bottom of the tie.)

Embroider

2. Use the ruler and fabric marker to find and mark the center of the waste canvas. To center the patterns without having to count the threads, work the patterns from the center.

3. Follow the stitch charts shown opposite, mixing and matching them to create your own design. (In the samples, the vest is stitched with Pattern 1; the tie is stitched from top to bottom with Patterns 2 through 14, with Pattern 6 doubled, and Pattern 2 repeated at the bottom.) Note: Each chart is made up of 24 or 25 stitches across, which is approximately 2½" of stitching when using 14-count waste canvas.

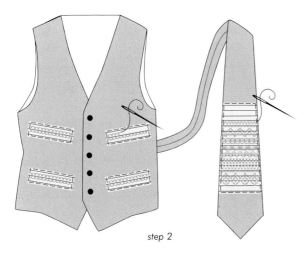

step 2

✳ *Tip: Test a pattern on scrap fabric before starting your project. This will give you a better sense of the scale and also help you become more comfortable with reading the line charts.*

Finishing

The vest:

4. Carefully remove the basting with the seam ripper and the waste canvas with tweezers (see page 15).

The tie:

5. Use the embroidery needle and sewing thread to slipstitch closed (see page 237) the center back seam of the tie.

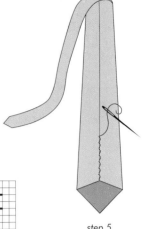

step 5

stitch charts

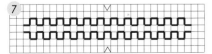

Daily Panties

level *1*

you will need

- White cotton panties (7 pairs)
- Sulky Tear-Away stabilizer
- DMC Six Strand Embroidery Floss, in peachy orange 352 ▧ (Sunday), light blue 3325 ▧ (Monday), sunny yellow 3822 ▧ (Tuesday), aqua green 954 ■ (Wednesday), light pink 3609 ▧ (Thursday), dark pinkish red 600 ■ (Friday), lilac 210 ▧ (Saturday) (1 skein each)
- All-purpose sewing thread, in contrasting color to panties
- Size 9 embroidery needle
- Embroidery scissors
- Regular scissors
- Seam ripper
- Sewing ruler
- Air-soluble fabric marker
- Iron
- Straight pins
- Daily Panties iron-on transfers (in envelope)

embroidery stitches

- Stem stitch (page 33)
- French knot (page 45)

techniques

- Using iron-on transfers (page 73)
- Using stabilizer (basting) (page 78)

This project mixes the sweet schoolgirl charm of assigning a day of the week to your underthings with the mature sexiness of French lace. Oooh la la! (If you wear the wrong day, you can pretend that "Tuesday" is your secret stripper name.) Embroidered with easy stem stitch—perfect for curvy cursive letters—these panties make a lovely gift for a bridal shower—or anyone who's a little naughty and nice. When you are done, start all over again on the front hem of your man's boxers.

Transfer the lettering to the panties

1. Use the fabric marker to mark center front of panties about ⅜" below the waistband. Using the mark, center the transfer and iron it onto the panties.

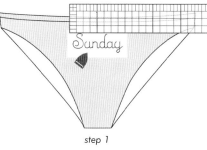

step 1

Warning: Heat will melt lace, and yes, I learned this the hard way! Cover any lace edging or detailing with a manila file folder to protect it while you iron.

Baste the stabilizer to the back of the lettering

2. Using regular scissors, cut a piece of stabilizer ½" larger than the lettering on all sides. (For example, cut a 3¼" × 1¾" piece of stabilizer for "Monday.") Pin the stabilizer to the wrong side of the panties, centered on the lettering. Baste all four sides using sewing thread and the embroidery needle; remove the pins.

Embroider the lettering

3. Using two strands of floss in the needle, embroider the lettering using a stem stitch. Note: Dot the *i* in Friday with a French knot.

4. When you're finished, carefully remove the basting with the seam ripper and gently tear away the excess stabilizer.

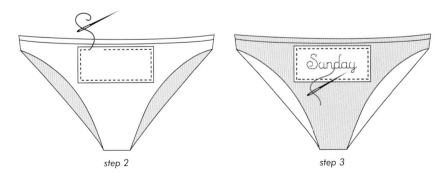

step 2   *step 3*

Needlework Necklace

Stitch up your own precious jewelry from scrap fabric you have lying around, and you can save a bundle. A big blue blossom resting just below your collarbone is the perfect accent for that smart cocktail dress. Or use the necklace to dress up a V-neck and jeans. So simple and quick to make—you can even use the same method to make a matching bracelet or earrings. Or make a necklace for every outfit or for every friend on your list!

Cut and interface the pendant front

1. Select a fabric with a floral motif similar in scale to the sample. (The point of overembroidery is to create unique art out of existing materials, so explore your scrap stash!)

2. Place the fabric for the pendant right side up on your work surface. Use the fabric marker to outline the design you'd like to embroider. Cut ¼" beyond the marked outline (you'll trim away the excess later).

step 2

stitch diagram

A Straight stitches   C Bead embroidery

B Running stitch   D Seed stitch

B

A

3. Pin the adhesive side of the interfacing to the wrong side of the fabric.

4. Trim the interfacing following the outline of the fabric.

C

5. Place the fabric facedown on an ironing surface. Remove the pins. Fuse the interfacing to the fabric following the manufacturer's instructions.

D

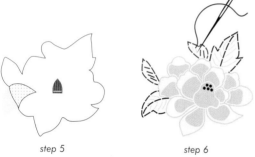

Embroider the motif

6. Embroider the motif as shown in the stitch diagram or according to your selected fabric. In the sample, 2 strands of floss were used for

step 5   *step 6*

working seed and straight stitches on the motif, and sewing thread was used to embroider the cluster of beads to highlight the flower's stamen.

Complete the pendant components

7. Use embroidery scissors to trim the motif to the edge of the embroidery.

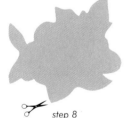

step 8

8. Place the wrong side of the motif on the wrong side of your backing. (If you're using felt, either side will do.) Trace the outline of the motif onto the backing and carefully trim along the marked line with embroidery scissors. The smaller blades make this detailed work easier.

9. Place the wrong side of the motif on the watercolor paper. Trace the outline of the motif onto the paper. Use regular scissors to cut the paper ¼" smaller, on all sides, than the outline. (The paper is stiff and will give the pendant weight, allowing it to hang nicely.)

step 9

Finish the raw edges of the pendant

10. Pin the motif to the backing.

11. Use two strands of floss and use a closely spaced overcast stitch to sew the motif to the backing. Stop halfway around the pendant.

step 11

✳ *Tip: When you work this stitch, the thread has a tendency to land on the stitch that came before it instead of on the fabric. To make your overcast stitches as even as possible, use your fingertips to coax the floss to the right spot.*

12. Insert the watercolor paper. Trim as needed with regular scissors.

13. Finish stitching around the pendant with the paper sandwiched between the motif and the backing.

Finish the necklace

14. Using a needle and thread, sew the jump rings to the upper edges, on either side, at the back of the pendant. Make at least three stitches around the bottom center to secure each jump ring.

15. Thread the cord through one jump ring and tie a knot at the bottom of the cord. Thread the cord through the second jump ring and try on the necklace in front of a mirror. (Note: The sample shown is approximately 22" long.) Adjust the cord to the desired length, tie a second knot, and snip off the excess cord.

16. Stitch through the knots of the cord using sewing thread to ensure they won't come undone.

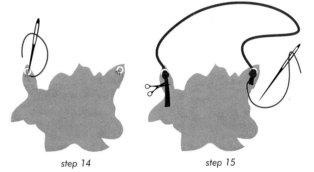

step 14   *step 15*

Beaded Dress

level *1*

you will need

- Plain dress with waist band
- Wool felt, in bright or light color (9" x 12")
- Brass flower bead caps: ½" diameter (5); ⅝" diameter (3)
- Semiprecious or glass seed beads: 9/0 (5); 4/0 (3)
- All-purpose sewing thread, to match dress
- Beading needle
- Embroidery needle (optional)
- Embroidery scissors
- Needle threader (optional)

embroidery stitch

- Straight stitch (page 30)

technique

- Bead embroidery (page 32)

love this project because it's another marriage of old and current styles. A simple dress can be rendered breathtaking with a mixture of semiprecious beads and vintage-looking brass flower embellishments.

My dressmaking guru (aka Mom) agrees that a beaded "corsage" of shiny flowers adds a sassy and sophisticated touch. But if you want a more involved project, go crazy and bead the whole waistband. Or how about along the hem? Substitute pearls or delicate vintage buttons for the metallics. Play! When you are done, dress it up with heels and a shawl for a swanky cocktail party, then wear it with flats and a tote bag to brunch the next day. (See? If you decide to spend the night, no Walk of Shame necessary!)

Bead the waistband

1. Lay the dress on your work surface and arrange the bead caps and beads along the waistband as shown, approximately ¼" apart. Take a picture or make a sketch of the arrangement noting the exact distance between each bloom. Use the illustration as your guide, or design your own embroidered embellishment.

2. Carefully remove the bead caps and beads and place them onto a sheet of felt for safekeeping. (This is a a jewelry designer's trick; the nap of felt stops beads from rolling off the table.)

3. Thread the beading needle and stitch each bead cap to the waistband by working small straight stitches between each petal of the bead cap as shown. Make two stitches at each location for reinforcement.

✳ *Tip: A single strand of thread stitched twice in the same place is neater than one stitch using a doubled strand.*

4. Using the beading needle, stitch the beads into the center of the bead caps. Stitch the small beads into the small bead caps and the large beads into the large bead caps. Stitch each bead twice to secure it.

✳ *Tip: If you're having trouble threading the tiny eye of the beading needle, try an embroidery needle. If the embroidery needle passes through the bead hole, you can use it instead. Or, try using a needle threader.*

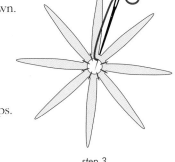

step 3

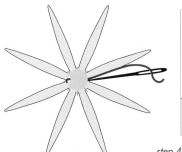

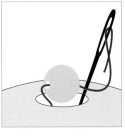

step 4

Stag Hoodie

step 2

f you want to let your buck know that he's yours, tag him and bag him with this Stag Hoodie. (But, please, do not tie him to the roof of your car!) First you embroider a "stag license," including his name, of course, for identification purposes. A black-on-orange color scheme will help you hunt him down in any crowd or forest. Even a city boy will feel like he owns a muddy pickup truck. Not a hoodie guy? Try his flannel shirt instead.

step 3

Transfer the artwork and prepare the materials for stitching

1. Using the ruler, rotary cutter, and mat, cut two 4" squares of stabilizer.

2. Transfer the stag motif—but not the lettering—close to the bottom of one piece of stabilizer using a warm iron.

3. Use the fabric marker to trace the date from the Font Library (page 243) at either side of the stag.

4. Use the embroidery needle and thread to baste the stag motif stabilizer to the center of the orange Ultrasuede. Baste near but not over any artwork.

step 4

level //

finished size

- 3" diameter

you will need

- Hooded sweatshirt in dark green
- Ultrasuede Soft, in orange 3324 and black 5813 (at least 4" square each)

- Sulky Tear-Away stabilizer
- DMC Six Strand Embroidery Floss, in orange 301 ■, black 310 ■ (1 skein each)
- All-purpose sewing thread, in black
- Size 9 embroidery needle
- Embroidery scissors
- Regular scissors
- Rotary cutter and mat, or fabric scissors

- Seam ripper
- Tweezers
- Quilting ruler
- Fabric marker
- Iron
- Straight pins
- Access to a photocopy machine
- Stag Hoodie iron-on transfers (in envelope)
- Stag Hoodie templates (page 105)
- Font Library (page 243)

embroidery stitches

- Backstitch (page 32)
- Split stitch (page 33)
- Running stitch (page 30)

techniques

- Using stabilizer (basting) (page 78)
- Using iron-on transfers (page 73)
- Using appliqué (page 43)

steps 5 and 6   step 7

step 8

A
#301

A
#301

B
#310

5. Trace the letters of your man's name from the Font Library (page 243) close to the top of the second piece of stabilizer using the placement guide provided on page 105.

6. Transfer the "stag license" below the name using a warm iron.

7. Repeat Step 4 to baste the lettering motif stabilizer to the black Ultrasuede.

Embroider the motifs

8. Use two strands of floss to work both parts of the license, following the stitches and colors indicated in the diagram. Note: Stitch two rows of backstitch for the "stag license" and one row of backstitch for the name.

9. Remove the basting with the seam ripper. Tear the stabilizer away from the embroidery, using tweezers as needed.

Trim the embroidery

10. Photocopy the Stag Hoodie template pieces on page 105 at 100%.

11. Cut out the template pieces using regular scissors.

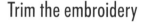

stitch diagram

- -

A Backstitch

B Split stitch fill

- -

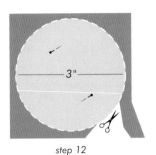

step 12

step 13

step 14

12. Pin the circular template to the stag motif and cut out using embroidery or fabric scissors. Remove the pins.

13. Repeat Step 12 using the stag cut-out template on the lettering motif.

Assemble the license and stitch it to the hoodie

14. Place the black lettering motif on the orange stag motif, matching the edges. Pin them together. Use a running stitch and thread to sew along the curved inside edges of the black motif, through both layers.

15. Use a running stitch and thread to sew the license to the chest of the hoodie.

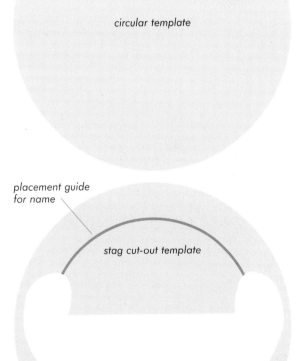

circular template

placement guide for name

stag cut-out template

step 15

Monogrammed Sneakers

Make your classic canvas kicks even more classic—with a neat, crisp monogram. They're so cute with summer shorts and a T-shirt. When you wear these to the Hamptons and leave them on the beach while you go for a walk, not only will you be the envy of all the prepsters for miles around, but potential prepster thieves will be deterred by the need to have your exact shoe size *and* initials.

Transfer the monogram to the sneaker

For light colors:

1. To make the heat transfer, trace the monogram onto tracing paper using the heat-transfer pencil (page 75). Use the sewing ruler for all straight lines. Cut out the traced monogram using regular scissors.

✱ *Tip: Use a regular pencil and ruler to draw a box with all sides equally spaced from the monogram. Use the lines of the box as a guide when positioning the monogram in the next step.*

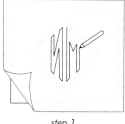

step 1

2. Pin the monogram to the right sneaker approximately ½" below the top eyelet and ¼" from the top edge or as desired.

3. Insert the rolled towel into the sneaker to support the area that is to be ironed. Transfer the monogram using a warm iron; remove the pins.

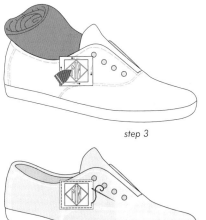

step 3

For dark colors (as shown):

1a. Use the fabric marker to trace the monogram onto the stabilizer. Use the ruler for all straight lines. Draw a box with all sides equally spaced from the monogram as in the tip, opposite. Repeat Step 2, above.

2a. Baste the stabilizer to the shoe using needle and thread. Remove the pins.

step 2a

3a. Outline the monogram with backstitch using needle and thread. Carefully remove the basting and stabilizer; use a seam ripper and tweezers as needed.

Embroider the monogram

4. Using two strands of floss, embroider in padded satin stitch. If you find that your fingers become sore pulling the needle through the thick fabric of the sneaker, try using a needle puller. Note: For a neater monogram, remember to separate the strands before you stitch (see page 21).

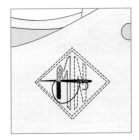

step 4

Folk Art Skirt

level //

you will need

- Denim skirt
- DMC Six Strand Embroidery Floss, in dark pink 3607 ▮, blue 322 ▮, bright red 3801 ▮, coral 351 ▮, light green 958 ▮, kelly green 699 ▮, yellow 725 ▯, blanc ▯ (1 skein each)
- Size 9 embroidery needle
- Embroidery scissors
- Iron
- Straight pins
- Needle puller (optional)
- Folk Art transfer (in envelope)

FOR DARK COLORS

- Sulky Tear-Away stabilizer
- All-purpose sewing thread in a contrasting color
- Regular scissors
- Seam ripper
- Tweezers

embroidery stitches

- Backstitch (page 32)
- Padded satin stitch (page 41)
- French knot fill (page 45)
- Stem stitch (page 33)
- Closed fly stitch (page 39)

techniques

- Using iron-on templates (page 73)
- Using stabilizer (basting) (page 78)
- Thread tracing (basting) (page 77)

have long admired the bold flowers of traditional Hungarian embroidery—they're like something a nana from the old country would wear on her apron. But I don't wear a lot of aprons, and this stitching is far too pretty to keep in the kitchen. So here's a version for your denim skirt. Once you transfer the pattern, it's like filling in a coloring book with basic satin stitch and French knots, plus a couple of other stitches for outlines and leaves. The bright colors really pop against dark denim. You can also stitch up a denim tote or adapt the pattern for your jeans—embroider a few flowers on your front pockets. How very *csinos!* (That's "pretty" in Hungarian.)

step 1

steps 1a and 1b

Transfer the artwork

For skirts in a light color:

1. Pin the Folk Art transfer to the skirt front. Transfer using a warm iron. (In the sample shown, the design is approximately 4½" from the left side seam, and 2¾" above the hem.)

For skirts in a dark color (as shown):

1a. Use a warm iron to apply the transfer to the stabilizer. Then trim the stabilizer to 1" around the edges of the design and baste it to the skirt, placing it as in Step 1.

1b. Trace the outline of the design using thread and backstitch.

1c. Carefully remove the basting and stabilizer; use a seam ripper and tweezers as necessary.

Embroider the design

2. Follow the diagram, opposite, for the floss colors and stitches used. Use four strands of floss for all stem and closed fly stitches. When working the padded satin stitch, use two strands of floss for the backstitch and padding, and one strand for the satin stitch. French knots were stitched with two strands. (If you're using the thread tracing method as in Step 1b, make sure you cover the thread with floss in this step.)

✳ *Tip: If your fingers start to feel sore, use a needle puller (a rubber disc that helps you grip and pull the needle through thick fabric)!*

stitch diagram

- A *Backstitch*
- B *Padded satin stitch*
- C *French knot (fill)*
- D *Stem stitch*
- E *Closed fly stitch*

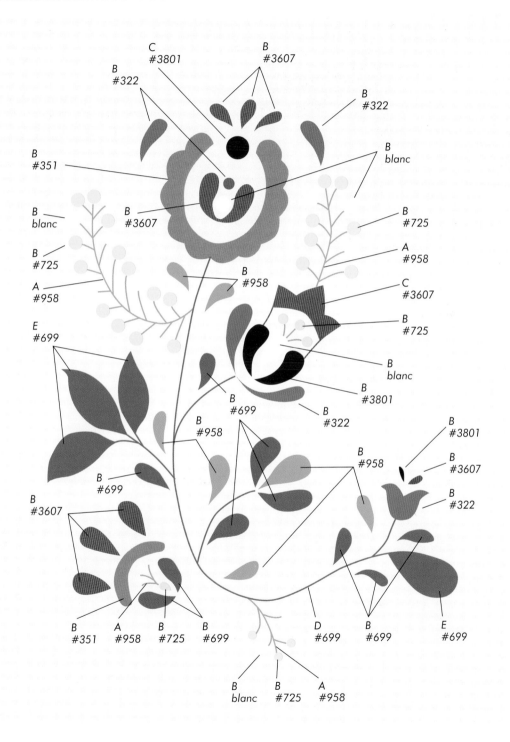

C
#3801

B
#3607

B
#322

B
#322

B
blanc

B
#351

B
#3607

B
blanc

B
#725

B
#725

A
#958

A
#958

B
#958

C
#3607

B
#725

E
#699

B
blanc

B
#699

B
#958

B
#3607

B
#3801

B
#3801

B
#3607

B
#322

B
#699

B
#322

B
#958

B
#699

B
#958

B
#3607

B
#351

A
#958

B
#725

B
#699

D
#699

B
#699

E
#699

B
blanc

B
#725

A
#958

Bargello Belt

- Belt buckle (2")
- Zweigart 14 mesh monocanvas (desired length + 6") (see Steps 1 and 2 below)
- Grosgrain ribbon for backing (1½" wide; 1½ yards)
- Paternayan Persian Yarn in gray 237 (2 skeins); blue gray 564 ▨, grape 310 ■, pale plum 323 ▨, navy 572 ■, dark khaki green 640 ■ (1 skein each)
- All-purpose sewing thread, to match ribbon
- Size 9 embroidery needle
- Size 22 tapestry needle
- Embroidery scissors
- Regular scissors
- Measuring tape
- Sewing ruler
- Black fine-tip permanent marker
- Artist tape

- Florentine stitch (page 56)

- Preparing a canvas (frames, page 18)
- Following a needlepoint chart (page 59)
- Basting (page 77)
- Finishing with overcast stitch, aka whipstitch (page 235)

f you thought that needlepoint was just for the parlor, you've got another think coming! Inspired by the zigzag patterns of Missoni's knitted fabrics (which were actually inspired by bargello designs), this belt takes needlepoint to a new place. Wear it slung over a cardigan or slipped through the loops of your jeans. When you apply this stitch (named for a set of seat cushions found in the Bargello, a museum in Florence, Italy), be prepared for your faux leather belt from The Gap to wilt with envy.

Calculate the belt length

1. Thread the measuring tape through the belt loops of a pair of well-fitting pants to determine the belt length. Then add 6" to the measurement to get x.

Prepare the canvas for stitching

2. Cut a strip of canvas 6" wide by x" long.

3. Tape the raw canvas edges with artist tape.

4. Write "top" on one long edge of the canvas with the permanent marker.

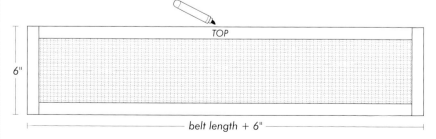

step 4

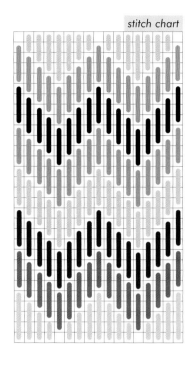

stitch chart

Needlepoint the design

5. Using two strands of yarn in the colors shown in the stitch chart, stitch the Florentine pattern. Begin stitching 3" in from one end and finish 3" from the other end.

Finishing the belt

6. Using regular scissors, ruler, and the permanent marker, measure, mark, and trim the worked canvas, leaving a ½" seam allowance of unstitched canvas around all four sides. Make sure to cut exactly along the threads of the canvas so the raw edges are straight.

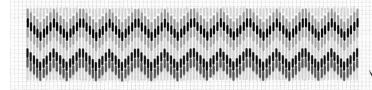

step 6

7. Turn the long unstitched edges of the canvas toward the wrong side of the belt. Using thread and an embroidery needle, baste the edges in place. Check that the stitches don't show on the right side!

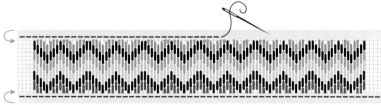

step 7

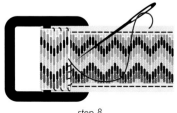

step 8

8. Slide one short end of the canvas through the buckle to the wrong side of the belt so 1" overlaps. Fold the unstitched canvas to the inside and, using the embroidery needle and thread, whipstitch the short end in place (see page 235).

9. On the remaining short end of the canvas, fold the ½" of unstitched canvas to the wrong side and press. Using thread and the embroidery needle, whipstitch the folded edge in place so the stitches do not show on the right side.

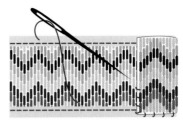

step 9

10. On one short end of ribbon, fold 1" to the wrong side and press.

11. Place the folded ribbon edge of the ribbon so it meets the end of the stitched edge of the belt without overlapping, as shown.

12. Using thread and the embroidery needle, whipstitch the ribbon to the inside back of the belt along the long and short edges.

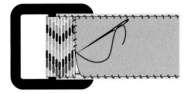

steps 11 and 12

* *Tip: Pull the ribbon slightly as you stitch to prevent it from puckering when the belt is curved around your waist.*

13. Finish the belt end by folding back 1" of wrong side. Then whipstitch along the fold as before.

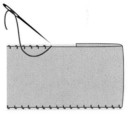

step 13

Feather-Stitched Scarf

level /

you will need

- Woven wool scarf in gray
- Anchor Tapestry Wool, in dark brown 9666 ■, bright red 8198 ■ (2 skeins of each)
- Size 22 chenille needle
- Embroidery scissors
- Sewing ruler
- Air-soluble fabric marker

embroidery stitches

- Feather stitch (page 38)
- Straight stitch (page 30)

Upgrade a plain wool scarf into something Maria might wear in *The Sound of Music* as she hikes, all ruddy-cheeked, through the Alps. Here's a project you can finish by the fireplace in an hour or two—especially if it's snowing outside. The results look great from both sides of the scarf, so you don't have to worry about how you wrap it. And it's so easy and quick, you can whip up a batch for holiday gifts. Try embellishing a hat to coordinate. Then find the nearest mountaintop and start yodeling!

Draw the stitch guides on the scarf

1. Use the fabric marker and ruler to draw guidelines on the scarf. Draw a line ½" from each long edge. Draw a second, parallel line ½" from the first. If the ink disappears as you're stitching, reapply the lines and continue to embroider.

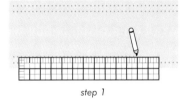

step 1

Stitching the scarf

2. Following the drawn lines, use 1 strand of dark brown tapestry wool and the chenille needle to embroider feather stitches along the long edges of the scarf. Note: If you want the feather stitches on both edges to run in the same direction, start stitching each edge from the same end of the scarf.

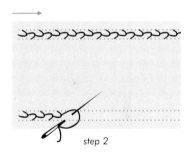

step 2

3. Finish the tops of the feather stitches with straight stitches made with 1 strand of bright red tapestry wool. The feather stitching on the back of the scarf will look like herringbone stitches.

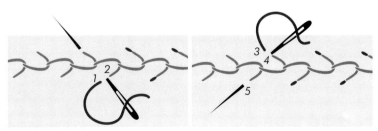

step 3

The straight stitches will look like herringbone stitch on the back of the scarf. (The feather stitches will be obscured.)

117

Crewel But Kind Giraffe

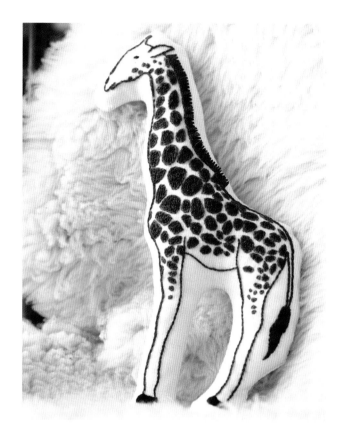

Flat stuff is for walls and museums. I like to make my stitching 3D—who can say no to a project you can play with? Crewel work is an ancient embroidery style done with wool on a plain, tightly woven background. The feel of wool in the hand is so satisfying that I thought a stuffed crewel giraffe would be great and grabbable. Fill him, sew him shut, and set him free in the nearest playroom.

level ///

finished size

- Approximately 11½" tall x 4½" wide

you will need

- Linen fabric in buff (for giraffe front/back; ½ yard)
- Muslin fabric or similar (for lining; ¼ yard)
- Faux-suede dark brown trim (for mane; at least ¼" wide and 10" long)
- Fiberfill (approximately 12 oz.)
- Beanbag fill (less than 8 oz.)
- Paternayan Persian Yarn in white 261 ▢, rust 440 ▨, brown 430 ▦, dark brown 459 ▨, black 220 ■ (1 skein each)
- All-purpose sewing thread (to match linen)
- Size 22 chenille needle
- Size 9 embroidery needle
- Embroidery scissors
- Fabric scissors
- Rotary cutter, cutting mat, and quilting ruler (optional)
- Sewing ruler
- Heat-transfer pencil (optional)
- Tracing paper (optional)
- Air-soluble fabric marker or similar
- Straight pins
- Hoop
- Crewel But Kind Giraffe iron-on transfers (in envelope)
- Iron
- Binder clip (optional)
- Sewing machine (optional)

embroidery stitches

- Satin stitch (page 40)
- Split stitch (page 33)
- Split stitch fill (page 33)
- Straight stitch (page 30)

techniques

- Cutting fabric on-grain (page 14)
- Using iron-on templates (page 73)
- Using a heat-transfer pencil (optional) (page 75)
- Finishing with slipstitch (page 237)

Cut the fabric and transfer the giraffe

1. Measure, mark, and cut the linen into two 13" × 17" rectangles for the sides of the giraffe. Use the selvage of the fabric as a guide to ensure that the fabric is cut on-grain. *Optional:* Use a quilting ruler, rotary cutter, and mat to make this step easier.

2. Repeat Step 1 with the lining and cut two 11" × 15" rectangles.

3. Transfer the giraffe pattern to one piece of linen using a warm iron.

4. To transfer the giraffe in reverse (for the second side), trace the iron-on transfer with a heat transfer pencil and tracing paper (see page 75). Transfer it to the second piece of linen using a warm iron. *Optional:* Save time and effort by embroidering just one side of the giraffe (one piece of the linen) and leave the other side plain.

Embroider the giraffe

5. Fit one giraffe side onto the hoop. Embroider as shown in the stitch diagram (page 120) using the chenille needle and 1 strand of yarn. Work the outline of the giraffe in split stitch. Outline the spots with split stitch then fill the interior of the spots with split stitch fill.

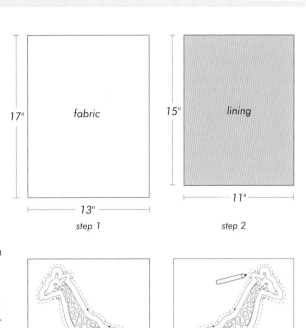

17" fabric 13"

step 1

15" lining 11"

step 2

step 3

step 4

step 5

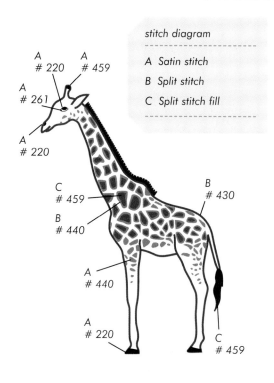

stitch diagram

A Satin stitch
B Split stitch
C Split stitch fill

A # 220
A # 459
A # 261
A # 220
C # 459
B # 440
B # 430
A # 440
A # 220
C # 459

Make the mane

6. Make ⅛" deep notches in the shape of small *V*'s along one long edge of the faux suede. Use embroidery scissors and be careful not to cut too deeply. Cut the suede strip in half to make two 4" strips. (Note: If you've chosen to embroider only one side of the giraffe, only one side of the mane is needed.)

7. Pin each mane to the neck of one giraffe side. Sew in place, along the unnotched edge, using a single strand of dark brown yarn. (In the sample, small vertical straight stitches were made about ¼" apart, but a running stitch would work just as well.)

8. Repeat Step 7 if you've embroidered both sides of the giraffe. Be sure both manes begin and end in the same location on the neck.

steps 6 and 7

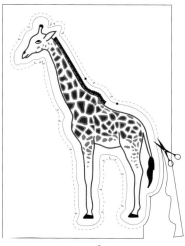

step 9

Trim giraffe sides and attach the interfacing

9. Use embroidery or fabric scissors to trim the giraffe sides following the dashed line. If you're making a giraffe that is embroidered on only one side, cut the remaining piece of linen to match. Pin the stitched giraffe to the second piece of linen and carefully cut around it to create a mirror image of the stitched side.

10. With wrong sides together, pin each giraffe side to a rectangle of lining fabric. Trim the lining to match each giraffe side.

11. Keeping a ¼" seam, backstitch each giraffe side to its lining with the embroidery needle and thread. Note: This step may also be completed on a sewing machine.

Prepare the giraffe sides for assembly

12. Clip small notches along the giraffe's edges as indicated on the heat transfer. Make sure they are no more than ⅛" deep. (The notches will help to ease the fabric around the curves in the giraffe.) Press back the seam allowances to the wrong side along the seam line.

Assemble the giraffe

13. With lining sides facing, pin and then slipstitch (see page 237) the giraffe sides together using a doubled strand of thread and the embroidery needle. Leave a 1½" opening in the center of the back of the neck. Leave your needle and thread attached.

14. Beginning with the legs and neck, stuff the giraffe with a combination of beanbag fill and fiberfill. Use the binder clip to close the opening if you want to double-check your work without spilling the beanbag fill. An unsharpened pencil is handy for stuffing fiberfill into hard-to-reach areas such as the head and the legs.

15. To finish the giraffe, slipstitch the back opening closed.

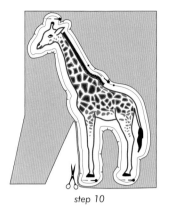

step 10   step 11

step 12   step 13

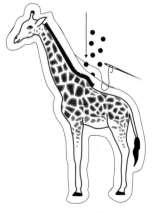

steps 14 and 15

Patch'Em Ups

Turn your feller out to sea with a shipshape patch. An anchor looks great on a sweater or a hoodie, and hand-stitched patches look serious and old-school—like something Napoleon would wear on his uniform. Mix that old-world feel with a modern design and you've got a winner. Patches are not just decorative; they can also cover rips and holes. Put a stitched bandage where your jeans have a boo-boo or sew a safety pin where your backpack is falling apart. Satin stitch on felt means easy sewing, quick going—you don't even need an embroidery hoop. Make a set of all five designs and give them to your favorite roughhousing ruffian.

Make the patch

1. Apply the Patch 'Em Ups transfer to the felt using a warm iron.

2. Embroider using two strands of floss. Use padded satin stitch for the anchor, safety pin, star, and heart. (Refer to the photographs for the direction in which the padded satin stitch should be worked.) Use running stitch for the bandage and French knots for the embellishments. For the safety pin, use split stitch where shown in photograph. Always separate and then recombine single strands of thread for neater stitching.

3. Trim the felt to ⅛" of the motif.

step 1

step 2

step 3

Attach the patch

4. Use the needle and thread to make appliqué or running stitches and apply the patches wherever you'd like.

step 4

Smocked with Love Dress

A fancy way of gathering fabric to form a pattern, smocking was common in the Middle Ages as a way to shape a garment and make parts of it warmer (gathered fabric = thicker = warmer). In more recent history (ten years ago, that is), my mom and I spied a gorgeous little girl's dress with a honeycomb-like smocked yoke at a Paris flea market. She bought it for my niece Zoe, but that dress stayed in my mind, long after Zoe outgrew it. It is the inspiration for this project.

Determine the fit of the dress

Note: Ideally, to ensure a good fit, you'll want to measure the child who will be wearing it; if this isn't possible, please refer to the sizing chart below. If you're unsure of the length you need, measure an existing dress in the correct size.

1. Measure the chest. Wrap the tape measure around the child at the high chest. Do not pull the tape too tightly so the dress will fit comfortably. Write this measurement down.

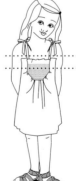

.... high chest
.... chest

Chest	Size
21"	2
22"	3
23"	4
24"	5

Cut the dress fabric

2. Add 3" to the chest measurement taken in Step 1. For example, 22" chest + 3" = 25".

125

3. Measure the child from her underarm to 1" below her knee. Add 1" to this length for the hem allowance. (The sample is 15¾" long and was made to fit a three-year-old girl.)

4. Find the selvages. Mark and then cut the fabric so the length measurement runs with the grain and the chest measurement runs against the grain (see page 14). Use the selvage of the fabric as a guide to ensure that the fabric is cut on-grain, but measure and mark the fabric so the selvages get cut away. *Optional:* Use a quilting ruler, rotary cutter, and mat to make this step easier.

selvage

crossgrain = width

cut to desired size

grainline = length

selvage

step 4

Sew the center back seam

5. Fold the fabric in half widthwise, right sides together. Draw a ½" seam allowance onto the fabric with the fabric marker and ruler. (Having a line to follow will make for a perfectly stitched seam.)

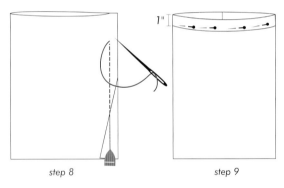

1"

step 8   step 9

6. Pin the raw edges of the fabric together to keep the fabric from shifting as you sew.

7. Using the embroidery needle and thread, backstitch along the center back seamline. Note: This step may also be completed on a sewing machine.

8. Open the seam allowances and press flat on both the wrong and right sides to set the stitching.

Finish the top of the dress

9. Using the sewing ruler or sewing gauge as a guide, fold under 1" along the cut edge to the wrong side and press. Along the same edge, fold under another 1" to the wrong side, press again, and pin.

10. Whipstitch the folded edge in place (see page 235). Press.

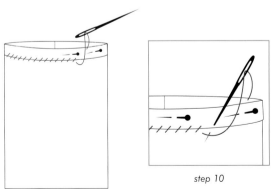

step 10

Finish the hem

11. Using the sewing ruler or sewing gauge as a guide, turn under 1" along the bottom hem edge to the wrong side, and press. Tuck the raw edge into the fold to make a ½" double-turned hem. Pin.

12. Whipstitch the hem in place. Note: This step may also be completed on a sewing machine. Press.

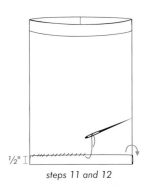

½" 𝕀

steps 11 and 12

Prepare and mark the fabric for smocking

13. Lay the dress flat on a table. Using the ruler, find the center front of the dress and mark the spot with the fabric marker.

14. Make a mark 1¼" down from the center front mark. This indicates where the smocking will begin.

15. Using the natural grid of the gingham fabric as a guide, mark a horizontal row of 19 evenly spaced dots on either side of the center smocking mark you made in Step 14 (see stitch chart, page 128). (The 38 centered dots will be the basis for the 19 stitches in the top row, Row 1a.) Move down one row on the gingham pattern and mark a horizontal row of 18 evenly spaced dots on either side of center to create Row 1b. Moving down one row on the gingham pattern at a time, repeat Rows 1a and 1b (combined Row 1) five times to create Rows 2–6. Mark 17 dots on either side of center to create Row 7a; mark 16 dots on either side of center to create Row 7b. Continue marking Rows 8a–10b, subtracting 1 dot from either side of center in each row.

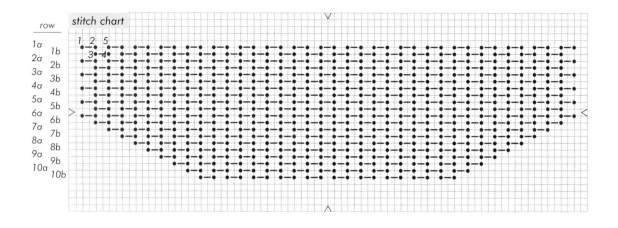

Smock the fabric in the center front of the dress

16. Using the embroidery needle and 3 strands of embroidery floss, backstitch the honeycomb smocking pattern on the grid of marked dots. (Backstitch twice into the fabric, gathering it together to make each pleat.) When stitched, Row 1 (Row 1a + Row 1b) becomes one completed row of honeycomb smocking. Stitch all 10 rows to complete the smocking.

17. Working on the wrong side of the fabric, use the embroidery needle and thread to sew a line of running stitch ⅛" in from the top of the dress to connect and hold together the tops of the pleats created by the smocking; if they are not stitched together, the smocking will not lie flat. Press to set the stitching.

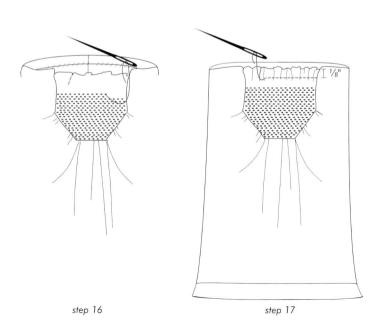

step 16

step 17

Make the shoulder straps

18. Cut the grosgrain ribbon into four equal lengths (7½" each).

19. Fold back ½" at one end of each piece of ribbon. Press. Cut the unpressed ends on the diagonal to help prevent fraying.

20. Turn the dress inside out and lay it flat with the back seam facing up. Use the ruler and a fabric marker to measure and mark 2" to the right and left of the top of the back seam. Pin one pressed edge of a ribbon to the outside of each mark, 1" down from the top of the dress. (The back ribbons should be 4" apart.)

21. Flip the dress so the inside front is facing up. Find the center front again (or refer to the mark made in Step 14) and mark 3" to the right and left of center along the top edge. Pin the ribbons as in Step 20. (The front ribbons should be 6" apart.)

22. If possible, have the child try on the dress again for fit and adjust the location and length of the straps if necessary. (If a fitting isn't possible, loosely baste the straps in place for finishing later. The fit will vary with each child.)

23. Use backstitch or overcast stitch (whipstitch) to sew the folded ends of the pinned straps to the dress fabric. Remove the pins. To wear, tie the ends of the straps over the shoulders.

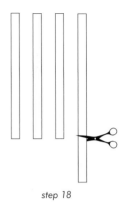

step 18

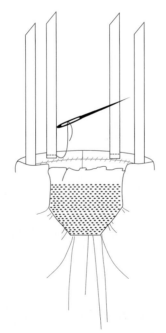
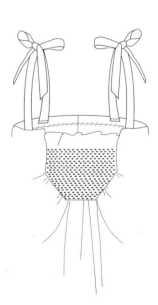

step 23

you will need

FOR FLOWER 1

FOR FLOWER 2

FOR FLOWER 3

embroidery stitches

technique

- Fabric flower hairpins (or make your own, opposite)
- Embroidery scissors

FOR FLOWER 1

- Pale pink flower (1½" diameter)
- DMC Six Strand Embroidery Floss, in bright pink 3708 ■ (1 skein)
- Size 9 embroidery needle

FOR FLOWER 2

- White flower with black polka dots (1½" diameter)
- 9/0 seed beads in red and turquoise
- All-purpose sewing thread, to match seed beads
- Beading needle

FOR FLOWER 3

- Medium pink flower (1½" diameter)
- 3 mm flower-shaped sequins in pale pink
- 9/0 seed beads in pearly pink
- All-purpose sewing thread, to match sequins and seed beads
- Beading needle

embroidery stitches

- Blanket stitch (page 36)
- Straight stitch (page 30)

technique

- Bead embroidery (page 9)

for kids

Bejeweled Blossoms

Get that hair out of your face! These fabric flowers should do just the trick. They're pretty little things that look like they've been kissed by a little embroidering bee. Start with flowers from the mall, and embellish them with a few blanket stitches along the petals. Or sew on beads that sparkle like drops of dew. Once you've gathered all the materials, you can complete all the stitching faster than you can say "geranium" or "heliotrope." Tuck one of these blossoms just above a little ear or at the base of a ponytail (maybe even yours!). Then buzz over to a botanical garden and wait for people to admire the foliage.

How to make

Flower 1

Use a single strand of floss and the embroidery needle to work tiny blanket stitches along the edges of each petal.

Flower 2

Use thread and the beading needle to sew the beads to the polka dots with small straight stitches.

Flower 3

Place a single flower-shaped sequin on the edge of each petal. Then sew a seed bead into the center using the beading needle and thread.

Make Your Own Flower Hairpins

YOU WILL NEED

- Fabric flower
- Felt (any color)
- Embroidery scissors
- Hot glue gun and glue
- Hairpins

1. Cut a felt circle for the backing about ⅜" smaller in diameter than the flower. (You don't want to see the felt from the front, so trim it until it's hidden.) Cut a second circle slightly smaller than the first.

2. Glue the large felt circle to the center back of the flower and allow it to cool.

3. Glue the end of the hairpin to the center of the felt backing. Then center the smaller circle over the end of the hairpin and glue. Allow it to cool before wearing.

Book for Baby

This is really my way of introducing kids as early as possible to loving embroidery (and reading, too, of course). This fabric book is super touchable, so even teeny-tiny babies can enjoy the textures and the cute critters. When the bambinos get bigger, they can learn their color words and start to spell them. There's a dedication page in the front for personalization, and fusible batting between the pages makes the book become puffy like a quilt—and cuddly like a bunny. With so much to love, it'll easily replace baby's blankie!

level ///

finished size

- 7½" x 7" square

you will need

- Corduroy fabric in periwinkle for cover (at least 45" wide; ½ yard)
- Cotton fabric for pages (at least 45" wide) in white (½ yard); in green, black, brown, yellow, gray, and red (¼ yard each)
- Pellon fusible fleece (¼ yard)
- Magic Cabin wool felt, in shell (at least 9" x 12")
- Sulky Tear-Away stabilizer
- DMC Six Strand Embroidery Floss, in black 310 ■, darkest brown 3371 ■, peacock blue 3765 ■, purple 3834 ■, mocha brown 3781 ■, rust 400 ■, gold 3829 ■, medium brown 433 ■, coffee 3781 ■, bronze 680 ■ (1 skein each)
- Paternayan Persian Yarn, in dark gray 201 ■, black 220 ■, cream 261 ☐, rusty orange 860 ■, butterscotch 700 ■, yellow 773 ☐, apple green 692 ■, turquoise 581 ■, grape 310 ■, very dark brown 415 ■, medium brown 460 ■, bronze 740 ■, light gold brown 741 ■, grayish white 246 ☐, kelly green 630 ■, mint 686 ☐, dark green 690 ■, bright green 699 ■, golden brown 733 ■, goldenrod 711 ■, neon yellow 760 ☐, light yellow 763 ☐, primary yellow 772 ☐, light gray 212 ☐, medium gray 202 ■, light pink 325 ☐, pinkish tan 475 ■, black dark brown 420 ■, dark red orange 850 ■, bright red orange 852 ■, dark red 968 ■ straw gold 700 ☐, white 262 ☐ (1 skein each)
- All-purpose sewing thread, in white
- Size 9 embroidery needle
- Size 22 chenille needle
- Embroidery scissors
- Rotary cutter, ruler, and mat, or fabric scissors
- Seam ripper
- Point turner (optional)
- Quilting ruler
- Water-soluble fabric marker
- Straight pins
- Iron
- Sewing machine (optional)
- Book for Baby iron-on transfers (in envelope)

embroidery stitches

- Straight stitch (page 30)
- Running stitch (page 30)
- Backstitch (page 32)
- French knot (page 45)
- Stem stitch (page 33)
- Split stitch (page 33)
- Chain stitch (page 34)
- Satin stitch (page 40)
- Eyelet wheel stitch (page 41)
- Cross-stitch (page 44)

techniques

- Cutting fabric on-grain (page 14)
- Using iron-on transfers (page 73)
- Using interfacing (page 239)
- Using stabilizer (basting) (page 78)
- Thread tracing (basting) (page 77)
- Backstitching a seam (page 237)
- Finishing with slipstitch (page 237)

Cut the fabric, fusible fleece, and felt

Note: Whenever you cut fabric, use the selvage as a straight edge so it's cut on-grain. Don't know what the heck I'm talking about? See page 14 for more info.

1. Using the ruler, rotary cutter, and mat, cut the corduroy fabric into a 17½" × 8¼" rectangle. This fabric piece will become the book's cover. Repeat with the gray fabric for the backing.

2. Cut the white fabric into eight 7¼" squares.

3. Cut a 7¼" square in each of the brown, green, black, yellow, gray, and red fabrics.

4. Cut two 17½" × 8¼" rectangles and thirteen 7¼" squares of fusible fleece. Note: You won't be applying the fusible fleece to the wrong side of the fabric "pages" until after the hot-iron transfers are applied, but it's easier to cut everything at once.

5. Mark and then cut one 7" × 4¼" rectangle from wool felt for the book's title page and one 5⅝" × 4½" rectangle from wool felt for the book's dedication page.

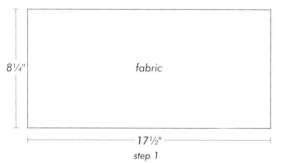

8¼"

fabric

17½"

step 1

7¼"

fabric

7¼"

steps 2 and 3

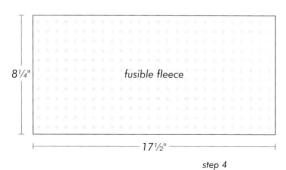

8¼"

fusible fleece

17½"

step 4

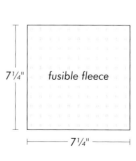

7¼"

fusible fleece

7¼"

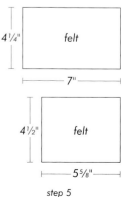

4¼"

felt

7"

4½"

felt

5⅝"

step 5

Transfer the artwork to the book pages

6. Center, pin, and apply the "what colors?" transfer to the center of the 7" × 4¼" felt title page using a warm iron.

step 6

step 7

7. Center, pin, and apply the bookplate art to the center of the remaining felt with a warm iron.

8. On the felt dedication page, use the fabric marker to write in the baby's name, date of birth (optional), and your name.

✳ *Tip: Use a water-soluble marking pen since an air-soluble fabric marker may disappear before you have a chance to embroider on top of it.*

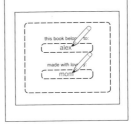

step 8

step 9

9. Working one motif at a time, center, pin, and apply each animal image (squirrel, frog, bear, butterfly, bunny, and fox) onto one white fabric "page" using a warm iron.

10. Then apply the green, yellow, gray, and red color name transfers onto the center of each light-colored fabric square "page" of the same color.

step 11

step 10

11. For the dark-colored fabric squares, cut two 4" × 3" pieces of stabilizer. Center the brown color name transfer onto the stabilizer and pin. Apply the transfer with a warm iron.

12. Baste the printed stabilizer to the center of the brown fabric page using the embroidery needle and regular sewing thread.

13. With needle and thread, trace the design with stitches (see page 77 for more on this method). Remove the basting with a seam ripper and tear away the stabilizer.

14. Repeat Steps 11–13 with the "black" color name transfer and matching cotton fabric "page."

step 12

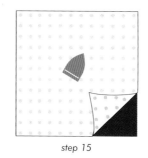

step 15

Apply the fusible fleece

15. Pin and then attach the glue side of each fusible fleece square to the wrong side of each fabric square. (One of the white fabric squares will not have an image on it; if the fabric is reversible, you can use either side.)

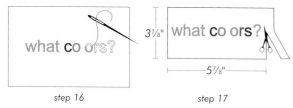

step 16

step 17

Embroider the title page

16. Using a single strand of wool yarn, the chenille needle, and the padded satin stitch, work the "what colors?" design as shown in the stitch diagram on page 138.

17. Carefully trim the stitched felt to measure 5⅞" wide by 3⅛" high.

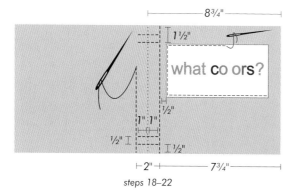

steps 18–22

Stitch the spine and attach the title page

18. Lay the corduroy cover fabric flat on a table horizontally with right side up. Measure and mark the center of the fabric lengthwise with a vertical line (your mark should be about 8¾" from both sides).

19. Measure and mark a vertical line parallel to and 1" on either side of the line made in the previous step.

20. Perpendicular to the previously drawn lines, draw a horizontal line ½" from the bottom of the book and 2" long. Draw another 2" line ½" above and parallel to the first. Repeat at the top edge of the cover as shown.

21. Using a single strand of medium brown wool yarn #460 and the chenille needle, cover the lines drawn in Steps 19 and 20 with a running stitch.

22. Place the "what colors?" title on the front cover ¾" to the right of the spine stitching and 1½" down from the top edge. Check placement with the ruler, and pin. Then, using the embroidery needle and matching thread, sew the felt to the fabric using slipstitch (see page 237).

Finish the book cover

23. Place the corduroy book cover on a table right side up. On the wrong side of the blank rectangular lining fabric, draw a ¼" seam line around all four sides. Lay the gray backing fabric on top of the cover, right sides together (you should be looking at the fleece side, the wrong side). Pin around all four sides close to the raw edge(s).

24. Using the embroidery needle and all-purpose thread, and starting at the center bottom, backstitch the lining and cover fabrics together with a ¼" seam allowance. Leave a 2" opening for turning. Note: This step may also be completed on a sewing machine.

25. Press the seam allowances open, including the seam opening. Trim the corners as shown.

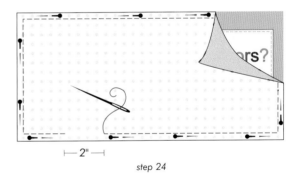

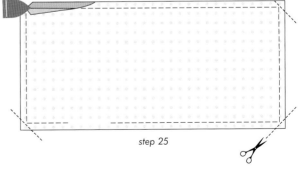

step 24

step 25

stitch diagram

A Satin stitch	G French knots (fill)
B Stem stitch	H Cross-stitch
C Chainstitch	I Eyelet wheel stitch
D Backstitch	J Split stitch
E Backstitch fill	K Split stitch fill
F Straight stitch	L Running stitch

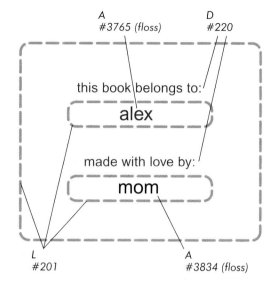

A
#3765 (floss)

D
#220

this book belongs to:

alex

made with love by:

mom

L
#201

A
#3834 (floss)

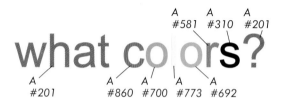

A
#581

A
#310

A
#201

A
#201

A
#860

A
#700

A
#773

A
#692

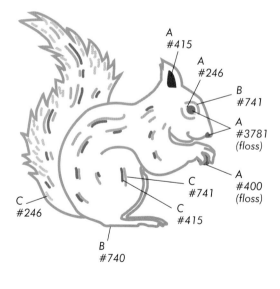

A
#415

A
#246

B
#741

A
#3781
(floss)

C
#741

A
#400
(floss)

C
#246

C
#415

B
#740

A
#261

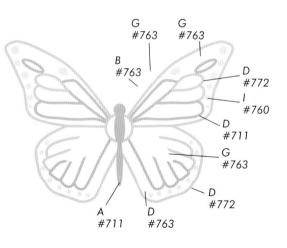

G
#763

G
#763

B
#763

D
#772

I
#760

D
#711

G
#763

D
#772

A
#711

D
#763

A
#261

26. Turn the cover right side out by pulling the fabric through the opening. Use a point turner or similar tool to gently poke out the corners. Press.

27. Slipstitch the opening closed along the pressed seam allowance.

Embroider the pages

28. Embroider the dedication page as shown in the stitch diagram on page 138, except for the running stitch outline.

29. Center the felt dedication page on a white fabric square. Pin. Use running stitch to sew around the edge in medium gray yarn #201.

30. Using the chenille needle with a single strand of wool and the embroidery needle with 2 strands of yarn, embroider all of the remaining designs as shown in the stitch diagrams on pages 138 and 140. On the brown and black pages, stitch over the designs you traced in Step 13.

Sew the pages together

31. With right sides together, pin together the pages in the following combinations: blank white fabric page with brown, squirrel with green, frog with black, bear with yellow, butterfly with gray, bunny with red, and fox with blank white.

✳ *Tip: If you plan to backstitch the pages together by hand, use the fabric marker to draw a ¼" seam line onto each set of pages before pinning in Step 23. This will help you make perfectly straight stitching.*

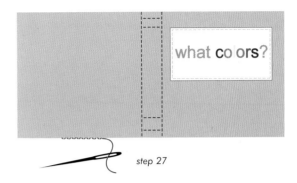

step 27

step 28

step 30

stitch diagram

A Satin stitch	G French knots (fill)
B Stem stitch	H Cross-stitch
C Chainstitch	I Eyelet wheel stitch
D Backstitch	J Split stitch
E Backstitch fill	K Split stitch fill
F Straight stitch	L Running stitch

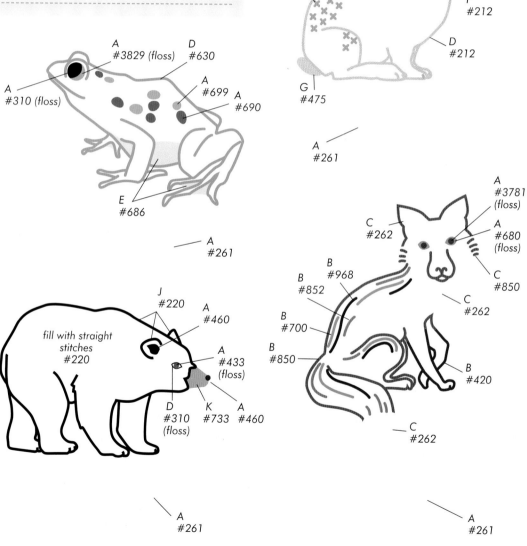

Rabbit:
A #3781 (floss)
A #3371 (floss)
E #325
H #202
D #325
F #212
D #212
G #475
A #261

Frog:
A #3829 (floss)
D #630
A #310 (floss)
A #699
A #690
E #686
A #261

Bear:
J #220
A #460
fill with straight stitches #220
A #433 (floss)
D #310 (floss)
K #733
A #460
A #261

Fox:
A #3781 (floss)
A #680 (floss)
C #262
C #850
C #262
B #968
B #852
B #700
B #850
B #420
C #262
A #261

32. Starting with one set of pages, use regular sewing needle and thread to backstitch around all four sides with a ¼" seam allowance, leaving a 2" opening at the center of the right-hand side of each page. Note: This step may also be completed on a sewing machine.

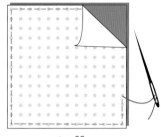

step 32

33. Press the seam allowances open and trim the corners. Turn the fabric right side out, pulling the fabric through the opening, and then poke out the corners with the point turner. Press again and slipstitch the opening closed as for the book cover (see Steps 25–27).

34. Repeat Steps 32 and 33 with each set of fabric pages.

Stitch the binding

35. Stack the pages in the correct order; the correct color names should be facing the correct animal motif. The correct order is: dedication page/brown, squirrel/green, frog/black, bear/yellow, butterfly/gray, bunny/red, and fox/blank page.

36. Thread the embroidery needle with a double strand of sewing thread and tie a knot. Sew the stack of pages together with backstitches on the left side of the page, making five evenly spaced stitches over the "spine" as shown. Repeat each backstitch a few times for reinforcement.

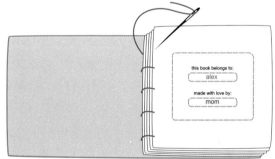

step 36

37. Lay the corduroy book cover on the table with the title page facedown. (You should see a white "page" inside of the cover.) Center the pages right side up on top of the cover; you should see the dedication page.

38. Thread the embroidery needle with a single strand of sewing thread and tie a knot. Slipstitch the inside of the front and back covers to the binding of the pages to complete the book.

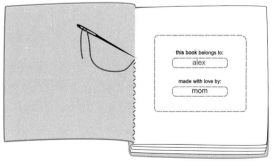

step 38

Kimono Baby Booties

This project will expand your horizons—and skill set! It allows you to play dressmaker—or really, shoemaker—as well as embroiderer. Booties are easy to stitch and since the scale is small, they're very quick. (One of the advantages of sewing baby projects.) Embellishing store-bought booties is a cinch, but if you make these yourself, you can hide the not-so-pretty backside of your stitches. I started with polka-dot fabric, cut out the bootie pieces according to a free online pattern (noted at left), and decorated each dot with an outline and cross-stitches in bright colors. Embellish your bootie fabric any way the itty-bitty spirits move you. (No machine required!) New moms will swoon, and babies will enjoy their comfy new kicks.

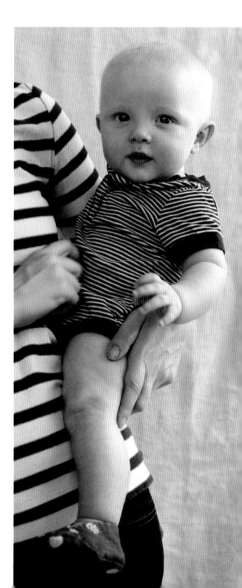

Embroider the booties

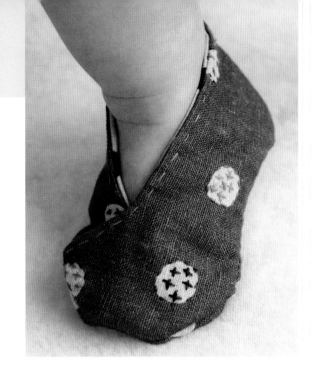

* *Tip: If you make your booties, embroider the outside pattern pieces first so the wrong side of the stitching is hidden behind the lining.*

1. How you decorate these tiny baby booties is up to you! Think of the booties as a blank canvas. Use two strands of floss throughout and in contrasting colors as shown. In the sample, the polka dots are first filled with a sprinkling of three to six upright cross-stitches. Running stitch is then worked around each polka dot.

2. Embroider the upper edge of the booties with a contrasting running stitch.

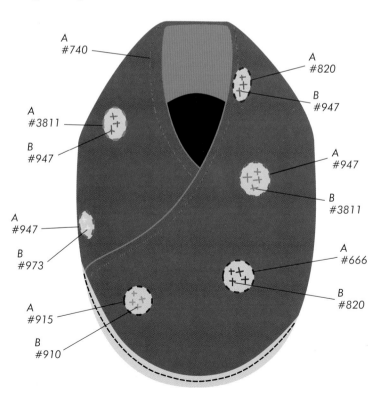

A
#740

A
#820

B
#947

A
#3811

B
#947

A
#947

B
#3811

A
#947

B
#973

A
#666

B
#820

A
#915

B
#910

---

stitch diagram

A *Running stitch*

B *Upright cross-stitch*

Baby Bird Bib

When your favorite baby human wants to be fed, shield his shirt with extra cuteness. These three baby birds will cheep-cheep-cheep for breakfast along with him and catch all the spills. You can bring these appliqué birdies to life in an afternoon. Just cut out the wool felt birdies and branches and sew them on with a simple running stitch. No fancy needlework required. The dimensional, somewhat sculptural result is very satisfying. Repeated washings will soften the raw edges. (Note: Felt will pill and shrink if not laundered correctly, so swap out felt for other fabric scraps if you prefer.)

If making a set of bibs, vary them by arranging the birdies in a different pattern or using different color combinations for each one. Now fly away to your sewing kit and get stitching.

level

finished size

- Approximately 8½" x 12" as shown

you will need

- Bib (approximately 8½" x 12")
- Scraps of Magic Cabin wool felt sufficiently sized to fit the motifs (3 birds, nest, and branch) in 5 colors: lilac, lemon, and aqua (birds); green pea (nest); and ginger brown (branch)

- Scrap of Sulky Tear-Away stabilizer (optional)
- DMC Six Strand Embroidery Floss, in light purple 3836 ■, light yellow 728 ■, teal 3809 ■, blue green 3850 ■, dark purple 3837 ■, bright orange 946 ■, orange spice 721 ■, olive green 581 ■, rusty brown 975 ■ (1 skein each)
- Size 9 embroidery needle
- Embroidery scissors
- Regular scissors

- Sewing ruler
- Air-soluble fabric marker
- Straight pins
- Access to a photocopy machine
- Baby Bird Bib templates (page 146)

IF USING FABRIC APPLIQUÉS INSTEAD OF FELT

- Fusible interfacing (¼ yard)
- Iron

embroidery stitches

- Running stitch (page 30)
- French knot (page 45)
- Backstitch fill (page 32)
- Blanket stitch (page 37)

techniques

- Using interfacing (page 239) (optional)
- Using appliqué (page 43)
- Thread tracing (basting) (page 77)

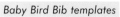

Areas to be stitched
(backstitch fill)

Copy the motifs to make pattern pieces

1. Photocopy (or scan and print) the artwork on the facing page at 100% to create a paper copy of the template motifs.

2. Using regular scissors, cut around the outlines of the paper pattern pieces, and then pin the pieces to the felt.

3. Using embroidery scissors, cut the birds, wings, nest, and branch from the felt. (The short blades will make cutting easier.)

For fabric appliqués:

4. Repeat Step 3 with fabric, right side up, and fusible interfacing. Be sure to pin and cut the templates with the glue side facing up.

5. Pin the wrong side of the fabric to the glue side of the interfacing shapes.

6. Iron the interfacing and fabric shapes together (see page 239).

Sew the appliqué motifs to the bib front

Note: Use two strands of floss for this project. For neater stitching, separate two single strands from the 6-strand skein and then put the two strands back together before threading the needle.

7. Pin the wing pieces to each bird. Using the embroidery needle and two strands of floss (in the colors indicated on the stitch diagram), sew them in place with a running stitch. Make French knots on each bird for the eyes.

8. Using the ruler, find the center front of the bib and mark this spot with the fabric marker.

9. Using the mark made in Step 8 as a guide, center the birds on the bib. After you have them nicely arranged, use the ruler to confirm that the group is centered; make any necessary adjustments before pinning each bird in place.

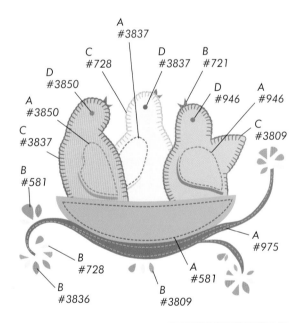

A #3837
C #728
D #3837
B #721
D #3850
D #946
A #946
A #3850
C #3809
C #3837
B #581
A #975
B #728
A #581
B #3836
B #3809

stitch diagram

A Running stitch
B Backstitch fill
C Blanket stitch
D French knot

147

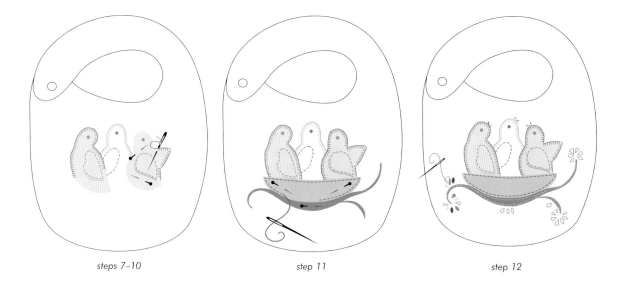

steps 7–10   step 11   step 12

10. Using the embroidery needle and two strands of floss, sew the birds to the bib with the blanket stitch (page 36).

11. Lay the nest in place on top of the birds. As before, you'll want to make sure the nest is centered before pinning it. With a running stitch, sew the nest to the bib as shown. Repeat with the branch.

Embroider the remaining design elements

12. Stitch the beaks on the birds and the flowers around the branch with backstitch fill. In the sample, these shapes were drawn freehand directly onto the bib with the marker and then filled in with backstitch. If you're not comfortable transferring the art this way, simply trace the beak and flower illustrations onto the stabilizer and do a thread trace (see "Basting," page 77). Note: If you're bothered by being able to see the wrong side of the stitching on the back of the bib, hide it by applying a piece of fusible interfacing cut ½" larger than the design area.

Art of Conversation Pillows

I n Jane Austen's day, silhouettes cut from black paper were *all* the rage. These pillows reinterpret that art for the parlor where you sit chatting over tea and scones. Channel your own Austen pillow talk as you needlepoint away the afternoon: "Why, Miss Price, what lovely piping you have." "Oh now, stop! You are too forward." Place them gently on your drawing room settee, or toss them on the bed for a cozy look, like two lovers canoodling. Note: This project is very time-intensive; to simplify, use appliqué (page 43) for the silhouettes.

level ///

finished size

- 16" square each

you will need

(FOR BOTH PILLOWS)

- Pillow forms (two 16" square; down pillows are the nicest!)
- Linen fabric for pillow backs (1 yard)
- Zweigart 16 mesh monocanvas (two 18" squares)
- Cotton fabric-covered piping (3 yards)
- 24" extra-tack frisket (4 yard roll) (available in art supply stores)
- Poster board (two 16" squares)
- Medium body acrylic paint
- ¾-inch flat paintbrush
- Vineyard Silk yarn, in French blue C-114 ■ (6 skeins)
- Vineyard Merino Wool yarn, in natural C-110 □ (24 skeins)
- All-purpose sewing thread, to match pillow backs
- Size 9 embroidery needle
- Size 22 tapestry needle
- Embroidery scissors
- Rotary cutter and mat, or fabric scissors
- Regular scissors
- Seam ripper
- Utility knife
- Hobby knife
- Quilting ruler
- Black fine-tip permanent marker
- Iron (optional)
- Straight pins
- Artist tape
- Repositionable glue stick
- Newspaper
- 2 stretcher bar frames (18") and needlepoint tacks
- Access to a photocopy machine
- Sewing machine (optional)
- Art of Conversation silhouette templates (page 153)

embroidery stitches

- Basketweave (page 54)
- Encroaching gobelin stitch (page 56)

techniques

- Preparing a canvas (frames, page 18)
- Using a stretcher bar frame (page 18)
- Painting a canvas (page 79)
- Cutting fabric on-grain (page 14)
- Basting (page 77)
- Backstitching a seam (page 237)
- Finishing with slipstitch (page 237)

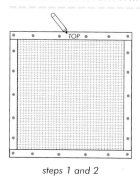

steps 1 and 2

Prepare the canvas

1. Tape the raw edges of the canvases with artist tape. With the marker, mark one edge as "top."

2. Attach the canvases to the stretcher bar frames using tacks. Set them aside.

Create the stencils

3. Copy the Art of Conversation Pillows silhouette templates on page 153 at 500%. Cut out the templates, making sure the registration marks are still visible.

4. Using the ruler, utility knife, and cutting mat, measure and cut two 18" squares of poster board (one for each silhouette).

5. Mark the 9" center point along each side of one square, then draw a horizontal and vertical line connecting opposite marks. Repeat with the second square.

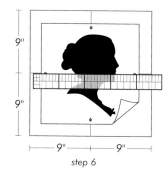

step 6

6. Spread glue across the back of one template, then center and press it onto a poster board square, aligning the registration marks with the lines drawn in Step 3. Check that the artwork is correctly centered. Repeat with the second template and square.

7. Peel the opaque paper backing from the frisket film and press the film to the right side of one of the templates (over the artwork). Smooth out any wrinkles and trim it to the edges of the square.

8. Use the ruler and marker to trace the registration lines onto the film.

9. To prevent shifting, tape the film and template assembly along all four sides to the cutting mat.

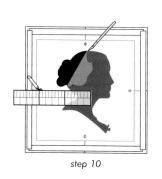

step 10

10. Using the craft knife with a new sharp blade, trace the contours of the silhouette to cut through the frisket film. For precision, use short strokes and apply even pressure.

11. Repeat Steps 7–10 with the second template and square. Then move the prepared canvases (from Step 2) near your work surface.

12. Carefully peel away the artist tape and film to separate it from the cutting mat and poster board. (The taped frame from Step 9 should still be there.)

Apply the stencil to the canvas

13. Align the registration marks on the film stencil with the center marks on the canvas and press down the stencil, smoothing out any wrinkles. Use the ruler to check that the art is centered on the canvas horizontally and vertically and reposition the stencil if needed. Burnish the cut edges of the stencil with your hand to secure them to the canvas.

14. Repeat Steps 12 and 13 with the second template and square to prepare the second silhouette stencil.

Paint the canvas

15. Lay out the newspaper and place the framed canvases on top.

16. One canvas at a time, apply a light amount of paint evenly to the surface, brushing it from about 1" outside of the edge of the stencil toward the center (brushing out risks damaging the stencil line). Fill in the entire stencil, making sure that the paint is uniform. Note: Test the paint on a scrap of canvas to determine how much paint to use. Too much paint will prevent the needle from passing through the canvas. If you notice paint filling in the mesh of the canvas, insert a tapestry needle into the hole to avoid clogging.

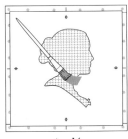

step 16

17. Carefully remove each stencil. (Note: To save the stencil or do multiple canvases, tape the stencil to the edge of a table and allow the paint to dry before using it again.) Allow the canvases to dry completely.

Stitch the silhouettes one at a time

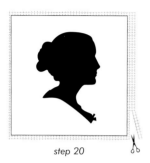

step 20

18. Work the background of the silhouette in encroaching gobelin stitch using the natural wool.

19. Stitch the silhouette onto the canvas using basketweave stitch and blue silk.

20. Remove the stitched canvas from the stretcher bars and trim the canvas edge to ½" beyond the stitching, using the grid of the canvas as a guide for cutting a straight edge.

21. Repeat Steps 18–20 with the second silhouette design.

Cut the fabric for the pillow backs

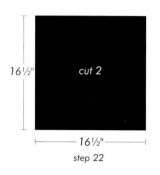

16½"

cut 2

16½"

step 22

22. If the fabric is wrinkled, press before cutting. Measure and cut two 16½" squares from the pillow fabric using the selvage as a guide to ensure that the fabric is cut on-grain.

Apply the piping to the pillow fronts

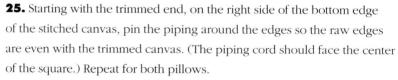

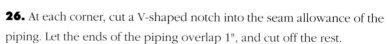

step 24

23. Cut the piping in half so you have two 1½-yard lengths.

24. Use the seam ripper to remove 1" of stitching from one end of the piping. Peel back the fabric and cut off 1" of the cording inside, being careful not to cut the fabric.

25. Starting with the trimmed end, on the right side of the bottom edge of the stitched canvas, pin the piping around the edges so the raw edges are even with the trimmed canvas. (The piping cord should face the center of the square.) Repeat for both pillows.

26. At each corner, cut a V-shaped notch into the seam allowance of the piping. Let the ends of the piping overlap 1", and cut off the rest.

steps 26 and 27

27. Baste the piping to the canvas along the stitching line of the piping. Repeat for both pillows. Note: This step may also be completed on a sewing machine with a piping foot.

Art of Conversation Pillows templates

Photocopy at 500%

Making the pillow

28. Place one pillow front right side up on a table. Lay the square of backing fabric on top of it, right sides together. Align each corner and the raw edges and pin.

29. Using the embroidery needle and thread, backstitch around all four sides so the stitches are close to the piping, ensuring that the raw canvas will not show, and leaving a 7" opening at center bottom. Note: This step may also be completed on a sewing machine with a piping foot.

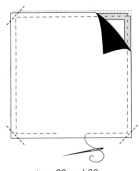

steps 29 and 30

30. Trim the corners and turn the pillow right side out. Insert the pillow form.

31. Sew the opening closed using a slipstitch.

32. Repeat Steps 28–31 for the second pillow.

step 31

Place Setting Place Mat

Confession: Even though I am a grown lady with good manners, I can never remember how to set a table. *(Which side does the knife go on? Where do you put the salad fork?)* So I designed this project as a cheat sheet—and it happens to be quite a charming cheat at that. Transfer the design or, for an exact outline, simply trace your own plate and silverware. Then embroider the lines with easy backstitch. The simplicity of dark thread on a white mat is striking—and white thread on a dark mat will look cool, too. Or stitch each mat in a different bright color to make a pack of 4, 6, or 8. This is perfect for a household where little kids are learning to set the table (or when big kids like me need a reminder).

level

you will need

- Fabric place mats in white (large enough to accommodate the 14½" x 9" motif)
- DMC Six Strand Embroidery Floss, in dark gray 3799 ■ (1 skein per place mat)
- Size 9 embroidery needle
- Embroidery scissors
- Iron
- Place Setting Place Mat transfer (in envelope)

embroidery stitch

- Backstitch (page 32)

technique

- Using iron-on transfers (page 73)

Prepare your place mat

1. Use a warm iron to apply the Place Setting Place Mat motif to the center of the place mat.

step 1

Embroider

2. Use the backstitch to embroider the design using 3 strands of floss and the embroidery needle. Keep the stitches even; the sample stitches are approximately ⅛" long.

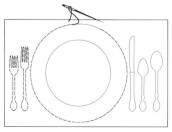

step 2

Color Theory Coasters

Wouldn't your martini feel right at home on a little piece of abstract art? While other folks are stitching, oh . . . maybe a goose wearing a bonnet, you can knock out these little square tributes to color theory in about one tenth the time and they're infinitely cooler. This is easy-to-do needlepoint because it is on plastic canvas. If you can count rows, you can do it. Be experimental and swap around the crayon-bright colors any way you like. Simple but sophisticated, these coasters make a wonderful hostess gift—just stitch 'em, stack 'em, and tie 'em up tight with a pretty ribbon.

level

finished size (each)

- 4" square

you will need

- Uniek 10-mesh clear plastic canvas (11" x 14"; 3 sheets)
- Magic Cabin wool felt, at least 4¼" square in each of the following colors: lemon, royal, wine, sky, cranberry, and leaf
- Anchor Tapestry wool (2 skeins each): Coaster 1: dark turquoise 8674 ■, wine 8204 ■, bright red 8198 ■; Coaster 2: berry 8402 ■, dark pink 8454 ■, medium pink 8452 ■, light pink 8484 □; Coaster 3: maroon 8426 ■, dark purple 8594 ■, light purple 8590 ■; Coaster 4: light blue 8686 ■, sage 9066 ■, ivory 8006 □, lime green 9152 □; Coaster 5: dark green 9104 ■, blue green 8820 ■, jade 8970 ■, light turquoise 8806 □; Coaster 6: yellow 8120 ■, orange 8166 ■, red 8202 ■

- DMC Six Strand Embroidery Floss (color to match felt; 1 skein each): Coaster 1: dark turquoise 995 ■; Coaster 2: cranberry 150 ■; Coaster 3: maroon 902 ■; Coaster 4: sky blue 813 ■; Coaster 5: dark green 890 ■; Coaster 6: golden yellow 972 ■
- Size 9 embroidery needle
- Size 18 tapestry needle
- Embroidery scissors
- Regular scissors

- Rotary cutter and mat, or fabric scissors
- Quilting ruler
- Air-soluble fabric marker
- Straight pins

embroidery stitch

- Continental (tent) stitch (page 52)

techniques

- Following a needlepoint chart (page 59)
- Finishing with overcast stitch, aka whipstitch (page 235)

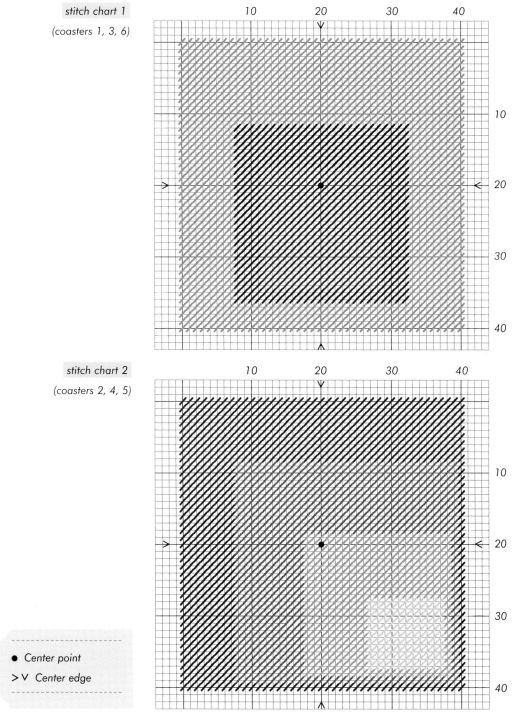

stitch chart 1
(coasters 1, 3, 6)

stitch chart 2
(coasters 2, 4, 5)

● Center point
> ∨ Center edge

Prepare the canvas and the backing material

1. Using the regular scissors, ruler, and fabric marker, measure, mark, and cut six 5" squares of plastic canvas.

2. Using the ruler, rotary cutter, and mat, cut six 4¼" squares from the felt.

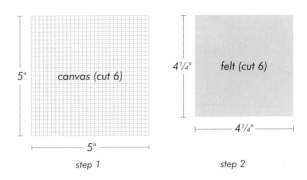

5" | canvas (cut 6)

5"

step 1

4¼" | felt (cut 6)

4¼"

step 2

Stitch the needlepoint coasters

3. Find the center of the canvas and mark or insert a pin at this point. Since the tent stitch is always worked from right to left, count over from center to determine where to place the first stitch of the smallest color block. Work one color block at a time. (Each grid square in the stitch charts is equal to 10 × 10 stitches.)

4. Using the tapestry needle and a continental (tent) stitch, needlepoint the coasters following the charts (opposite). Note: The grids show colors for Coasters 1 and 2; simply swap out the colors to make the other four coasters.

Finishing

5. Trim the canvas with regular scissors so there is only one row of unstitched plastic mesh.

6. Use an overcast stitch to finish the last row of canvas, taking three stitches at each corner to completely cover the plastic.

7. Using a single strand of matching floss and the embroidery needle, whipstitch the felt backing to the wrong side of the coaster.

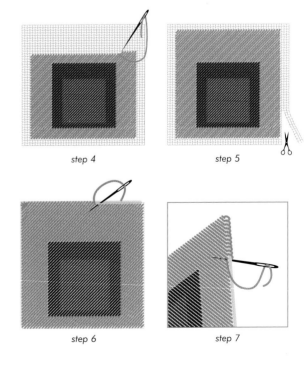

step 4

step 5

step 6

step 7

Greenmarket Tote

level 1

finished size

- 13½" x 15½"; 5½"
  bottom gusset;
  23" handles

you will need

- Canvas tote (sample is
  from ecobags.com.)
- Paternayan Persian
  Yarn, in dark Christmas
  green 705 ■, very dark
  peacock green 680 ■
  (2 skeins each)
- Size 22 chenille needle
- Embroidery scissors
- Iron
- Needle puller (optional)
- Recycling Symbol
  transfer (in envelope)

embroidery stitch

- Split stitch fill
  (page 33)

technique

- Using iron-on transfers
  (page 73)

Just say no to plastic bags. You can save the earth *and* be the cutest person buying Brussels sprouts at the market. Shop with this sturdy organic cotton tote . . . over and over and over again. The recycling symbol looks soft and sweet in green wool, the split stitch makes a nice textured filler, and the tote fabric is so stiff you don't need to use an embroidery hoop. If you want to take the recycling idea one step further, embroider the green arrows onto a tote you already have—even if there's text or a pattern on the bag. It'll give it new life!

✱ Tip: Canvas fabric comes in a variety of weights, measured in ounces. Lightweight is about 4 or 5 oz.; medium-weight is about 7 or 8 oz.; heavyweight is about 10 or 12 oz. I used a 4 oz. bag, which was a pleasure to stitch. If pulling the needle through your fabric takes a lot of effort, either use a needle puller (see page 3) or choose another bag. Trust me, your fingers will thank you!

Embroider the motif

1. Apply the Recycling Symbol transfer to the bag using a warm iron. I placed mine 1½" from the bottom of the tote and 3¾" from the right side seam. A word of caution: Be careful that your iron is set to the correct temperature setting—canvas will scorch if the iron is too hot.

2. Outline the motif with split stitch using a single strand of yarn. Refer to the stitch diagram for color placement.

3. Fill the motif with split stitch, working it parallel to the sides of the arrow to complete the design.

stitch diagram

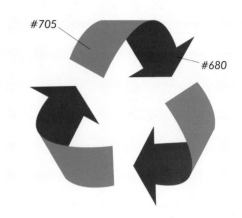

#705

#680

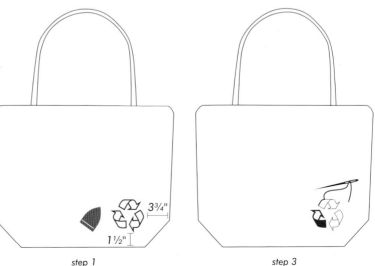

3¾"

1½"

step 1

step 3

Horsey Draft Dodger

When the wintry winds make your windowsills and doorsills drafty, don't just block the cracks with a rolled-up towel. This elegant and functional Horsey Draft Dodger—an homage to Eadweard J. Muybridge and his photographic study of horses in motion—problem-solves with style. Sew the horse silhouettes onto raw linen with a galloping, errr, running stitch. Then finish it and set it on its mark!

Prepare the pattern pieces

1. Photocopy the Horsey Draft Dodger Templates 1–6 (at right and on pages 166–167) at 100%. Using regular scissors, cut out each silhouette very close to the outer edges of the artwork (the reins will be stitched separately in Step 6).

horses 1, 6

level ///

finished size

- 36" x 4"

you will need

- Zweigart Edinburgh raw linen for pillow front (2½ yards)
- Magic Cabin wool felt in black (two 18" squares)
- 15-lb. bag Yesterday's News cat litter (dust-free and made from recycled newspapers)
  NOTE: If your draft dodger is in danger of getting damp, replace the litter filling with a combination of fiberfill and bean bag pellets.
- DMC Six Strand Embroidery Floss, in black 310 ■ (1 skein)
- All-purpose sewing thread, to match linen
- Size 9 embroidery needle

- Embroidery scissors
- Regular scissors
- Rotary cutter and mat, or fabric scissors
- Point turner (optional)
- Quilting ruler
- Air-soluble fabric marker
- Iron
- Straight pins
- Access to a photocopy machine
- Sewing machine (optional)

- Horsey Draft Dodger templates (above, pages 166–167)

embroidery stitches

- Running stitch (page 30)
- Backstitch (page 32)

techniques

- Using appliqué (page 43)
- Backstitching a seam (page 237)
- Finishing with slipstitch (page 237)

163

Cut the pillow fabric and the felt

2. If the fabric is wrinkled, press it before cutting. Using the ruler, rotary cutter, and mat, cut two 37" × 5" rectangles for the front and back.

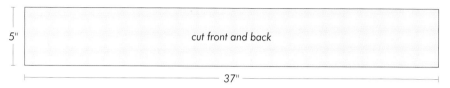

5"

cut front and back

37"

3. For each horse image, pin the image onto the felt right side up, as shown. Cut the felt around the edges. Repeat for each of the five horse images.

✳ *Tip: Use embroidery scissors or a pair of small scissors to cut out the felt shapes; the small blades will make it much easier to do.*

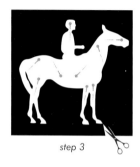

step 3

Mark the placement of the horses and pin them in place

4. Using the ruler and marker, draw a ½" seam allowance along both short ends of the pillow. Then mark the center on the pillow front to help place the horse motifs in the order shown. Note: An air-soluble fabric marker won't need to be washed out after the horses are stitched in place. Reapply if the lines disappear.

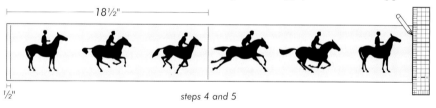

18½"

½"

steps 4 and 5

5. Using the marks as a guide, arrange the cutout felt horse motifs, wrong side down, to the right side of the pillow front. Pin them. Note: The distance between horses ranges between 1⅛" and 1⅞"; place them so they're visually balanced.

Stitch the appliqués to the pillow front

6. With the embroidery needle and two strands of floss, stitch around each felt horse motif with ⅛"-long running stitches placed ⅛" from the edge of the motif, hiding the knots on the back of the fabric. Backstitch the reins as indicated on the templates (pages 163, 166–167).

7. Repeat Step 6 for each felt motif to complete the design. Each time you finish and start sewing a new horse, check your work with a ruler. Don't wait until the end to find out there's a problem with the spacing!

step 7

Finish the dodger pillow

8. Place the pillow front right side up on a table. Using the fabric marker and a ruler, draw a seam line ½" inside all four edges of the wrong side of the backing fabric. Place the backing fabric on top of the front, right sides together and matching the corners. Pin all around the edges.

9. With the embroidery needle and thread, backstitch around all four sides of the pillow on the marked ½" seam line, leaving a 7" opening at the center bottom. Note: This step may also be completed on a sewing machine.

10. Press the seam allowances open along all four sides including the opening (in preparation for it being stitched closed). Trim the corners as shown.

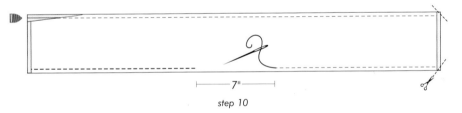

step 10

11. Turn the draft dodger right side out by pulling the fabric through the opening. Use a point turner or similar tool to gently poke out the corners. Press the right side of the fabric along the seam lines.

12. Fill the draft dodger with cat litter or fiberfill and beanbag pellets.

13. Using the embroidery needle and thread, slipstitch the opening closed (see page 237).

steps 12 and 13

horse 2

horse 3

horse 4

horse 5

Light-as-a-Feather Doorstop

Ever wondered if you could stop a whole door with a feather? Now you can. Not with magic or atomic manipulation—but with needlepoint. It's fun to decorate something heavy (in this case, a plain ol' brick) with something light and fluffy. Next time you or someone you love reaches for a big ugly rock to hold a door open, let this feather do the heavy work. For a feather you can throw, use this pattern to needlepoint a pillow front. Just expand the blue background to form a neat square.

Prepare the canvas

1. Tape the edges of the canvas with artist tape. With the marker, write "top" on one long side.

2. Attach the canvas to the stretcher bar frame with tacks (see page 18).

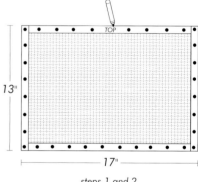

13"

17"

steps 1 and 2

level ///

finished size

- 8" x 4" x 2¼"

you will need

- Standard-size brick (8" x 4" x 2¼")
- Magic Cabin wool felt (at least 9" x 5"; since the doorstop will be on the floor and will get dirty, a dark color is best)

- Zweigart 12 mesh monocanvas (13" x 17")
- Paternayan Persian yarn, in cream 261 ▨, very light gray 203 ◼, dark gray 210 ◼ (1 skein each); sky blue 584 ◼ (6 skeins)
- All-purpose sewing thread, in light blue and to match felt
- Size 9 embroidery needle
- Size 20 tapestry needle
- Embroidery scissors

- Regular scissors
- Rotary cutter and mat, or fabric scissors
- Quilting ruler
- Black fine-tip permanent marker
- Artist tape
- Stretcher bar frame (same size as canvas) and needlepoint tacks

embroidery stitches

- Continental (tent) stitch (page 52)
- Brick stitch (page 57)

techniques

- Preparing a canvas (frames, page 18)
- Using a stretcher bar frame (page 18)
- Following a needlepoint chart (page 59)
- Blocking (page 238)
- Basting (page 237)
- Finishing with overcast stitch, aka whipstitch (page 235)

stitch chart

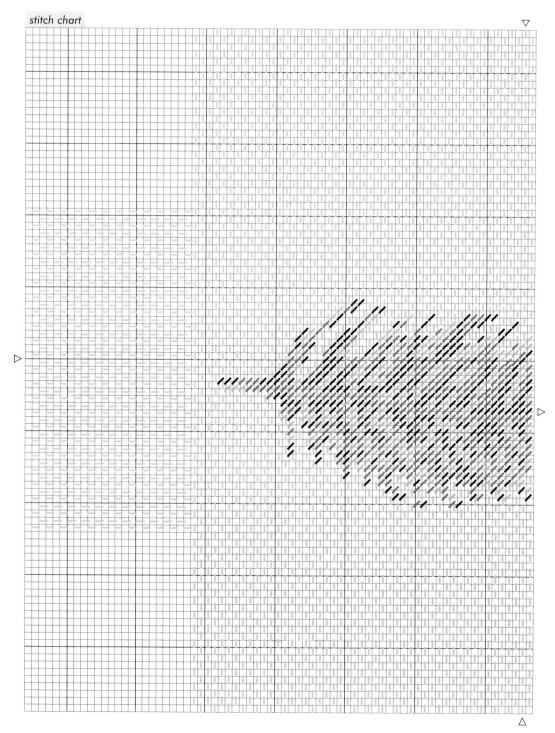

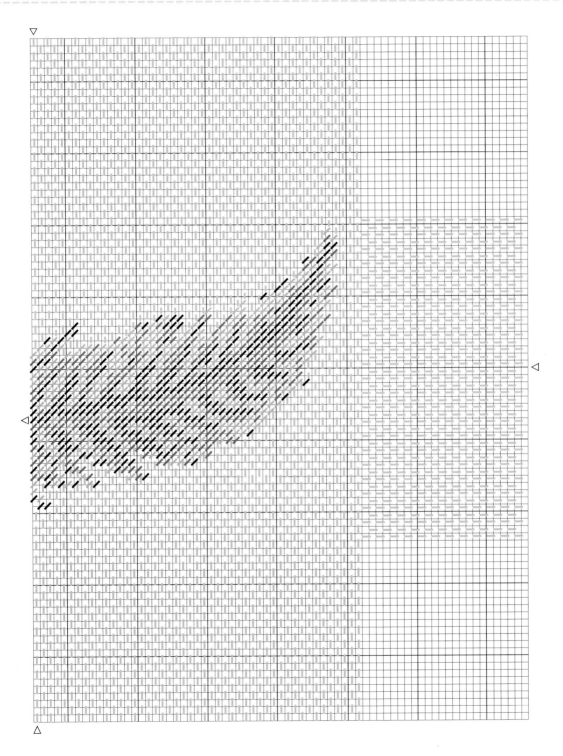

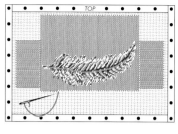

step 3

Stitch the canvas

3. Using the tapestry needle, two strands of yarn, and continental stitch, work the canvas following the stitch chart on pages 170–171. Stitch the feather first, working out from its center, then stitch the blue background.

Finishing the cover

4. Remove the canvas from the stretcher bars. Block if necessary.

5. Using regular scissors, trim the excess canvas around the design to ½".

6. Fold the edges of the raw canvas to the wrong side. Using the embroidery needle and light blue thread, baste the edges in place. (Make sure the stitches do not show on the right side of the canvas.)

7. Using the tapestry needle and sky blue yarn, fold up and whipstitch the short sides together on the right side of the canvas. Be sure to make the stitches small and discreet.

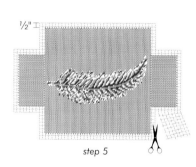

½"

step 5

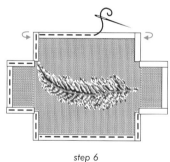

step 6

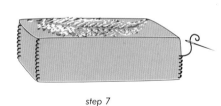

step 7

8. Place the canvas on a table wrong side up and insert the brick.

9. Using the ruler, rotary cutter, and mat, cut an 8⅛" × 5⅛" piece of felt.

10. Place the felt on the bottom of the brick cover. Using the embroidery needle, thread, and overcast stitch, sew the felt to the last row of the needlepoint cover, making small stitches so they're not visible when the doorstop is being used.

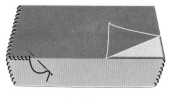

step 10

Dishwasher Sign

level //

finished size

- 7¾" x 2½"

you will need

- Zweigart 10 mesh monocanvas (20" x 4½")
- Uniek clear plastic canvas (at least 8" x 2½")
- Anchor Tapestry wool, in avocado 9200 ■, bright orange 8196 ■ (3 skeins each); natural 8034 □ (5 skeins)
- All-purpose sewing thread, in ivory
- Size 20 tapestry needle
- Sewing needle
- Embroidery scissors
- Regular scissors
- Sewing ruler
- Black fine-tip permanent marker
- Artist tape
- Stretcher bar frame (same size as cut canvas) and needlepoint tacks (optional)

embroidery stitch

- Continental (tent) stitch (page 52)

techniques

- Using a stretcher bar frame (page 18)
- Following a needlepoint chart (page 59)
- Blocking (page 238)
- Basting (page 77)
- Finishing with overcast stitch, aka whipstitch (page 235)

No more bellowing across the house, "Are these clean or dirty?!" Flip this handy sign to the proper side, revealing the answer in needlepoint. This will bring veritable *minutes* of family peace. To make it, you do the lettering and background in continental stitch (a basic tent stitch) and whipstitch it together with yarn. Though you'll be tempted to place the sign elsewhere—bookcase, TV screen, the laundry bin, your mind—keep it on the dishwasher. Just remember to use it.

Prepare the canvas

1. With regular scissors, cut the canvas in half widthwise to make two 10" × 4½" rectangular pieces of canvas, one for each side of the reversible sign.

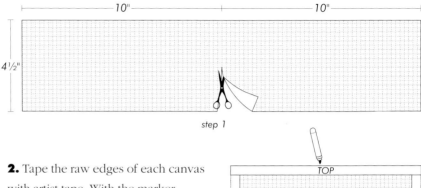

step 1

2. Tape the raw edges of each canvas with artist tape. With the marker, mark "top" on one of the long taped edges on each canvas. If desired, tack the canvas to a frame for stability and to minimize distortion (see page 18).

step 2

Stitch the signs

3. Using the tapestry needle, one strand of yarn, and continental stitch, stitch one needlepoint design (DIRTY and CLEAN) on each of the canvas pieces following the chart.

Prepare the canvas for finishing

4. If the canvas appears to be distorted, block both pieces.

5. Using regular scissors, trim the excess canvas around the design to ½".

step 5

stitch chart

6. Working on one side of the sign at a time, fold the excess canvas to the wrong side along the last stitched row of the design, and baste in place using the sewing needle and thread so the stitches aren't visible on the right side of the work. If they are, pull out the stitch (unthread the needle and gently pull out the thread), then restitch. Repeat for all four sides of each canvas sign.

Make a cord to hang the sign

7. Cut three 60" strands of the natural color yarn. Put the strands together and smooth out the yarn to make sure that the strands are even in length.

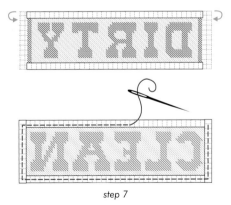

step 7

175

8. Tie one end of the yarns to a stationary object, like a door knob or other handle, and the opposite end to a marker or pencil.

9. Continually rotate the pencil clockwise, stopping when the yarn becomes very taut.

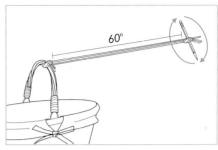

steps 9 and 10

10. Without losing the tautness, grasp the yarn cord at the center and fold it in half. Then release the cord from the fixed object, allowing the two halves of the cord to twist together. Tie a knot at the ends to keep the cord from untwisting. The twisted cord should be approximately 11" long.

step 11

Finish the sign

11. Place one sign right side down on a flat surface. Place the second sign on top of it, wrong sides together.

step 13

12. Rethread the tapestry needle with the natural color yarn. Starting at the center bottom of the sign, using an overcast stitch, sew only the bottom and the short sides together, making three stitches into each corner to cover the canvas completely.

13. Insert the plastic canvas between the two signs through the top opening. The plastic will stiffen the sign and add weight, which will help it hang evenly.

step 14

14. Insert each end of the twisted cord between the sign layers so the end is ½" below the top edge and 1¼" in from the sides. Finish by overcast stitching the opening closed using the tapestry needle and the natural color yarn, as in Step 12.

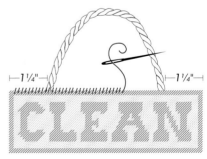

step 15

Voulez-Vous Pillowcase

Question: What is sexier than asking "Voulez-vous coucher avec moi?" Answer: Making the inquiry with embroidery on a soft, sensual pillow. And stitching the question in white, *on white,* is like whispering. Work this project in silklike floss using padded satin stitch and split stitch to keep the curves smooth and swoopy. When you're *fini,* you can toss this provocative gift on a loved one's bed, or keep it for yourself to put out when the night is right. Must be over eighteen to stitch. (Kidding! Sorta.)

Transfer the motif to the pillowcase

1. Pin the transfer to the center of the pillowcase front. Apply using a warm iron.

step 1

Voulez~vous

Embroider the motif

2. Outline the entire phrase in split stitch using two strands of floss. Use two rows of split stitch for areas that will be worked in padded satin stitch. It's easier to stitch the phrase from right to left, so start at the question mark and work backward to *Voulez*.

3. Starting from the right again, fill in the padded satin stitch areas as indicated in the diagram (below) using one strand of floss.

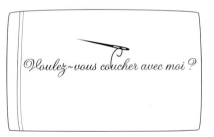

step 2

step 3

stitch diagram

- - - - - - - - - - - - - - - - - -
■ *Split stitch*
■ *Padded satin stitch*
- - - - - - - - - - - - - - - - - -

coucher avec moi ?

Old Country Tea Towel

My German ancestry inspired me to give the old country a textile shout-out with this traditional cross-stitch pattern. Stitch it in black and red floss on a linen tea towel, counting waste canvas threads to keep the X's uniform. This tea towel takes some patience to craft, but it'll look like an expensive antique when you're done. Sure, you can save it in a trousseau, or shelve it until the next tea party, but linen is a hardy fabric; use your tea towel to whisk a hot pie from the oven or wipe up a spill. Then toss it in the laundry and hang it from the oven door for more hot kitchen action. This craft project is at its best when it's handled and used to the max!

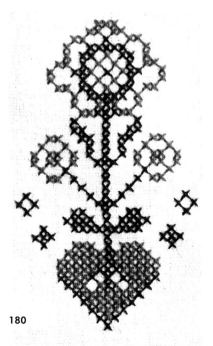

Prepare the fabric

✱ *Tip: You can count the threads of your linen tea towel, and skip the waste canvas, but waste canvas was used in this sample because the linen was 36-count and the threads were too tiny to see. If you prefer to count thread, choose a coarser linen with 28-count weave. You then have to work over two threads in each direction to make one cross-stitch. You can also use the waste canvas method described here to stitch the design onto a cotton tea towel.*

step 2

step 3

1. Cut a piece of waste canvas 10" × 6" using regular scissors.

2. Use the ruler to center the waste canvas on the front of the tea towel about 1¼" from the bottom of the towel (or desired location). Pin and baste in place using sewing thread and the embroidery needle (see page 77).

Embroider the design

3. Use three strands of floss. Work the center motif first, following the stitch chart. Begin with the center bottom stitch of the motif, about 1" or ten threads from the center bottom of the waste canvas.

4. Stitch the letters from the Font Library so they are centered vertically and spaced two stitches from either side of the center motif.

Finishing

5. Carefully tear out the basting stitches with the seam ripper.

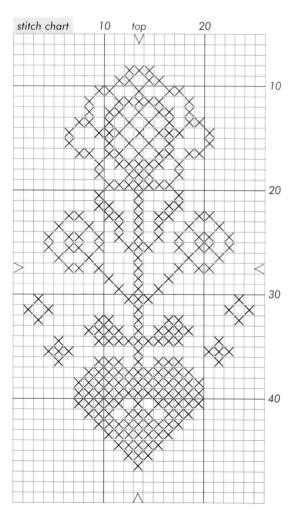

stitch chart

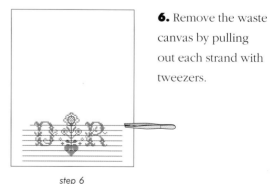

6. Remove the waste canvas by pulling out each strand with tweezers.

step 6

Peony Jewelry Box

level //

you will need

- Wood frame box with 5" square opening in lid (sample is Sudberry house "Betsy" box in white)
- Linen, in gray blue (at least 10" square)
- Batting (low-loft; size of box frame backing)
- Splendor Silk 12-ply silk floss, in yellow S909 , bright red S911 ■, primary red S820 ■, burgundy S826 ■, lime green S847 , dark apple green S1140 ■, sage S1100 ■, medium blue S1156 ■, light blue S862 ■ (1 skein each)
- Size 9 embroidery needle
- Embroidery scissors
- Rotary cutter and mat, or fabric scissors
- Quilting ruler
- Straight pins
- Artist tape
- Iron
- Hoop
- Peony Jewelry Box transfer (in envelope)

embroidery stitches

- Satin stitch (page 40)

techniques

- Using iron-on transfers (page 73)
- Hooping your work (page 25)

Peonies are my all-time fave flower. I planted them at my fiancé's family's farm and practically hover over them waiting for them to bloom. When I'm not hovering, I've been taking botanical illustration classes. I learned to draw a peony, and have translated my drawing into an embroidery design for you. Stitch 'er up in gorgeous reds and greens. You'll almost be able to smell the fragrant blooms every time you put away your bracelets for safekeeping. Or make your mom proud and present it to her on Mother's Day.

Prepare the fabric

1. Using the ruler, rotary cutter, and mat, cut a 10" square of linen fabric and batting.

2. Center the transfer on the linen, pin, and then apply using a warm iron. Remove pins.

3. Insert the fabric into the hoop.

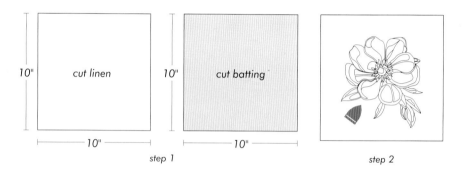

step 1

step 2

stitch diagram

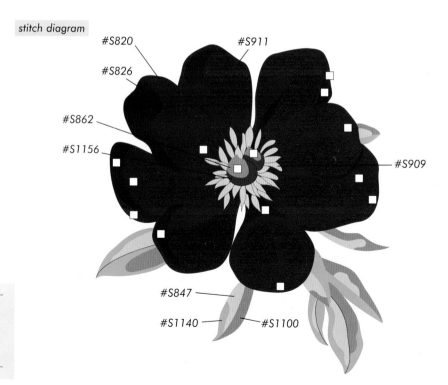

#S820

#S911

#S826

#S862

#S1156

#S909

#S847

#S1140

#S1100

Satin stitch (worked horizontally) except as noted with □, which are worked vertically.

Embroider the design

4. Stitch the peony in satin stitch using two strands of floss and the embroidery needle. (For neater stitching, separate the strands and then recombine them.) Follow the stitch diagram for color placement and the outline illustration for the direction in which the satin stitches should be worked.

step 4

Finishing

5. Remove the hoop and carefully press the fabric with a warm iron.

6. Lay the fabric, wrong side up, on your work surface. Open the box and remove back and the mat board behind it. Center the batting and then the mat board over the embroidery.

7. Fold the edges of the fabric onto the mat board and tape in place. The fabric should be smooth with no distortions.

8. Insert the embroidery assembly into the frame and check to make sure that your work fits. If necessary, adjust the position of the fabric or add more batting. Trim away any excess fabric to make the back of the work as flat as possible.

9. When finished, place the embroidery into the box lid and secure the backing over it.

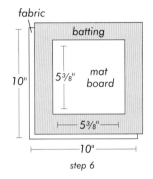

step 6

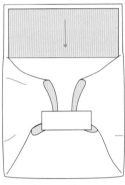

step 7

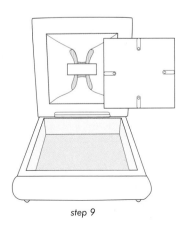

step 9

Lacy Parasol

you will need

- Leighton parasol or umbrella, in aqua
- DMC Six Strand Embroidery Floss, in lemon 444 ☐ (2 skeins)
- Size 9 embroidery needle
- Embroidery scissors
- Sewing ruler
- Air-soluble fabric marker
- Artist tape
- "Lace 1" pattern from TheArtfulStencil.com

embroidery stitches

- Backstitch (page 32)
- French knot (page 45)
- Straight stitch (page 30)
- Detached chain stitch (page 35)

t's the dog days of summer and there's not a spot of shade to be found. Oh, what to do? Why not make your own shade with this lacy parasol? Picture bridesmaids carrying them at a sunny wedding. Or pack one with the picnic basket or take one to a backyard garden party. Oh, you know who else would really like one of these? Your favorite little preteen girl. White on cream, red on cream, gold, pink, or blue will all look divine.

Trace the design on the parasol

1. Measure and mark ⅜" from the edge of the parasol.

2. Carefully line up the bottom edge of the stencil with the mark made in Step 1. Use the ruler to check the placement, then tape the stencil to the parasol.

3. Trace the stencil pattern with the marker to transfer the design to the parasol.

4. Remove the stencil from the parasol.

step 3

Embroider the design

5. Stitch the lace pattern following the chart below using two strands of floss. Keep the back of the work neat by trimming excess floss from knots as you go.

6. Repeat Steps 1–5 until the perimeter is completely stitched.

step 5

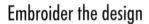

stitch diagram

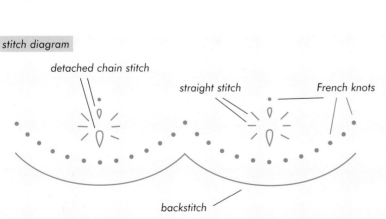

detached chain stitch

straight stitch   *French knots*

backstitch

Victorian Tic-Tac-Toe

Snooty, old-fashioned lettering meets silly fun kids' game with these decorative beanbags. They're serious multitaskers—great for playing tic-tac-toe on the road, on the beach, or on the carpet at home. You can juggle them, too, or just let them sit pretty in a bowl. And the letter *X,* of course, is an homage to the cross-stitch itself—one of the simplest stitches around. The thick Aida cloth background makes it easy to count threads, so the lacy crosses stay neat. Once you master the *X*s and *O*s, you can try cross-stitching other letters to make monograms. (Unless your name is Xavier O'Shea, in which case you're all set!)

Prepare the Aida cloth and the lining fabric

1. With ruler, chalk pencil, and rotary cutter and mat or fabric scissors, measure, mark, and cut eighteen 5" squares of Aida cloth.

2. Repeat Step 1 with the lining fabric, cutting on-grain (see page 14).

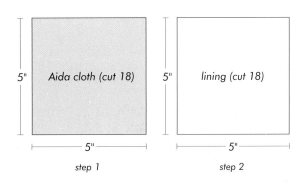

5" Aida cloth (cut 18)

5"

step 1

5" lining (cut 18)

5"

step 2

level

finished size

- 4" square (each)

you will need

- DMC 14-count Aida cloth, in black (20" x 30"—enough to cut eighteen 5" squares)
- Cotton fabric in black for lining (¼ yard)

- Beanbag fill (36 oz.; about 4 oz. for each beanbag)
- DMC Six Strand Embroidery Floss, in ecru ☐ (4 skeins) and black 310 ■ (1 skein)
- Size 9 embroidery needle
- Embroidery scissors
- Rotary cutter and mat, or fabric scissors
- Sewing needle

- Point turner (optional)
- Quilting ruler
- Chalk pencil, in white
- Straight pins
- Sewing machine (optional)

embroidery stitches

- Cross-stitch (page 44)
- Backstitch (page 32)

techniques

- Cutting fabric on-grain (page 14)
- Following a counted thread chart (page 65)
- Basting (page 237)
- Backstitching a seam (page 237)
- Finishing with slipstitch (page 237)

189

stitch charts

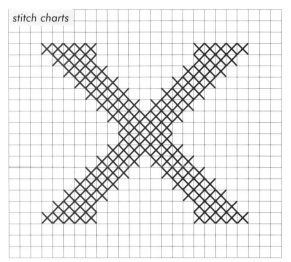

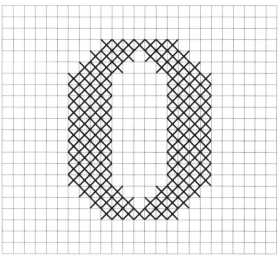

Embroider the designs

3. Using the embroidery needle and 3 strands of floss, cross-stitch the Aida cloth squares, 9 with the *X* pattern and 9 with the *O* pattern, following the stitch charts above. Be careful not to split the threads as you stitch; if this happens, unthread the needle, pull out the stitches, and restitch. Note: The cross-stitches in this project are twice as big as the 14-count fabric, which means you must insert the needle into *every other* hole.

The Wrong Side of Cross-Stitch

make a single cross-stitch on a scrap of Aida cloth and then take a look at the wrong side. Can you see that the stitches are straight and vertical in the back? (It'll be a bit messy, but still . . .) This means that instead of searching for the correct spot on the front of the canvas, you can simply take a straight stitch down into the next hole from the back (or in the case of this project, the second hole down). If you allow light to shine through from the back side of the fabric, it will help you guide your needle.

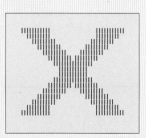

vertical stitches
on the wrong side

Baste the linings to the Aida cloth

4. Pin one piece of lining to the wrong side of each cross-stitched letter.

5. Using embroidery needle and a single strand of floss, baste the lining to the Aida cloth with a ⅜" (or narrower) seam allowance (see page 77). Note: This step may also be completed on a sewing machine.

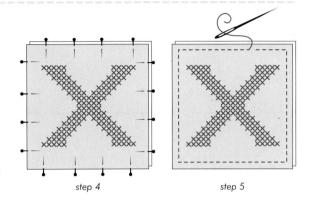

step 4   step 5

Sew the beanbag pieces

6. Arrange the *X*s and *O*s on a table with one *X* on top of one *O* and right sides together. Pin.

7. With a sewing needle and a single strand of black floss, backstitch the squares together with a ½" seam allowance. Leave a 2½" opening at center top as shown. Note: This step may also be completed on a sewing machine.

8. Trim the corners as shown, and trim the seam allowances to ¼" to reduce bulk.

9. Turn the beanbags right side out by pulling the fabric through the opening. Use a point turner or similar tool to gently poke out the corners.

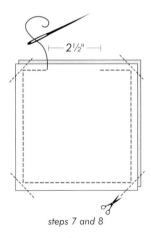

steps 7 and 8

Finishing

10. Fill the pillows about three quarters full with beanbag fill. (You'll need some space to sew the beanbag closed.)

✳ *Tip: Make a funnel using a taped piece of cardstock and pour the fill using a small plastic cup. It makes the job much easier!*

11. Using a sewing needle and a single strand of black floss, slipstitch the opening closed, adding more fill if needed before completely closing it up.

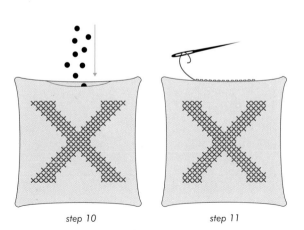

step 10   step 11

- 4⅝" x 2⅝"

- Luggage tag (3½" x 2") with openings
- Linen fabric (¼ yard)
- Fusible interfacing (at least 10" x 6")
- Sulky Tear-Away stabilizer
- DMC Six Strand Embroidery Floss, in medium red 321 ■, dark beaver gray 844 ■ (1 skein each)
- All-purpose sewing thread to match fabric
- Size 9 embroidery needle
- Embroidery scissors
- Rotary cutter and mat, or fabric scissors
- Seam ripper
- Tweezers
- Quilting ruler
- Pencil
- Fabric marker
- Iron
- Embroidery hoop (optional)
- Return-to-Sender Luggage Tag iron-on transfers (in envelope)
- Font Library (page 243)

- Backstitch (page 32)

- Cutting fabric on-grain (page 14)
- Using iron-on transfers (page 73)
- Using stabilizer (basting) (page 78)

for giving

Return-to-Sender Luggage Tag

Transform any old store-bought luggage tag into a frame for this very useful bit of artwork. Embroider your name, address, and any other crucial info— like your e-mail address or zodiac sign—in cute red backstitches. The design on the flip side is inspired by an old-fashioned rubber stamp. You'll be the envy of the luggage carousel. It also makes for a stellar bon voyage gift.

Prepare the fabric for stitching

1. Using the ruler, rotary cutter, and mat, cut two 7" squares of fabric using the selvage of the fabric as a guide to ensure that the fabric is cut on-grain.

2. Cut a 4" square of stabilizer.

3. Use a warm iron to apply the template for the luggage tag front (the hand) to the center of one of the squares of fabric.

4. Repeat Step 2 with the luggage tag back template (the lines) on the second square of fabric.

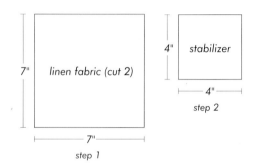

linen fabric (cut 2)

7"

7"

step 1

4" stabilizer

4"

step 2

RETURN TO SENDER

step 3

step 4

step 5

5. Lay the stabilizer on top of the alphabet (page 245) and use the pencil to trace the lettering for the back of the tag. Space the lines to match the luggage tag back motif. Note: You may also do this step freehand.

6. Baste the stabilizer to the motif, aligning the text to the lines of the motif. *Optional:* Use an embroidery hoop to keep your fabric taut.

Embroider the motif

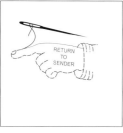

step 7

step 8

7. Backstitch the front of the tag using four strands of medium red floss to outline the hand; use two strands for the Return-to-Sender lettering.

8. Backstitch the lettering on the back using two strands of red floss. Remove the basting with a seam ripper, then gently tear away the stabilizer, using tweezers as needed.

9. Backstitch the lines with two strands of dark beaver gray floss.

Finishing

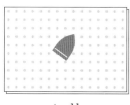

step 10

10. Trim the front and back pieces to fit into your luggage tag.

11. Cut the interfacing to match the trimmed pieces. Adhere the interfacing to the wrong side of each piece following the manufacturer's instructions.

12. Insert the pieces into the luggage tag.

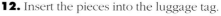

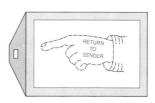

step 11

step 12

Baroque Paper Frame

level ❙❙

you will need

- 3" x 5" photo
- Pre-cut mat board frame with 3" x 5" window, in blue or desired color
- Mat board for backing (same size as frame)
- Cork board or cardboard scrap (at least 1" larger on all sides than mat board frame)
- DMC Pearl Cotton size 3, in white ▢ (1 skein)
- Size 22 chenille needle
- Bookbinder's awl or pushpin
- Hobby knife
- Artist tape
- Glue stick
- Access to a photocopy machine
- Baroque Paper Frame template (page 196)

embroidery stitch

- Backstitch (page 32)

Stitching on paper brings a special kind of satisfaction. It's unexpected. It reminds me of the sewing cards I played with as a little girl. Even the sound of thread pulling through paper is cool, and a nice change from working with fabric. Once you have the technique down, you never need to buy a card, Valentine, or gift tag again—simply stitch 'em!

Baroque Paper Frame template

Prepare the artwork

1. Photocopy the template, opposite, increasing the size as necessary to fit around the opening in your pre-cut frame. Note: Copying at 125% produces a template to fit around a 3" × 5" frame window.

Punch the stitching holes

2. Lay the mat board frame on top of the cork board or cardboard. Center the paper template around the opening of the frame. Tape it in position. Using the bookbinder's awl, punch holes where indicated by the dots. Keep the hole sizes consistent.

Embroider the frame

3. Remove the template and backstitch through the holes using the pearl cotton and the chenille needle.

Finishing

4. Place the photo on the back of the frame centered over the opening. Tape the corners.

5. Spread glue across the wrong side of the mat board backing. Press it to the back of the frame, lining up the edges, to adhere the pieces together.

step 2

step 3

step 5

Family Tree
Photo Album Cover

I f you like how embroidery connects you to the past, this is the project for you. Embroiderers have been stitching family trees for centuries. The apple tree is a very traditional motif inspired by a popular nineteenth-century design, and is perfectly suited to old-timey linen. If you have grandparents or even great-grandparents, here's a wonderful reason to sit down with them and chat about who's who (and find out the right names to stitch onto all those apples). After you attach your embroidery to a photo album and trim it with ribbon, show it to Granny and Gramps—they will be so tickled, since they sprouted the family tree in the first place!

level

////

finished size

- 9½" x 11½"

you will need

- Photo album (sample is a Kolo cloth album)
- Zweigart Belfast linen, in cream (½ yard)
- Muslin or similar fabric for lining (¼ yard)
- Fusible interfacing (¼ yard)
- ⅝" grosgrain ribbon, in dark brown (1¼ yards)

- ½" grosgrain ribbon, in cream (1 yard)
- DMC Pearl Cotton size 5, in dark brown 938 ■, medium brown 801 ■, dark rust 400 ■, light tan 437 ■, light green 502 ■, dark green 500 ■ (1 skein each)
- DMC Six Strand Embroidery Floss, in medium desert sand 3773 ■, medium garnet 815 ■, golden olive 832 ■, darkest brown 3371 ■ (1 skein each)
- All-purpose sewing thread, to match linen
- Size 9 embroidery needle

- Size 22 chenille needle
- Embroidery scissors
- Rotary cutter and mat, or fabric scissors
- Quilting ruler
- Air-soluble fabric marker
- Iron
- Straight pins
- Fabric glue
- Embroidery hoop
- Sewing machine (optional)
- Family Tree Photo Album Cover iron-on transfer (in envelope)

embroidery stitches

- Long and short stitch (page 42)
- Closed fly stitch (page 39)
- Satin stitch (page 40)
- Backstitch (page 32)

techniques

- Using iron-on templates (page 73)
- Hooping your work (page 25)
- Using interfacing (page 239)
- Basting (page 77)
- Cutting fabric on-grain (page 14)

C
#801

C
#437

C
#400

A
#815

D
#502

D
#500

C
#938

B
#400

B
#938

B
#801

A
#832

B
#437

A
#3773

stitch diagram

A Satin stitch

B Long and short stitch

C Backstitch

D Closed fly stitch

Prepare the materials and apply the artwork to the fabric

1. Using the ruler, rotary cutter, and mat, cut the cream-colored linen into a 14" × 15" rectangle. Use the selvage of the fabric as a guide to ensure that the fabric is cut on-grain.

2. Repeat Step 1 to cut a 7" × 11" piece of interfacing.

3. Repeat Step 2 to cut the lining fabric (muslin).

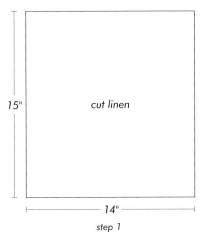

cut linen

15"

14"

step 1

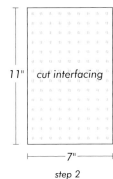

11" *cut interfacing*

7"

step 2

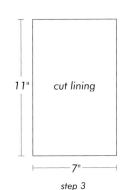

11" *cut lining*

7"

step 3

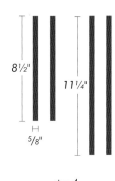

8½"

11¼"

⅝"

step 4

4. Cut the dark brown ribbon into two 8½"-long pieces and two 11¼"-long pieces.

5. Center and pin the Family Tree transfer art onto the linen fabric. Apply using a warm iron.

6. Insert the fabric into the embroidery hoop.

step 5

step 7

step 10

Embroider the design

7. Using one strand of pearl cotton with the chenille needle, and one strand of floss with the embroidery needle, stitch the design as shown in the stitch diagram (page 200).

Stitch the ribbons

8. Mark your relatives' names freehand about 2" apart onto the cream ribbon to customize it. (Note: Depending on the number of family members or length of names, you may need additional ribbon.) Using two strands of darkest brown floss #3371 and the embroidery needle, stitch over all the names using a backstitch.

9. Use the embroidery scissors to cut a small V-shaped notch on either side of each name (first practice this step on unstitched ribbon), to make little banners.

10. Place the name banners one at a time in the desired location on the tree, following the illustration. Using thread and the embroidery needle, make one small vertical straight stitch at each end of the ribbon to attach it to the tree.

Prepare the linen

11. Using the ruler, fabric marker, and fabric scissors, measure, mark, and cut the stitched linen fabric to measure 8" × 11", being sure the stitched tree is in the center.

12. Place the interfacing on the wrong side of the linen, aligning all edges, and apply with a warm iron.

13. Place the lining fabric on a flat work surface, wrong side up. Place the interfaced linen family tree on top of the backing, wrong sides together, and pin. Using sewing thread and needle, baste the linen to the backing with a ¼" seam allowance. Note: This step may also be completed on a sewing machine.

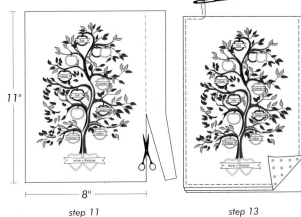

step 11

step 13

Attach and "frame" the motif

14. Place the photo album flat with the front cover facing up. Center the linen on the front cover.

15. Apply a small drop of fabric glue to each corner of the linen and adhere the fabric to the album.

16. Create the ribbon "frame." Place and then glue each precut length of dark brown ribbon onto the cover as shown, applying the two longer (vertical) pieces first, then overlapping the ends of the shorter (horizontal) pieces.

step 15

step 16

Old-Meets-New Gadget Cozies

level

finished size

- 3⅛" x 5⅛"

you will need

- Magic Cabin wool felt, in taupe and ice (at least 5" x 11" each per cozy)
  *Do not use acrylic craft felt; it will melt when transfer is applied.
- DMC Six Strand Embroidery Floss, in dark antique blue 930 ▨ (1 skein is enough to stitch all 3 designs)
- Paternayan Persian Yarn, in light brown 463 ▨ (1 skein)
- Size 9 embroidery needle
- Embroidery scissors
- Rotary cutter and mat, or fabric scissors
- Quilting ruler
- Air-soluble fabric marker
- Iron
- Straight pins
- Old-Meets-New Gadget Cozies iron-on transfers (in envelope)

embroidery stitches

- Backstitch (page 32)
- Blanket stitch (page 36)

technique

- Using iron-on templates (page 73)

Remember when headphones looked like something made by NASA? Let your e-gadgets know from whence they came—and keep them safe from scratches and spills. Store your cell phone, iPod, or digital camera in a felt cozy embroidered with their analog ancestors. Embroidering on felt is like stitching through butter. Here you use backstitch to draw the olde-tyme machinery in classic blue floss. And no hemming the edges! Looking for a project to do up for a dude? You have come to the right page. Every time he answers his phone he will look oh-so-smartly sophisticated.

Cut the felt to size

Note: Instructions are for a single cozy. Simply repeat to make the whole set!

1. Using the ruler, rotary cutter, and mat, cut a 3¾" × 5" rectangle from each felt color. Then cut two 3¾" × 2½" rectangles from each rectangle. You will have a taupe front and back and two ice lining pieces.

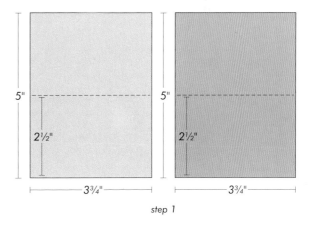

step 1

Apply the transfer

2. Center the transfer on one taupe felt half and pin. (Orient the motif horizontally or vertically, as shown in the photograph on page 204.)

3. Apply the transfer to the felt using a warm iron. Remove pins.

Embroider the design

4. Using two strands of floss and the embroidery needle, backstitch the design. These look best when the stitches are small and even; the stitches in the sample are only ⅛" in length.

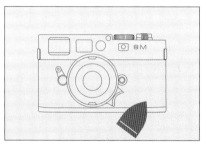

step 3

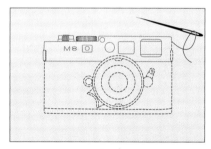

step 4

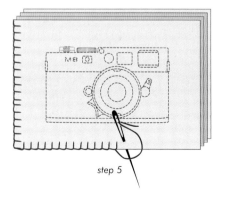

step 5

Finishing the cozy

5. Place the unworked piece of taupe felt on your work surface. Layer both pieces of ice felt, and then place the embroidered taupe front (right side up) on top. Align all the edges, and then pin the layers together to keep them from shifting.

6. Use blanket stitch and a single strand of yarn to sew through all layers along the long sides and the bottom.

7. At the top, separate the felt into two layers (taupe back and ice lining; and ice lining and taupe front) and work blanket stitch around them to create the opening.

8. Insert the gadget, and you're good to go!

Diamond Cuff Links

level

finished size

- ¾" diameter

you will need

- Linen in black (4" x 8")
- ¾" cuff link blanks (2)
- Size 30 (¾" diameter) Dritz flat cover buttons (2)
- Dressmaker's carbon paper, in contrasting color to fabric, with stylus or tracing tool
- DMC Six Strand Embroidery Floss, in bluish white 3756 ▢ (1 skein)
- Size 9 embroidery needle
- Rotary cutter and mat, or fabric scissors
- Embroidery scissors
- Regular scissors
- Pliers
- Quilting ruler
- Fabric marker (in a contrasting color to fabric)
- Straight pins
- Super glue that will adhere metal to metal
- Embroidery hoop
- Diamond Cuff Links iron-on transfers (in envelope)

FOR LIGHT COLORS:
- Iron

embroidery stitch

- Backstitch (page 32)

techniques

- Using dressmaker's carbon (page 78)
- Using iron-on transfers (page 73)
- Hooping your work (page 25)

Forget Tiffany's, here's a warmer, sweeter way to say "I love you." Stitch up a pair of elegant diamonds—these must be at least 50 karats—in white floss on black linen. Classy! Then turn them into covered buttons, which become handsome cuff links. You can make them for him in an afternoon. Next time you two lovebirds have a charity ball or dinner for two, give him these sparklers right before you head out the door. He'll beam like a little girl. Speaking of girls, you can switch the colors (emerald green on cream!) and make a set of jewels for all your friends. Covered-button kits can make rings or bracelets, too—a new take on a bridesmaid's gift!

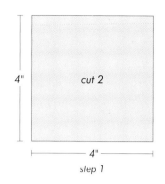

4"

cut 2

4"

step 1

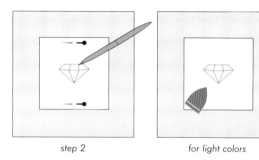

step 2   *for light colors*

step 3   *step 4*

step 6

Prepare the fabric

1. Using the ruler, rotary cutter, and mat, cut the fabric into two 4" squares.

2. Place the dressmaker's carbon paper facedown on one fabric square. Place the diamond transfer face up and centered on the carbon. Pin the layers together. Transfer the diamond shape using the tracing stylus. Repeat for the second fabric square.

For light colors:
Center the diamond transfer on a fabric square and pin. Use a warm iron to apply the design. Repeat for the second fabric square.

Embroider the design

3. Insert one fabric square into the embroidery hoop. Use backstitch to work the design using two strands of floss and the embroidery needle. Repeat for the second fabric square.

Covering the buttons

4. Remove the shank from each button backing by squeezing it with the pliers.

5. Draw a 1½" square centered around each diamond motif with the fabric marker.

6. Cut out the 1½" fabric circle template from the back of the button packaging with regular scissors.

7. Place the circle template on top of each diamond, centering it in the square. Trace the outline of the circle.

8. Use fabric or embroidery scissors to cut out traced circle.

✳ *Tip: The short blades of embroidery scissors make it easier to cut small shapes.*

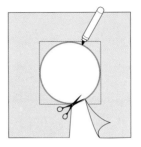

steps 7 and 8

9. Center the button cover on the wrong side of the fabric. Working from side to side and top to bottom, hook the fabric over the teeth of the button cover. Stretch the fabric for a tight, smooth fit; snap on the button backing.

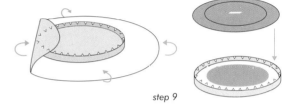

step 9

Finish the cuff links

10. Follow the glue manufacturer's instructions for adhering metal to metal. For each cuff link, adhere a button backing to the top of a cuff link blank. Allow the glue to dry before wearing.

step 10

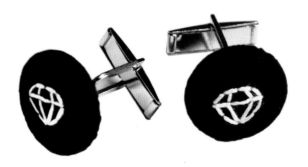

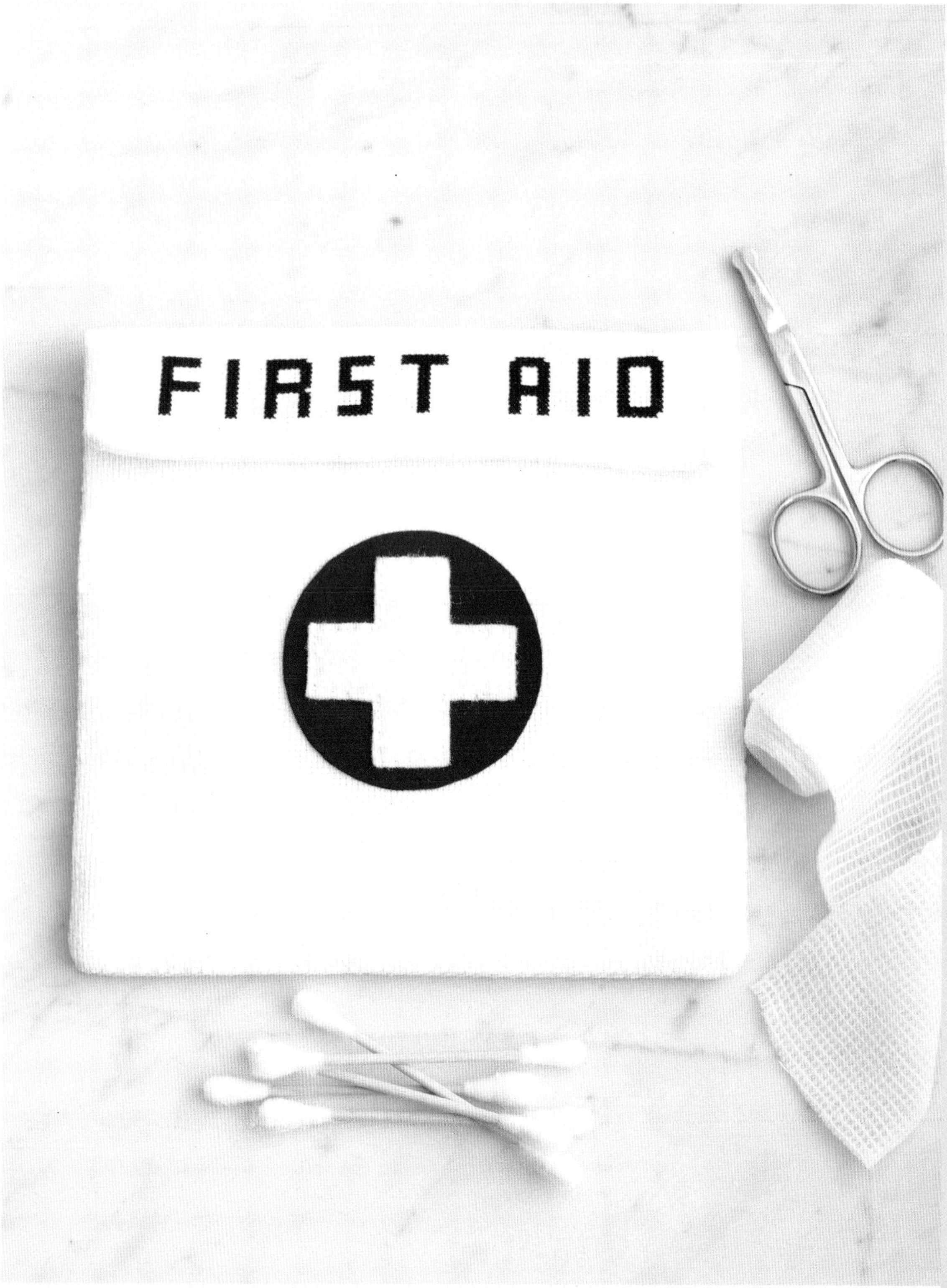
FIRST AID

Fancy First Aid Kit

Show off your style while you save the day by fetching a bandage, tweezers, or aspirin for a friend with a splinter. Perhaps said friend will forget his pain the moment he casts his eyes on your lovely handiwork. Easily worked in basic stitches on Aida cloth, you don't have to stitch the white background—you just do the fun parts. (You're welcome!) Then line your work with white cotton broadcloth and sew the front to the back to form an envelope. Fill with lotions, potions, and bandages, and then tuck it into your glove box or desk drawer. Florence Nightingale, eat your heart out!

Cut the Aida cloth and the lining fabric

1. Using the ruler, rotary cutter, and mat cut a 7" × 8¼" rectangle from the Aida cloth for the front, and a 7" × 7¼" rectangle for the back. Follow the grid of the fabric when cutting.

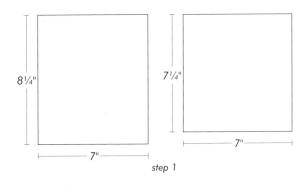

step 1

level //

finished size

- 6½" square

you will need

- Cotton broadcloth fabric in white for lining (¼ yard)
- Magic Cabin wool felt, in red (at least 9" square) and white (at least 3" square)
- DMC 18-count Aida cloth, in white (14" x 18")
- Size 3 snaps (2)
- DMC Six Strand Embroidery Floss, in apple red 666 ■ (3 skeins), black 310 ■ (1 skein), white ☐ (1 skein)
- Size 9 embroidery needle
- Embroidery scissors
- Regular scissors
- Rotary cutter and mat, or fabric scissors
- Point turner (optional)
- Quilting ruler
- Air-soluble fabric marker
- Tailor's chalk (in contrasting color)
- Straight pins
- Access to a photocopy machine
- Sewing machine (optional)
- Fancy First Aid templates (page 213)

embroidery stitches

- Cross-stitch (page 44)
- Running stitch (page 30)

techniques

- Cutting fabric on-grain (page 14)
- Following a counted thread chart (page 65)
- Finishing with overcast stitch, aka whipstitch (page 235)
- Backstitching a seam (page 237)
- Finishing with slipstitch (page 237)

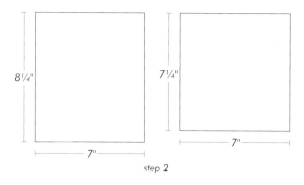

8¼" 7" 7¼" 7"

step 2

2. Repeat Step 1 with the lining fabric, using the selvage of the fabric as a guide to ensure that the fabric is cut on-grain.

Create the pattern templates and cut the shapes from felt

3. Photocopy the large cross, small cross, and circle templates, opposite, at 100%. Using regular scissors, cut around the outer edges of the paper templates.

4. Pin the large cross to the red felt. Using embroidery or fabric scissors, cut around the template.

5. Repeat Step 4, cutting the circle from the red felt.

6. Repeat Step 4, cutting the small cross from the white felt.

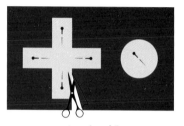

steps 4 and 5

step 6

Work the cross-stitched front

7. Using two strands of black floss and the needle, cross-stitch the words FIRST AID on the larger rectangle of Aida cloth, following the chart below, so the letter *F* is 1¼" in from the lower left-hand corner and 1" above the lower edge (to allow for the Aida cloth pieces to be sewn together with a ½" seam allowance after embroidering).

step 7

stitch chart

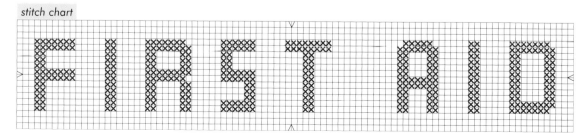

step 9

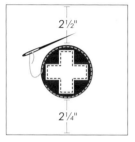

steps 10 and 11

Appliqué the felt shapes to the Aida cloth

8. Pin the large cross to the stitched Aida cloth so that it is centered 1" above the stitched letters. Use the ruler to double-check the placement.

9. Using one strand of red floss and the embroidery needle, attach the cross to the Aida cloth with a running stitch.

10. Center the white felt cross on top of the red cross felt circle and pin it into place. Using one strand of white floss and the embroidery needle, attach the small cross with a running stitch.

11. Place the completed circle/cross motif on the smaller (square) piece of Aida cloth and pin it 2½" down from the top. Using one strand of white floss and the embroidery needle, sew the motif to the Aida cloth with a running stitch.

Sew the lining fabric to the Aida cloth

12. On the wrong side of the larger cotton rectangle (the front lining), use the fabric marker and the ruler to draw a ½" seam line around all four sides and mark a 2" opening at the center bottom. Repeat with the wrong side of the smaller cotton rectangle (the back lining). Note: If the cotton fabric is reversible, simply choose a side to mark. This will make sewing straight a lot easier.

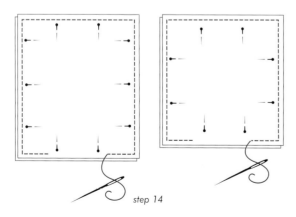

step 14

13. Lay the stitched front (red cross) on a table, right side up. Place the same-size lining fabric on top, right sides together (you should see the marked side of the facing), and pin them together. Repeat with the stitched back (red circle/white cross) and its corresponding lining fabric.

14. Using a single strand of white floss and the embroidery needle, backstitch over the seam lines, leaving the openings at the center bottom as marked. Note: This step may also be completed on a sewing machine.

15. Press the seam allowances open and flat, including the seam allowances along the openings of each piece (in preparation for being stitched closed). Trim the corners and trim the seam allowances to ¼".

16. Turn each piece right side out, pulling the fabric through the opening. Use a point turner or similar tool to gently poke out the corners.

17. Using a single strand of white floss and the embroidery needle, slipstitch each of the openings closed (page 237).

step 17

Stitch the back to the front

18. Lay the front/flap right side down on a table. Place the back on top of the front, with the lining fabrics together, so the bottom edges match (the flap with the words "First Aid" will extend beyond the back piece).

19. Using two strands of white floss and the embroidery needle, sew an overcast stitch, starting at the top of one side and following around three sides, leaving the top open.

Attach the snaps

20. Snaps come in two parts: a ball and a socket. Using a single strand of white floss and the embroidery needle, sew each ball to the inside of the flap ¼" down from the top edge and ⅜" in from each of the sides. Be neat; you don't want the stitching to show on the outside. (You'll need to insert your needle to the back of the canvas but not through the lining fabric.) Make several straight stitches through one of the holes, and then run the thread under the snap to the next hole and repeat.

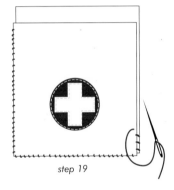

step 19

21. Rub chalk on the snap balls and close the flap. The chalk will mark where to place the snap sockets. Fold the flap over and press on the balls to transfer the chalk.

22. Center the snap sockets over the chalk marks and sew them in place the same way you sewed the snap balls.

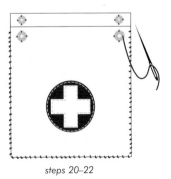

steps 20–22

Scissors Chatelaine

Back before women had purses, they kept their essentials on a chatelaine, which held keys, a buttonhook, scissors, and what have you. Now we carry handbags the size of boats, but it's still handy to have your little scissors around your neck when you're stitching. A stylish case keeps the tips protected and sharp. I whipped this one up in Brighton stitch (fun fact: there are almost as many needlepoint stitches as embroidery stitches), and beads can be added for texture and fun. A silk cord or pretty chain makes it a chatelaine. Enjoy, and then pass on to your child as a crafty heirloom!

Cut the canvas and lining

1. Tape the edges of the canvas using artist tape.

2. With the permanent marker, write "top" on the tape along one long edge. With the air-soluble marker, draw a line down the center of the canvas from one 12" side to another.

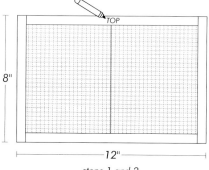

steps 1 and 2

level !!!

finished size

- 2¾" x 4½"

you will need

- Zweigart 18-mesh monocanvas (12" x 8")
- Cotton fabric for lining (¼ yard)
- Faux suede cord, in navy blue (⅛" x 2¼ yards)

- Paternayan Persian Yarn, in purple 312 ■, sage 679 ■, lilac 304 ■, medium brown 441 ■, light mustard 712 ▨, orange 701 ■, medium rose 903 ■, medium gray 210 ■, salmon pink 846 ▨, light steel gray 204 ■, rusty rose 932 ■, gold 752 ▨, periwinkle 344 ▨, rust 440 ■, light blue 505 ▨, light khaki 644 (1 skein each); true navy 570 ■ (2 skeins)
- All-purpose sewing thread, in muslin and navy

- Size 22 tapestry needle
- Size 9 embroidery needle
- Embroidery scissors
- Regular scissors
- Rotary cutter and mat, or fabric scissors
- Quilting ruler
- Black fine-tip permanent marker
- Air-soluble fabric marker
- Artist tape
- Sewing machine (optional)

embroidery stitches

- Brighton stitch (page 58)
- Upright cross-stitch (page 44)

techniques

- Preparing a canvas (frames, page 18)
- Cutting fabric on-grain (page 14)
- Following a needlepoint chart (page 59)
- Backstitching a seam (page 237)
- Finishing with overcast stitch, aka whipstitch (page 235)

216

front   back

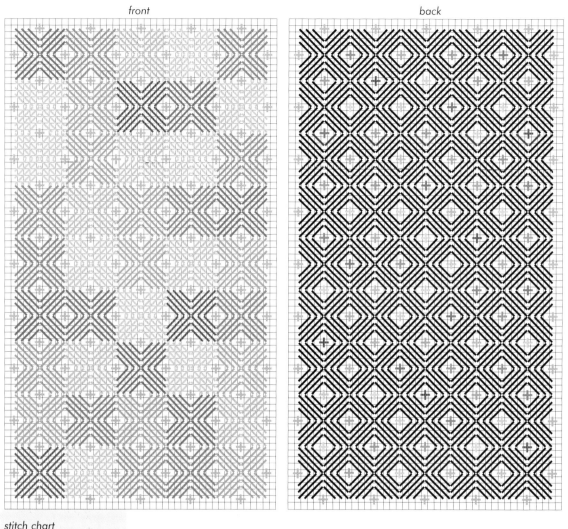

stitch chart

■ 312	▨ 304
▨ 712	■ 903
▨ 846	▨ 932
▨ 344	▨ 505
■ 570	■ 441
▨ 679	■ 210
■ 701	▨ 752
▨ 204	▨ 644
■ 440	

3. Using the ruler, rotary cutter, and mat, cut a 2½" × 9" piece of lining fabric. Use the selvage of the fabric as a guide to ensure that the fabric is cut on-grain.

Work the design

4. Using one strand of yarn and the tapestry needle, needlepoint the canvas with Brighton stitch. Start 2" down and over from the top left corner and follow the stitch chart above. Begin stitching the back at least 1" to the right of the front.

9"   lining

├─ 2½" ─┤

step 3

Cut the excess canvas away and then finish the raw edges

5. Cut the canvas in half widthwise to separate the two sides of the needlepoint.

6. Using regular scissors, trim the excess canvas around all four edges of each piece to ½" from the stitching.

7. For each needlepoint piece, fold the longer edges of the canvas to the wrong side along the last row of needlepoint stitches. Using the embroidery needle, whipstitch the edges in place with muslin thread on the front and navy blue thread on the back. Make sure the stitches do not show on the right side.

8. Fold the two shorter edges of the canvas (the top and bottom) to the wrong side and whipstitch in place as in Step 7 and as shown.

Stitch the sides of the chatelaine together

9. Place one stitched canvas right side down on a table. Place the other stitched canvas on top, wrong sides together.

10. Using 1 strand of navy blue yarn and the tapestry needle, whipstitch together the two long sides and one short end (which will become the bottom of the chatelaine).

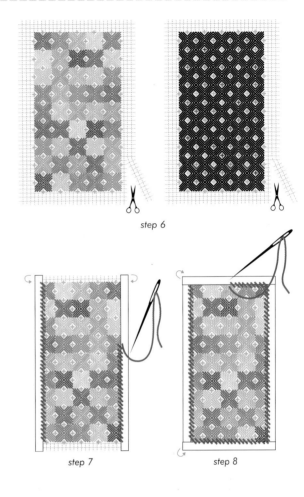

step 6

step 7

step 8

step 10

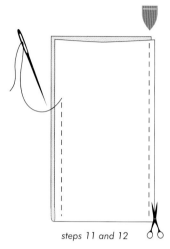

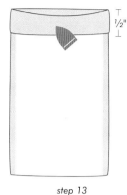

steps 11 and 12

step 13

step 14

Make the fabric lining

11. Fold the lining in half lengthwise, right sides together. Draw seam lines ¼" along the two long sides with a fabric marker and ruler. Using muslin-colored thread and the embroidery needle, backstitch along the two lines in a ¼" seam. Note: This step may also be completed on a sewing machine.

12. Press the seam allowances open and flat. Trim the seam allowance to ⅛" using embroidery or fabric scissors.

13. Fold over ½" along the open edge toward the wrong side of the fabric and press.

14. Slide the fabric lining into the needlepoint chatelaine, wrong sides together. With the muslin-colored thread and the embroidery needle, whipstitch together the top edges of the needlepoint and lining.

Finishing

15. Cut a 6" length of faux suede trimming. Starting at one side seam, and using the embroidery needle and navy blue thread, sew vertical straight stitches to attach the trimming to the top (open) edge of the chatelaine so that it covers the seam joining the lining to the needlepoint. Make the first stitch ⅛" in from the end of the trimming and then make a stitch every ½". Be sure to work each stitch several times, that is, several stitches on top of each other, so it will be securely attached. Cut away any excess trimming before stitching the last end in place.

16. Hold the chatelaine upside down in your nondominant hand so you're looking at the bottom edge. Starting at the center, place one end of the remaining piece of trimming flat against the chatelaine, covering the seam. Using the embroidery needle and blue thread, sew the trimming to the needlepoint with a straight stitch, making the first stitch ¼" in from the end of the trimming. As in Step 15, make several stitches in the same exact spot. Work around the chatelaine, continuing to sew the trimming over the seams, making a stitch every ½", until you reach the top of one side.

17. Decide how long you want the strap to be by wrapping the loose trim across your body, shoulder, or neck (I made mine hip-length so I can wear it across my chest, and it's approximately 44" long). Add at least 6" to the strap length (for finishing the opposite side and bottom) and then cut away any excess trimming.

18. Leaving the strap length unattached, continue stitching the rest of the trimming to the remaining side and bottom as before, until all sides of the chatelaine are covered with trim as shown.

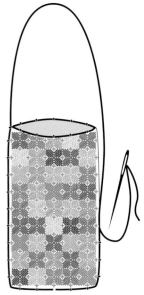

steps 15–18

finished size

- 2" x 1"

you will need

- Raw linen (at least 3" square)
- Magic Cabin wool felt in coral and blush (each at least 3" square)
- Fusible interfacing (at least 3" square)
- Fiberfill or catnip
- ⅛" leather cord for tail, in brown (2½" long)
- DMC Six Strand Embroidery Floss, in black 310 ■, dark charcoal 645 ■, ecru □ (1 skein each)
- All-purpose sewing thread, in ecru
- Size 9 embroidery needle
- Embroidery scissors
- Regular scissors
- Straight pins
- Iron
- Access to a photocopy machine
- Li'l Mouse Cat Toy templates (facing page)

embroidery stitches

- Upright cross-stitch (page 44)
- French knot (page 45)
- Straight stitch (page 30)

techniques

- Using interfacing (page 239)
- Finishing with overcast stitch, aka whipstitch (page 235)
- Finishing with blanket stitch (page 37)

Li'l Mouse Cat Toy

You don't have to be a cat to want to bat this li'l critter around with your paws. Less than two inches nose-to-tush, you can fill him with catnip and cotton fluff. Let your cat have at him or keep him safe on your windowsill. Purposely sew wonky cross-stitches onto a half-moon of raw linen, then tack down tiny pink ears and make French knot eyes before assembling the pieces—leather tail, too—with hand stitchery. Make a bunch of these critters at once and you'll have what's called a "mischief of mice"!

Create the pattern templates, cut the mouse pieces, and apply the interfacing

1. Photocopy the mouse template pieces at 100% and cut them out using regular scissors.

2. Fold the linen in half. Pin the body side template to the linen and use embroidery scissors to cut out the shape. You will have two pieces that are mirror images, one for each side of the body.

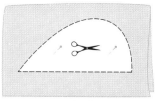

step 2

3. Repeat Step 2 with the interfacing.

step 4

4. Pin the ear template to the coral felt and cut out. Repeat to make two ears.

5. Pin the body bottom template to the blush felt and cut it out.

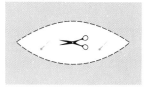

step 5

6. Use a warm iron to apply the adhesive side of the interfacing pieces to the wrong side of the body sides following the manufacturer's instructions. (If the fabric is reversible, pick a side.) Interfacing the fabric will give it more body, make it easier to stitch, and reduce fraying.

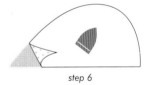

step 6

Li'l Mouse Cat Toy templates

ear

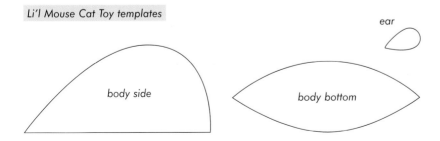

body side

body bottom

223

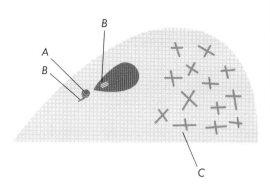

stitch diagram

A   French knot
B   Straight stitch
C   Upright cross-stitch

Embroider the mouse

7. Stitch following the diagram, using two strands of floss. Use dark charcoal floss for the upright cross-stitches. After stitching the black French knots for the eyes, add a tiny black straight stitch in the direction of the nose to create a teardrop shape.

8. Stitch each ear to the body sides with a few straight stitches in ecru floss.

Finishing

9. Place the interfaced sides of body sides together. Use blanket stitch to sew them together along the back from nose to tail, using ecru thread.

10. Sew the body bottom to the body sides, leaving a 1" opening.

11. Stuff the body with catnip or fiberfill.

12. Use overcast stitch to sew the opening closed.

13. Attach the tail to the bottom of the center back with a few straight stitches.

step 9

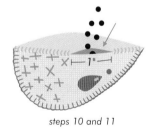

steps 10 and 11

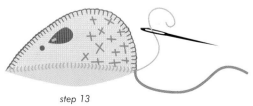

step 12   step 13

Something Blue Hanky

The name says it all: one of those four essentials for a bride's big day. You start out with an ordinary hanky, but you finish with a masterpiece as beautiful and delicate as a piece of Delft china—that's better for blowing your nose. I'm not gonna lie . . . the floral design will put a stitcher through her paces. There are French knots, couching, satin stitch, detached chain stitch, and more. Think of it as a sampler with a purpose. If you want to make it extra special, add the bride's initials and wedding date. Maybe the happy couple will be so moved that they name their firstborn after you.

level //

finished size

- 14¾" x 13½"

you will need

- Hanky (I used a fancy one made of Irish linen)
- 1" twill tape (one package)
- DMC Six Strand Embroidery Floss, in sky blue 813 ■ (3 skeins)
- Size 9 embroidery needle
- Embroidery scissors
- Iron
- Straight pins
- Embroidery hoop
- Something Blue Hanky transfer (in envelope)

FOR MONOGRAM (OPTIONAL):
- Heat-transfer pencil
- Tracing paper
- Monograms in Font Library (page 243)

embroidery stitches

- Backstitch (page 32)
- Stem stitch (page 33)
- Straight stitch (page 30)
- Chain stitch (page 34)
- Detached chain stitch (page 35)
- Closed fly stitch (page 39)
- Couching stitch (page 46)
- Padded satin stitch (page 41)
- Eyelet wheel stitch (page 41)
- French knot (page 45)

techniques

- Using iron-on transfers (page 73)
- Using a heat-transfer pencil (page 75)
- Hooping your work (page 25)
- Monogramming etiquette (page 49)

stitch diagram

A Backstitch

B Stem stitch

C Straight stitch

D Chain stitch

E Detached chain stitch

F Lazy daisy stitch

G Closed fly stitch

H Couching stitch

I Padded satin stitch

J Eyelet wheel stitch

K French knot

L French knot fill

All stitches are worked with 2 strands unless indicated otherwise.

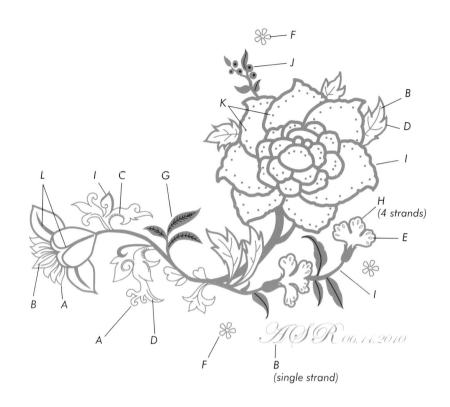

Transfer the motif to the hanky and prepare the hoop

1. Place the transfer on the hanky in the desired location and pin. (In the sample, the design was positioned 1½" inches from both the bottom and right side.) Apply the motif to the hanky using a warm iron.

step 1

2. Wrap the twill tape around the embroidery hoop and stitch the end in place. Then insert the fabric into the hoop.

Monogram (optional)

3. Trace the bride's monogram and the wedding date using the heat-transfer pencil and tracing paper. Apply to the hanky as in Step 1. (In the sample, the monogram was positioned ½" to the right of the lowest detached chain stitch and 1¼" above the bottom edge of the hanky.)

4. Using one strand of floss, stitch with stem stitch, backstitch, or a stitch of your choice.

Embroider the design

5. Follow the stitch diagram for stitch placement. Use two strands of floss except for the couching stitch, which is four strands couched with two strands. For French knot fill, make closely spaced clusters of French knots.

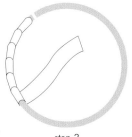

step 2

step 4

227

Skeleton Key Ring

Unless you live in a tent and travel by skateboard, you need a key ring. Here's to stitching up an awesome project that is small enough to tackle in an afternoon. The design is a simple, eerie skeleton key—a key that opens any door. If you chant "Skeleton Key, open for me" like a mantra while you stitch, your completed ring may well have magical powers or at least the power to keep your keys together! If a goth-style key doesn't turn your dead bolt, try a monogram, a little matchbox-size car, or a house.

Prepare the materials

1. Using the ruler, rotary cutter, and mat, cut a 3" × 7" rectangle of felt.

2. Repeat Step 1 with regular scissors to cut the stabilizer.

3. Trim the plastic canvas to 1⅛" × 2¾" with regular scissors. Set aside. (This will be inserted between the layers of felt to make the key ring tag stiff; see Step 11.)

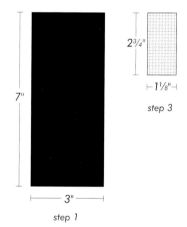

2¾"

1⅛"

step 3

7"

3"

step 1

level

finished size

- about 1¼" x 4¼" (including the ring)

you will need

- Wool felt in black (at least 3" x 7")
- Plastic canvas (at least 2" x 3")
- Sulky Tear-Away stabilizer

- ⅝" suede ribbon, in black (2")
- Split ring (1")
- DMC Six Strand Embroidery Floss, in old gold 833 ▨, black 310 ■ (1 skein each)
- All-purpose sewing thread, to match gold floss
- Size 9 embroidery needle
- Embroidery scissors
- Regular scissors
- Rotary cutter and mat, or fabric scissors

- Seam ripper
- Tweezers (optional)
- Quilting ruler
- Air-soluble fabric marker
- Iron
- Straight pins
- Skeleton Key Ring transfer (in envelope)

embroidery stitches

- Backstitch (page 32)
- Padded satin stitch (page 41)

techniques

- Using stabilizer (basting) (page 78)
- Thread tracing (basting) (page 77)
- Backstitching a seam (page 237)

228

Transfer the motif to the stabilizer

4. Transfer the motif to the stabilizer using a warm iron. Position the keys end to end as shown, spaced ¾" apart.

Baste the stabilizer to the felt

5. Place the stabilizer on the felt, matching the edges, pin, and then baste in place with the embroidery needle and thread. Remove pins.

Tracing with thread

6. Trace the outline of keys with backstitch using all-purpose thread.

7. Use the seam ripper to remove basting. Carefully tear away the stabilizer, using tweezers if necessary.

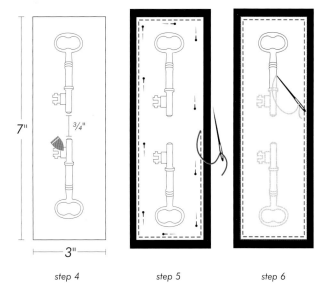

step 4   step 5   step 6

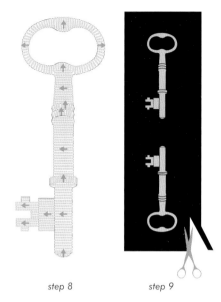

step 8 *step 9*

Embroider the design

8. Work padded satin stitch as shown in diagram using two strands of floss. (Separate and then recombine the two strands for neater stitching.) Follow the arrows on the illustration for the direction of the satin stitches.

Trim the felt to its final size

9. Trim the stitched felt to 1¼" × 6".

Finishing

10. Fold the felt in half, matching the short edges. Sew one side together using two strands of black floss and closely spaced backstitch. Pause when you reach the open end.

11. Slide the plastic canvas between the layers of felt.

12. Fold the ribbon in half, matching the cut ends. Insert the cut ends between the layers of felt, approximately ⅜" from the top edge and centered left to right. Pin.

13. Continue stitching as in Step 10 to sew the top end (securing the ribbon loop in place) and remaining side. Remove pins as you stitch.

14. Open the split ring and slide it onto the folded ribbon.

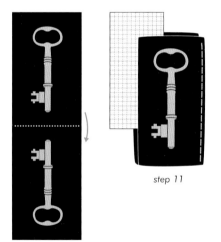

step 10 *step 11*

steps 13 and 14

Pet Portrait

I decided to celebrate my lovely and loyal dog, Rita, turning fourteen with an official canine portrait. You don't have to be a great artist to pull this one off. My alter ego, Trace-y Tracerton, does wonders with translucent paper and a pencil. Just enlarge a photo of your subject to a size and scale you like, trace, and transfer to fabric. Then

embroider over the lines using basic embroidery stitches and you'll have a drawing that speaks (or meows, barks, or tweets) volumes. Add in as much or as little detail as you wish. (Don't get bogged down in shading unless you feel like it.) You can apply the same technique to stitch portraits of friends with less fur and a bigger vocabulary— which they'll use to say "Thank you!"

level

finished size

• 5½" x 7"

you will need

• A photo of your pet
• Fabric (in a light color; if you'd like to use a dark color, follow the Tracing with Thread method on page 77)

• DMC Six Strand Embroidery Floss, in ivory 3865 ■, light shell pink 225 ■, light dusty rose 778 ■, dark desert sand 407 ■, light beige 3033 ■, medium beige brown 840 ■, darkest brown 3371 ■, black 310 ■ (1 skein each)

Note: These are just the colors I chose; feel free to try any color or type of thread you desire!

• Size 9 embroidery needle

• Embroidery scissors
• Rotary cutter and mat, or fabric scissors
• Quilting ruler
• Heat-transfer pencil
• Tracing paper
• Iron
• Straight pins
• Scotch tape
• Embroidery hoop (optional)
• Photo editing program (optional)
• Access to a photocopy machine

embroidery stitches

• Stem stitch (page 33)
• Seed stitch (page 31)
• Straight stitch (page 30)
• Backstitch (page 32)
• Satin stitch (page 40)

techniques

• Using a heat-transfer pencil (page 75)
• Hooping your work (page 25)
• Framing your work (page 241)

step 1

A high-contrast photo is easiest to trace.

Create the artwork for the design

1. Place the tracing paper over the photo and tape it so it doesn't shift. Trace using the heat-transfer pencil. *Optional:* This technique reverses the image in the photo when it is transferred onto the fabric. To have an image on the fabric that is the same as in the photo, you must reverse the photo first with a computer editing program or photocopy machine. Alternately, you could also tape the photo facedown on a sunny window and trace from the back of the photo to create a mirror image.

step 3

Transfer the artwork to the fabric

2. Using the ruler, rotary cutter, and mat, cut a piece of fabric at least 4" taller and wider than the traced image.

3. Center, pin, and apply the traced design to the fabric using a warm iron.

stitch diagram

A Stem stitch

B Seed stitch

C Satin stitch

D Back stitch

E Straight stitch

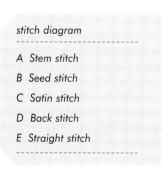

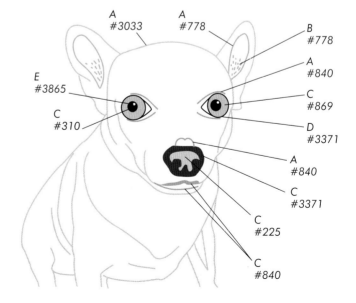

Embroider the design

4. Follow the stitch diagram for recommended stitches for the outline, eyes, nose, mouth, and ears. In the sample, six strands of floss were used to work the outline of the design with stem stitch. The eyes and nose were embroidered using satin stitch. *Optional:* Use an embroidery hoop to keep your fabric taut.

step 4

Finishing

5. Turn to page 241 for finishing tips and instructions for framing your completed work of art.

Finishing Up

ike anything else, embroidery requires some follow-through. What's the point of making a great hit if you're not going to run the bases? Follow-through, in my opinion, is what separates the good from the great. And for some of the embroidery pieces that you're about to tackle, it simply means doing a bit of hand sewing. This is good news! Why? Because hand sewing is really a form of embroidery. It isn't there to show off—it's simply there to hold stuff together. If you've mastered the basic freehand embroidery stitches in Chapter 3 (pages 28–47), you're already building good stitching habits that will only make your embroidering life easier—and your projects sturdier.

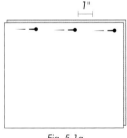

1"

Fig. 5.1a

Get Pinned

There are some projects that require you to pin fabrics together (or pin fabric to interfacing or stabilizer). Pins should be placed at intervals of about 1 inch (fig. 5.1a), and even closer together if the fabric is slippery or the project is small in scale or has lots of curves. For hand sewing, you may place your pins perpendicular to the edge or parallel with the pinheads facing toward you so that you don't get pricked.

I have three rules when it comes to pins:

1. They must be rustproof (so that they don't leave any rusty marks that can stain fabric).

2. They must not have plastic heads. Plastic-head pins often melt under an iron. Instead, stick with ones that are headless, have T-shaped heads, or have heads made of glass (fig. 5.1b). (Of those options, I like the glass-head pins because they're prettiest!)

3. They must be size-appropriate. This means that you'll want to use a very thin pin on a delicate fabric, since a thick one will likely leave a mark when the pins are removed. If you're not sure about the pin-size-to-fabric-heft ratio, stick a pin into a discreet area or scrap of the fabric you're stitching and then remove it to see if it leaves a hole.

Fig. 5.1b

Hand Sewing Tips

Since embroidery *is* hand stitching, the hand sewing required in any of the projects in this book will be second nature.

1. Cut your sewing thread between 18 inches and 24 inches long, just like you would with an embroidery thread or yarn (see page 21). Any longer than that, and you're inviting tangles.

2. Unless the instructions indicate otherwise, stitch from right to left if you are right-handed, and from left to right if you're a southpaw.

3. Err on the side of loose, even tension in order to avoid puckering the fabric.

4. Bring the needle through the fabric from the wrong side to the right side in order to keep the knot at the end of your thread from showing. When you're making a hem, start your thread underneath the inner folded edge.

Stitches to Finish What You Started

Overcast Stitch (aka Whipstitch)

There are two ways to use an overcast stitch in embroidery: edging and hemming.

✳ **Edging:** This is the best method for using thread or yarn to hide an edge. Draw the needle through your fabric or canvas from the wrong side, pull the thread through, and then draw the needle through again (from the wrong side) directly next to the last stitch (fig. 5.2). The length of the stitch is a design choice and therefore up to you, but it's a good idea to match the weight of the thread

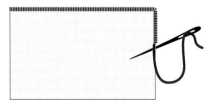

Fig. 5.2

to the size of the stitches. The heavier the thread, the bigger you'll want to make the stitches and vice versa. You're basically encasing the edge in a satin stitch. Knot the thread at the back of your work, or leave a 2-inch tail and secure it under your first stitches.

Fig. 5.3

* **Hemming:** You'll find this stitch at the bottom of many a pair of pants—but only if you look inside at the wrong side of the fabric. From the right side, the overcast stitch looks nearly invisible. To start, fold your hem to the wrong side of the fabric and press it in place. Overcasting the edge of your folded-over hem is just like overcasting any edge except that, with each stitch, you pick up a single thread on the wrong side of your embroidered work. Anchor your knot close to the raw edge of the hem. Sew under one thread of the main fabric to which the hem is to be secured. Then insert your needle ⅛ inch from the raw edge of the hem and ⅛ inch from the first stitch. Space the stitches about ⅛ inch apart, and start and end ⅛ inch below the raw edge of the hem. Hold your needle perpendicular to the hem as you go and you'll end up with neat, diagonal stitching (fig. 5.3).

Double-Turned Hems

he simplest way to make a hem is to fold the raw edge of your fabric up 1 inch and (A), press the fold, then tuck the raw edge of the fabric into the fold and press it again

(B), making a ½-inch seam. For projects that require double-turned hems, such as the Smocked with Love Dress on page 125, I indicate how much you need to fold. After pressing

and pinning the folds in place (C), use overcast stitch or slipstitch at the folded upper edge of the hem to attach it to the main fabric.

A hem is a method of finishing a raw edge of fabric by turning it under twice and stitching.

Basting Stitch

In hand sewing, basting is a temporary stitch made to hold two or more layers of fabric in place; in embroidery, it can also be used to transfer designs onto fabric (as described on page 77). The basting stitch is basically the same as the running stitch (see page 30) except that the stitches are longer—from ¼ inch to ⅜ inch—and you can have larger spaces between them (fig. 5.4). Because these stitches are only meant to be around for the short term, you don't need to worry about them being very tidy. Note: Use a contrasting colored thread so that it's easier to spot when it's time to tear it out.

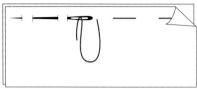

Fig. 5.4

Backstitch

Remember your friend the backstitch? You met him on page 32. This is the sturdiest stitch for hand-sewn seams. Bring your needle up through the fabric at 1 and make one stitch (about 1⁄16 inch long) to the right at 2. Bring your needle back up two stitch lengths to the left at 3, and then bring it down through the fabric again at 1 (fig. 5.5). Continue in this way and you'll have a strong straight line of stitching to hold a seam together. When completed, the stitches on the top should look like sewing machine stitches, and the ones on the underside should overlap and be twice as long.

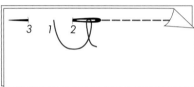

Fig. 5.5

Slipstitch

The slipstitch is a very discreet stitch that can be used for sewing a hem, applying an appliqué, or attaching one folded edge to another. It's also known as a blindstitch because, when done correctly, it's virtually invisible from both the right and wrong sides of the fabric. To start, bring the needle out through one folded edge so the knot is hidden inside the seam. Make a small horizontal stitch in the opposite folded edge by slipping the needle into the fabric close to the top of the fold without going through both layers. (You're actually stitching through the seam allowance fabric to keep the stitches hidden.) Pull the needle and thread through the fabric, then slip the needle about ¼ inch over into the first folded edge (fig. 5.6). Continue to stitch small horizontal stitches across alternating folding edges, about ¼ inch apart. Every three stitches or so, pull the thread gently to close the opening.

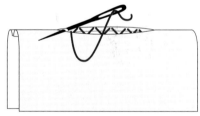

Fig. 5.6

So Wrong, It's Right!

As I've mentioned, there are two sides to every fabric. When a two-sided fabric comes in contact with another two-sided fabric, you need to think about how they should touch. Here's a guide to how to place your pieces.

Place fabric pieces right to right when you're attaching fabric where the seam will be hidden from view. With the Art of Conversation Pillow on page 149, for instance, you'll have the right sides of your work together as you stitch four sides, leaving a 7" opening. Then you will turn the work right side out so that the wrong sides are facing each other and you'll close off the opening with a slipstitch.

Place fabric pieces wrong to wrong if you're inserting a stiffening material between two pieces. This is the technique to use with the Needlework Necklace on page 97. Then you'll use overcast stitching to hide the unfinished edges from view.

Place fabric pieces wrong to right when doing appliqué, such as the deer motif on the Stag Hoodie (page 103). The back of your appliqué fabric piece will be stitched to the right side of your base fabric.

Other Odds and Ends

Some finishing steps do not require a needle and thread. The following techniques will help make your piece be all it can be.

Getting Things Straight and Flat

Fig. 5.7a

Fig. 5.7b

Embroidery fabric can usually be pressed or steamed on the wrong side to remove creases in the fabric without flattening the stitching, but canvas work usually needs to be blocked, which is the process of returning the stitched needlepoint (fig. 5.7a) back to its original size and alignment (fig. 5.7b). Here's the scoop:

* **Steam press (aka quick blocking):** This technique works best on canvases with only a little distortion. Put the canvas with wrong side facing up on a padded surface. Cover your work with a white, slightly dampened cloth or towel, and then steam-press lightly from corner to corner—press the entire canvas: the needleworked area as well as the unstitched border (fig. 5.8). Stretch the canvas in the direction opposite the distortion and pin to an ironing board or towel. After you've left the piece to dry flat, it should have a more desirable shape.

Fig. 5.8

* **Blocking:** Although you can make your own blocking board,
I recommend buying a ready-made one at a craft or needlepoint shop.
It will cost somewhere in the neighborhood of $40 to $70 depending
on the size. To use it, start by dampening your canvas or fabric
with a spray bottle or sponge with warm water on the wrong
side (fig. 5.9a), place it facedown on the blocking board, and
gently pull it into square, using
the guidelines on the board.
Insert pins perpendicular to
the fabric's edge and then
let the whole piece dry
flat (fig. 5.9b).

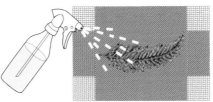

Fig. 5.9a

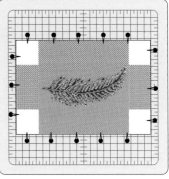

Fig. 5.9b

Interfacing

Although it's always hidden from view, interfacing is a valiant warrior that
comes to the rescue in many a sewing battle. It can be used to stick one fabric
to another fabric, and/or to add a degree of stiffness to a project, and/or to
protect the stitches from fraying or getting bothered in any way. (It's a good
idea to use interfacing if there's a chance that threads on the back of a piece
could be scratchy and bothersome when in contact with skin.)

There are different types of interfacing. For the projects in this book (like
the Needlework Necklace on page 97 and the Family Tree Photo Album Cover
on page 198), I recommend using fusible interfacing (shown on page 5) that is
adhered using a dry iron.

To start, simply pin the adhesive side of the interfacing to the wrong side
of the embroidery and trim the interfacing edges close to the embroidery. Set
the iron to the temperature setting appropriate for your fabric and then press
the fusible interfacing following the manufacturer's instructions (fig. 5.10).
Usually fifteen seconds will do the trick, but time and temperature can vary, so
be sure to follow the directions that come with the interfacing you're using.

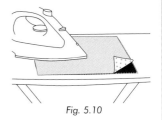

Fig. 5.10

Presentation Touches

Is your work ready to be shown off in a gallery in New York City? Or at least
the gallery on the fridge door? Either way, you will want to show it off as best
you can. Here are a few methods for showing off your super skills.

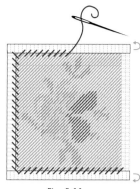

Fig. 5.11a

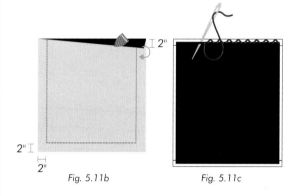

2" ⊥
⊢⊣
2"

Fig. 5.11b   *Fig. 5.11c*

Finishing Your Needlepoint Masterpiece

A work on canvas can be lined with another piece of fabric to keep the back of the work protected. Note: This shouldn't be done until after you've blocked your work (see "Getting Things Straight and Flat," page 238).

1. Fold the excess canvas to the wrong side. Go ahead and pin it in place if it won't stay down on its own. Discreetly baste the edge of the excess canvas to the stitches on the back of needlepoint. Fold the corners neatly and secure with a few stitches (fig. 5.11a).

2. Use a suitable color yarn to sew whipstitches around the perimeter of the canvas in order to cover any exposed canvas threads.

3. Cut a lining fabric, such as felt, wool, or burlap, that is 2 inches larger than your work on each side.

4. Fold the extra 2 inches of the lining to its wrong side and iron (fig. 5.11b).

5. Slipstitch the lining to the back of the canvas (fig. 5.11c).

Fig. 5.12a

Hanging

Create a casing or tunnel of fabric at the top of your stitched masterpiece and slide a dowel through it, just like a curtain on a curtain rod.

1. Measure the circumference of the dowel you plan to use and add 1 inch for ease and the seam allowance, or pin the fabric around the dowel and add 1 inch to this amount.

2. To begin the casing, fold the top edge of your work ½ inch to the back and press. Be sure to use a ruler or sewing gauge to measure the fabric as you iron; you want the hem to be perfectly even and straight.

3. Fold the pressed edge to the wrong side of the fabric by the amount calculated in Step 1, and pin the pressed edge in place. Insert the dowel into the fabric and make any necessary adjustments.

4. Stitch down the casing using a ⅛-inch seam allowance. Sew by hand with backstitch or whipstitch or use a sewing machine. Press.

5. Repeat Steps 1–4 on the bottom edge as shown if desired.

6. Insert dowel(s) (fig. 5.12a). Cut a length of wire or cord twice the length of one dowel. Tie to each end of the top dowel and hang (fig. 5.12b).

Fig. 5.12b

Mounting

Measure the needleworked area and purchase stretcher bars for canvas, in those dimensions, at an art supply store. Then assemble the stretcher bars. Lay your work facedown and place the stretcher strip assembly centered over your piece. Turn up the sides of the canvas or fabric and staple them to the bars (fig. 5.13). (You will need a staple gun for this.) Make neat triangular folds at the corners.

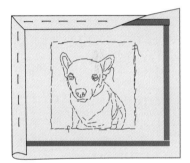

Fig. 5.13

Framing

Find a frame with an extra rabbet cut or step inside to prevent the glass from actually touching the needlework. Another option is to place an acid-free archival mat between the fabric and the glass. To avoid moisture damage to your work, make sure your frame is sealed on all sides.

I often have my work professionally framed, but I have to do the following steps before it's ready for framing:

1. Cut a piece of mat board (or have it cut for you at an art supply store) larger than the opening of your mat but small enough so the edges of the fabric can wrap over the edge of the mat board and onto the back.

2. Using a ruler and a pencil, measure and mark the center of each edge of the mat board (fig. 5.14a). Then find and mark the center point.

3. Mark the center of each edge of the design with a pin (fig. 5.14b).

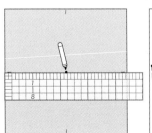

Fig. 5.14a

Fig. 5.14b

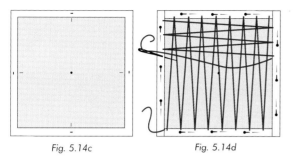

Fig. 5.14c   Fig. 5.14d

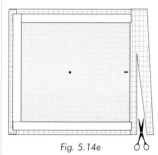

Fig. 5.14e

4. Lay the design facedown on a table. Place the mat board on the back of the fabric and line up the center marks (fig. 5.14c).

5. For embroidery on fabric: Use pins to secure the center of each edge of the fabric to the corresponding edge of the mat board. With a strong sewing thread and needle and starting at the center, lace the edges of the fabric together from one side to the other every inch as shown. Fold the fabric or canvas neatly at the corners so they are smooth and flat (fig. 5.14d).

For needlepoint on canvas: Cut the overage canvas to 1½ inches. Trim the corners diagonally so you can fold the edges back. Use artist tape to attach the canvas to the mat board (fig. 5.14e).

6. Center the mounted design under the mat and then tape them together on the back with artist tape.

Cleaning

I've mentioned this before but it is worth repeating: Always prewash your fabric. If it's going to shrink, let it shrink before you've poured love and sweat and tears into stitching it! After working on a piece for a few weeks, the oils—and maybe dirt—on your hands may show up on formerly clean canvas or fabric. When it's absolutely necessary, I swish my piece around in a basin of slightly soapy cold water, then roll it in a towel to blot the excess moisture. When all else fails, I go slouching to the dry cleaner.

Label Lover!

I like making personalized labels for projects I'm proud of. A little MADE AT MAKE or BY DIANA is the perfect finishing touch to a gift. (Hey, I take credit for my hard work!) I like to stitch tags on felt or thick satin or grosgrain ribbon. To do it yourself, use a fabric marker to draw your signature onto a piece of removable stabilizer, pin it to the tag, and stitch through both layers. Then tear off the stabilizer to reveal your signature.

For Stag Hoodie, *page 103*

A B C D E F G H I J K L M
N O P Q R S T U V W X Y Z
0 1 2 3 4 5 6 7 8 9

For Monogrammed Sneakers, *page 106*

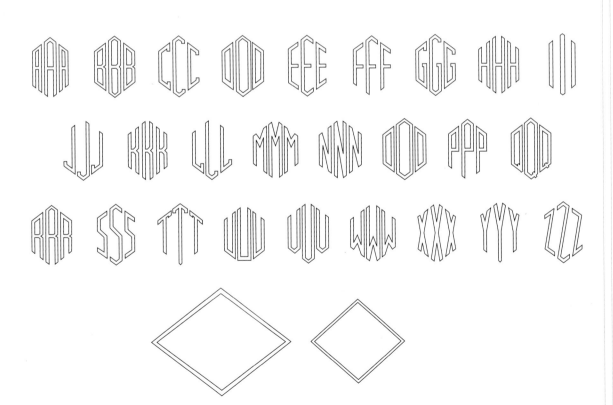

For Old Country Tea Towel, *page 180*

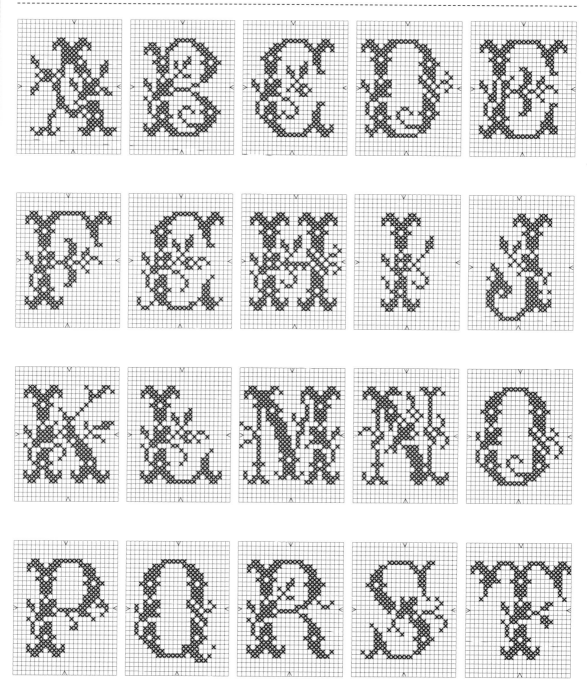

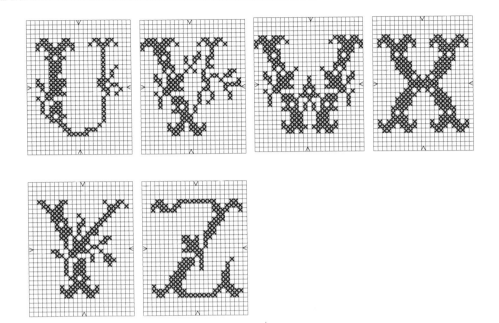

For Return-to-Sender Luggage Tag, *page 192*

a b c d e f g h i j k l m n o p q r s t u v w x y z
A B C D E F G H I J K L M N O P Q R S T U V W X Y Z
1 2 3 4 5 6 7 8 9 0 # @

For Something Blue Hanky, *page 225*

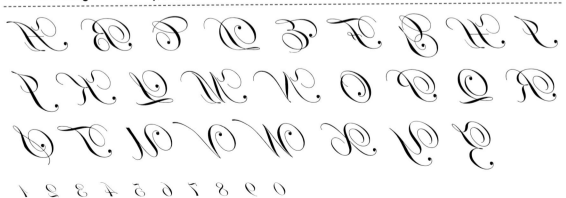

Resources

The following manufacturers and retailers provided or were the source of the materials used to create many of the projects in this book.

Anchor Yarn

A Westminster Fibers knitting brand specializing in yarn for canvas embroidery. Yarn is available in nearly 500 shades, is colorfast, and mothproof.

needlepoint.com

Beads World

A NYC-based spot for beads, beading needles, sequins, and silk cord (Needlework Necklace, page 97, and Scissors Chatelaine, page 216).

beadsworldusa.com

Clover USA

Makers of quality embroidery, sewing, and craft supplies including fabric markers, dressmaker's carbon, thimbles, and handy smocking stickers that you can apply to fabric as a stitching guide.

clover-usa.com

Colonial Patterns

This company sells Aunt Martha's transfers and a variety of hard-to-find vintage-style embroidery base materials.

colonialpatterns.com

DMC

The number one source for embroidery floss, pearl cotton, waste canvas, and many other needlework supplies ranging from Aida cloth to thread organizers.

dmc-usa.com

Eco-Bags

A site dedicated to selling reusable containers, and my source for the plain canvas "Organic Cotton Shopping Tote" (in natural) used for the Greenmarket Tote, page 160.

ecobags.com

Futai USA

Where to buy the Leighton Tiffany parasol (aka the Lacy Parasol, page 186).

leightonumbrellas.com

Gingher

The go-to brand for embroidery scissors and dressmaker's shears.

gingher.com

Magic Cabin

Makers of my favorite wool felt. The colors are so pretty and it doesn't melt when you apply heat transfers to it.

magiccabin.com

M & J Trimming

Premier trimming resource since 1936. I shopped here for the belt buckle (Bargello Belt, page 112), piping (Art of Conversation Pillows, page 149), and ribbon (Smocked with Love Dress, page 125 and Skeleton Key Ring, page 228).

mjtrim.com

Metalliferous

Metal, tools, and supplies for jewelry making. This is where I purchased the cuff link blanks, bead caps (for the Beaded Dress, page 101), and the split ring (for the Skeleton Key Ring, page 228).

metalliferous.com

My Homespun Threads

A personal craft blog and source of the free downloadable pattern for the Kimono Baby Booties (page 142). Visit the website and search for "Kimono Baby Shoes."

myhomespunthreads.blogspot.com

Paternayan

A quality Persian yarn for needlepoint and crewel embroidery made by JCA. Comes in more than 400 colors.

jcacrafts.com

Prym Consumer USA Inc.

Manufacturers of pretty much every notion you'd ever need for embroidery and sewing. I used their air- and water-soluble markers, heat transfer pencil, sewing gauge, pin cushion, covered button kits (for the Diamond Cuff Links, page 207), and more!

dritz.com

Sudberry House

Fine wood accessories for needlework since 1967—and the source for the "Betsy" box for the Peony Jewelry Box on page 183.

sudberry.com

Sulky of America

The maker of every type of stabilizer you can imagine plus heat transfer pens in a rainbow of colors.

sulky.com

Transfer-Eze

This water-soluble stitchable film makes transferring an embroidery pattern so easy!

createforless.com

Treglown Designs

The makers of the amazing Charley Harper painted needlepoint canvases (shown on page xviii).

treglowndesigns.com

Ultrasuede

Washable, durable, environmentally friendly, and cruelty-free fabric and cording material.

ultrasuede.com

Zweigart

The premier maker of needlepoint canvas, Aida cloth, linen, and many other types of needlework fabrics for more than 120 years!

zweigart.com

Illustrations by Sybille Schenker.

All principal photography by Jim Franco.

age fotostock: Image Asset Management p. xx bottom; **Alamy Images:** imagebroker p. xix top right, © INTERFOTO p.11 top; **The Art Archive:** Superstock p.47; **Jenna Bascom:** p. ii, p. xiii, p. xiv, p.1, p.2, p.4, p.5, p.8, p.9 bottom, p.10, p.12, p.13, p.15 bottom, p.32 top, p.33 bottom two, p.34, p.35 top, p.36, p.37, p.38, p.39 top, p.40, p.41 bottom, p.43, p.44 top and bottom, p.45, p.46, p.47 top, p.48, pp.52–58, p.63, p.67, p.69, p.86, p.115, anchor p.122, p.187, p.194, p.221, p.227; **Janette Beckman** dog p.iii, p.145; **Bridgeman Art Library:** ©Boltin Picture Library p. xvii bottom right, © Dreweatt Neate Fine Art Auctioneers Newbury Berks UK p. xx top, National Gallery London UK p.18, © Museum of London UK p.xix bottom, Private Collection p.xvi top, Private Collection p.68, Smithsonian Institution, Washington DC USA p. xvii bottom left; **Getty Images:** Spencer Arnold p. xi, Danita Delimont p.9 bottom, Japanese School p. xv, ©S.Stone 2010 retrovertigo.etsy.com p.51 bottom, Silver Screen Collection p.51 top; **Kim Johnson/www.desiretoinspire.net:** p. xviii right; **Melissa Lucier:** stars p. iii, p.9 top, p.15 top, p.29, p.31, p.33 top, p.41 top, p.42 top, p. 50, p.149; **New England Quilt Museum, Lowell, MA:** p. xvii top; **StitchesApp.com** p.80; **Courtesy Richard Saja:** p. xvi middle; **Courtesy ©Estate of Charley Harper,** "And One To Grow On" canvas is produced and marketed by **Treglown Designs** p. xviii middle; **Courtesy of Brandon Eggena and Diana Rupp:** p. vi, p. viii top and bottom, p. ix, p. x, p. xvi bottom, p.7, p.16, p.19, p.32 bottom, p.35 bottom, p.39 bottom, p.49, p.59, p.64 top and bottom, pp.70–79, p.81, p.151, p.209, p.234, p.236, p.242; **Courtesy of the Lacis Museum of Lace and Textiles:** p. xix top left; **Courtesy www.MarieGraceDesigns.com:** p. xviii left; **©V&A Images:** p.42 bottom.

Keep Your Hoop in the Loop

fter you stitch a project or two, let me know how you're doing! I'd love to see how your projects turn out. Please send digital photos to me via my website at makeworkshop.com so I can share them with the Make community—it's likely that your project will serve as inspiration for others. I'll be posting updates and alternate versions of the projects, too, so check back often.

—Diana